Clear and Present Safety

CLEAR AND PRESENT SAFETY

THE WORLD HAS NEVER BEEN BETTER AND WHY THAT MATTERS TO AMERICANS

MICHAEL A. COHEN
AND MICAH ZENKO

Yale
UNIVERSITY PRESS

New Haven and London

Published with assistance from the Louis Stern Memorial Fund.

Yale University Press books may be purchased in quantity for educational, business, or promotional use. For information, please e-mail sales.press@ yale.edu (U.S. office) or sales@yaleup.co.uk (U.K. office).

Set in Gotham and Adobe Garamond type by IDS Infotech, Ltd.
Printed in the United States of America.

Library of Congress Control Number: 2018954947

ISBN 978-0-300-22255-5 (hardcover : alk. paper)

A catalogue record for this book is available from the British Library.

This paper meets the requirements of ANSI/NISO Z39.48-1992
(Permanence of Paper).

10 9 8 7 6 5 4 3 2 1

To Isadora and Scarlett
—MC

To Michael and Denise
—MZ

Contents

Acknowledgments

This project began in 2011, when Michael was writing a short piece on the twentieth anniversary of the end of the Soviet Union with the counterintuitive argument that the world is actually far safer now than it was then. He called Micah to talk about that thesis, and a friendship and book idea were born.

Over the next several years, we found ourselves repeatedly asking why the world was so overwhelmingly characterized by U.S. politicians, pundits, military officials, think tankers, and the media as one of perpetually greater dangers, darkness, and chaos. Correspondingly, we recognized that these same voices portrayed the United States as facing ever-graver and growing foreign threats, while ignoring the real threats and harms that Americans face every day. Our in-boxes are still filled with emails we have sent to each other over the years of "can you believe he/she said that" statements from threat-mongering politicians and pundits, tales of amazing and unreported global development progress, and chronicles of challenges yet unmet.

This book represents the culmination of our exploration into this subject, and like most books that cover multiple disciplines, it was only possible with the original analysis, guiding insights, and feedback from many scholars, analysts, and colleagues. These include Steven Pinker, John Mueller, Chris Preble, Christopher Fettweis, Rebecca Friedman Lissner, Sean Kay, Michael Hanna, Peter Krause,

John Schuessler, Fredrik Logevall, John Glaser, Heather Hurlburt, Adam Zenko, Barry Posen, Paul Miler, Steve Walt, Elizabeth Economy, Adam Segal, Amelia Mae Wolf, and Courtney Lobel. We are also particularly thankful to Justin Vogt and Gideon Rose at *Foreign Affairs*, who agreed with us that an article examining why the world is actually safer than we have been led to believe would make for a provocative and important argument. They helped us turn that idea into the article that became the inspiration for this book.

A special thanks is also extended to Jenn Wilson of the Council on Foreign Relations (CFR) for contributing invaluable research, critical recommendations, and editing. We could not have completed this book without her assistance. Several CFR interns, including Dan Alles, Susanna Kalaris, Caroline O'Leary, and Max Friedman, also provided research support throughout the writing process. Of course, all errors of fact or analysis are our own.

We also are grateful for the institutional backing that we received throughout the past seven years, including from *Foreign Policy*, CFR, and as the Whitehead Senior Fellow in Chatham House's U.S. and the Americas Program for Micah. Over the years, Michael was able to preview some of the research for this book in his regular column for the *Boston Globe*, which his editor, Marjorie Pritchard, affectionately and jokingly called his "good news" pieces. Michael is indebted to the *Globe* and to Marjorie, in particular, for her steadfast support of his work over the past four years.

We also must thank our outstanding agent, Geri Thoma, for helping us find a publisher, and Jaya Aninda Chatterjee at Yale University Press and Andrew Katz for bringing the manuscript to print.

On a more personal note, as we put together the final edits for the aforementioned article in *Foreign Affairs*, Michael's daughter Isadora was born. In fact, in late December 2011, the two of us sat in a hospital room on New York's Upper East Side with Michael holding his new baby in one arm and the final edits of that article in the other. Michael now has two children, Izzy and her younger sister, Scarlett. He dedicates this book to them—as a reminder of the extraordinarily hopeful world in which they will come of age but also the vigilance that they must maintain in order to ensure that it remains that way for them, for their children, and for their children's children.

Micah dedicates the book to his parents, Michael and Denise, who have provided a lifetime of love and support, for which he will always be grateful.

Clear and Present Safety

Introduction

Neither a man nor a crowd nor a nation can be trusted to act humanely or to think sanely under the influence of a great fear.

—*Bertrand Russell*

On a crisp January day in 2016, in the small hamlet of Pittsfield, New Hampshire, several hundred voters were gathered for what is a quadrennial rite of passage in the Granite State: listening to a politician make his or her pitch to be the next president of the United States. The speaker this day was Chris Christie, who was then the Republican governor of New Jersey and one of more than a dozen presidential candidates campaigning across the state.

Christie discussed everything from illicit drugs and immigration to the federal budget and the U.S. war against the self-proclaimed Islamic State. "He was pretty good," one woman unenthusiastically shrugged after he finished. But as she struggled to say anything of substance, it seemed clear that Christie had not made much of an impression. When asked, though, if any specific policy issue took on particular importance, her face lit up: "ISIS. I'm really worried about ISIS." The thought of her kids and grandkids growing up in a world where groups like the Islamic State would be threatening their future seemed to cause her genuine and palpable concern.[1]

The woman's anxieties were sincere, but her fear could not have been more misplaced. The Islamic State had yet to launch even one direct terrorist attack within the United States, and if the group had drawn up a list of potential targets, the chances that Pittsfield, New Hampshire—an hour's drive north of Manchester—would be high on that list were decidedly slim. At a time of ever-widening income inequality, stagnant wage growth, gun violence, and a raging opioid epidemic that in the previous year had claimed 422 lives in New Hampshire alone, this woman considered a shadowy terrorist group that had not killed a single American on U.S. soil one of the biggest challenges facing the country.[2] She was far from alone. Public opinion polling consistently shows that Americans have long exaggerated the danger that terrorism represents to the United States. Since 9/11 the average number of Americans killed yearly in a terrorist attack is twenty-seven—and 90 percent of them were in Afghanistan or Iraq. Yet, in 2018, 81 percent of Americans ranked "cyberterrorism" as the most critical threat facing the United States, followed by international terrorism at 75 percent.[3] Eighty-three percent of voters expect that a major terrorist incident with large numbers of casualties is likely to occur in the near future. Remarkably, in November 2017, more than half (52 percent) of Americans thought the United States was less safe then than it was before 9/11—as if the trillions spent on homeland security and fighting terrorists in Iraq and Afghanistan had done nothing to make America less vulnerable to international terrorism. Seventeen years after September 11, the outsized fears of another 9/11-style terrorist attack provided compelling—and depressing—evidence that terrorist groups had succeeded, beyond their wildest imaginations, in transforming American society.[4]

It is not just armed jihadists that scare Americans. A 2012 poll showed that six out of seven Americans agree that "the United States faces greater threats to its security today than it did during the Cold War"—a time when the United States found itself in the crosshairs of approximately ten thousand nuclear weapons, each with a destructive power up to fifty times that of the nuclear bomb that was dropped on Hiroshima.[5]

How Americans, such as this woman from a small town in the "Live Free or Die" state, became convinced that the United States faces such acute and harmful foreign threats is, at its core, the story of this book. The American public is being fed, by politicians and pundits alike, a steady diet of threat inflation that has made them deeply fearful of the world outside their borders. They have become convinced that overseas menaces are perpetually becoming more likely, lethal, and complex. The world is forever on fire; America is always getting weaker; and its citizens are facing a constant drumbeat of tremendous and unceasing risks. The pervasiveness of threat inflation is such conventional wisdom that alternative—or even less threatening—descriptions of the world are largely nonexistent in foreign policy debates. As a result, most Americans are simply unaware of the extraordinary and unprecedented political, economic, and social progress that has taken place in virtually every corner of the globe over the past three decades.

On that January day in New Hampshire, while alluding to the national debate on the balance between security and privacy, Christie declared ominously, "You can't protect civil liberties from a coffin." Pittsfield voters who had watched the most recently aired Republican presidential debate would have heard former Florida governor Jeb Bush tell them that the Islamic State had formed "a caliphate the size of Indiana with . . . 30,000 to 40,000 battle-tested soldiers that are organized to destroy our way of life."[6] They would have heard candidate and former pediatric neurosurgeon Ben Carson claim that dirty bombs and cyberattacks are, "in fact, an existential threat to us."[7]

Those following the Republican primaries would have heard Donald Trump, the eventual Republican nominee and president of the United States, tell them that the only way to keep America safe was to ban all Muslims from entering the country, torture suspected terrorists, and "take out" (murder) their families.[8]

As regular consumers of news, Republican voters might have heard South Carolina senator Lindsey Graham tell Americans, "The world is literally about to blow up," in January 2014 (spoiler: it did not).[9] They might have caught Sen. John McCain, who, having been born in 1936, had lived through conflicts that killed an estimated sixty million people and had fought in one of those wars, say in 2015, "We are probably in the most serious period of turmoil in our lifetime."[10] Perhaps in the spring of 2017, they caught secretary for homeland security John Kelly claiming, "Make no mistake—we are a nation under attack" and "We are under attack every single day. The threats are relentless."[11] Or, in the summer of 2018, they might have heard his boss, President Trump, warn that "people coming in from the Middle East" would come across the border by using "children to get through the lines."[12]

This incessant, default threat-mongering is neither a partisan issue nor a habit reserved for elected officials. Those Americans tuning in to CNN in October 2014 might have the chyron asking the hypothetical question "Ebola: 'The ISIS of Biological Agents?' "[13] Maybe they saw local reporting on defense secretary Chuck Hagel saying, "Cyber threats . . . are just as real and deadly and lethal as anything we've ever dealt with," or New York senator Kirsten Gillibrand calling Iran an "existential threat" to America, or perhaps Arkansas senator Tom Cotton warning that the Islamic State, in coordination with Mexican drug cartels, could infiltrate the border and "attack us right here."[14]

Even if viewers missed all that, they would have found it far more difficult to avoid the nonstop news coverage of the latest terrorist attack in Paris, Barcelona, or London.

Even more important than what Americans hear from the nation's leaders is what they do not hear. They do not hear that terrorism harms fewer Americans each year than falling televisions and furniture, bathtub drownings, and lightning strikes do. Annually, more Americans lose their lives from these three rare killers—roughly thirty-three, eighty-five, and forty fatalities, respectively—than at the hands of wild-eyed Islamic jihadists.[15] These numbers pale next to the number of Americans killed each year prematurely by preventable, noncommunicable diseases (more than 2.5 million), suicide (44,100), and gun homicides (14,400).

In short, Americans do not hear that America is unusually safe and secure from foreign threats. Part of this is a function of geography, but it is also true that the United States faces no serious great-power rival and no near-term political or economic competitor.

So it should not be surprising that 86 percent of Americans view Russia's military power as either an important or a critical threat to America, even though Russia is hemmed in by NATO, has a moribund economy, and has no enduring military partnerships in South Asia, the Middle East (outside of Syria), or the Western Hemisphere. Nor should it be surprising that 87 percent of Americans are concerned about China's military power even though China faces its own pressing social, economic, and environmental challenges—and its primary near-term interest is maintaining Communist Party rule, not directly challenging the United States. Nor should it be surprising that 75 percent of Americans called the development of nuclear weapons by Iran a "critical threat"—even though Iran has surrendered its nuclear fuel and has allowed invasive inspections of its nuclear facilities through at least 2030.[16]

Finally, we should not be surprised that half the American people believe that U.S. armed forces are not the number-one military in the world, even though the United States spends more on national defense than the next nine nations combined, is allied or has mutual defense treaties with five of those countries, enjoys long-term security partnerships in every region of the world (outside Antarctica), and is, quite simply, the world's most dominant nation and more secure than any other great power in history.[17]

In addition, the Republican primary voters in Pittsfield—or those who voted for a president who regularly told them "the world is a mess"—almost certainly did not hear that the world today is cumulatively more peaceful, freer, healthier, better educated, and wealthier than at any point in human history.[18] Like most Americans, they would not have heard that in the year 2015 the proportion of people living in extreme poverty (on less than two dollars a day) dropped to below 10 percent of the global population, the lowest level ever and down from close to 50 percent in 1981.[19] They are likely unaware that AIDS deaths have declined for more than fifteen years in a row, global life expectancy has increased by seven years since 1990 alone, and child mortality rates (for children under five years old) has been halved over that same period. Unbeknownst to them and the overwhelming majority of Americans, improvements in polio vaccines and delivery methods have practically eradicated the disease (just eleven active global cases by July 2018), saving more than 650,000 lives since 1988.[20] What is most remarkable about all these positive developments is that they are uncontestable—the data are simply that strong.

This fundamental disconnect between what Americans have been encouraged to believe about the world and the reality of global affairs is the most critical foreign policy issue facing the United States today. The American people are being sold a dangerous bill of goods that is distorting our foreign policy choices and leading politicians and policy makers to focus more on the threats that Americans perceive, rather than the ones that actually exist. This strategic misdiagnosis has led to consistently mistaken foreign (and domestic) policy choices that are diverting resources and attention away from the actual dangers that Americans face in their homes, neighborhoods, and workplaces. Every dollar spent bombing and then rebuilding Middle Eastern countries, modernizing a duplicative nuclear weapons arsenal, or building the next generation of combat aircraft that are intended to fight yesterday's enemies means less money for America's greatest domestic challenges. This includes America's underperforming schools; a health care system that performs far worse than those of other affluent countries; crumbling roads, bridges, and water systems in places like Flint, Michigan; inadequate preparation for the inevitable and irreversible effects of climate change; and a tattered social safety net that is a far cry from those enjoyed by other developed countries.

Pointing out that foreign threats pose a relatively insignificant risk to Americans compared to vastly greater domestic dangers and systemic harms is not to suggest that the United States should pull up the drawbridge and abandon its global role. If anything, at a time of relative peace and stability in the world, smart American leadership and active involvement in global affairs are more important than ever. In the seventy-plus years since the end of World War II, the United States, along with its allies and partners, has helped construct an international system that limits large-scale interstate conflict; encourages democratization, adherence to the rule of law, and respect for human rights; and advances human development. The challenge for the next generation of U.S. policy makers is to solidify the gains that have been made and to ensure that this extraordinary progress is not reversed.

For that to happen, Americans must change the ways they think and talk about foreign policy and national security—and the first step is to acknowledge that foreign-threat inflation and the corresponding policy choices that it encourages are a problem. Americans need to think about the world in a whole new way, one that is more accurate and more uplifting than the dystopian view promoted by politicians and pundits. In the following six chapters, we will spell out how this paradigm shift might occur.

First, there must be greater recognition that potential rivals and complex issues—frequently portrayed as dangers to Americans—are, in reality, relatively minor threats to Americans. Great-power wars have disappeared, interstate wars have become vanishingly rare, and the world is a safer and freer place than it has ever been in human history.

Second, there needs to be better appreciation of the extraordinary global progress that has been made over the past several decades—and why it benefits the American people. The world today is healthier than would have been scarcely imaginable decades ago and is far richer and better educated than ever before. It is also more united and interconnected through travel, communications, economic links, and diplomatic relations. These trends make this current era of relative peace, safety, and prosperity not a momentary blip but, more likely than not, the future reality of global affairs.

Third, it is imperative that Americans rethink what "national security" means and focus on the systemic dangers that diminish economic opportunities and the American people's basic quality of life. From noncommunicable diseases to gun violence to crippling political dysfunction, the things that actually injure and kill us receive rare moments of national attention, while foreign terrorists and other outside threats perpetually occupy our minds. Political attention, policy changes, and expanded government resources can significantly—and cost-effectively—reduce these risks, but that will happen only if Americans recognize the need to address them.

Fourth, the loose collection of politicians, government officials, pundits, private security firms, think tankers, academics, cable news hosts, and news editors that we call the Threat-Industrial Complex demands far greater scrutiny. These are the individuals—and institutions—who shape public perceptions about international relations and promulgate a false narrative of danger and insecurity.

Fifth, our modern era of threat inflation must be placed in a larger political and historical context: namely, as an enduring feature of American politics and foreign policy debates since World War II. From "missile gaps" and the "domino theory" to the "evil empire" and "evildoers," foreign threats have been consistently manipulated both in times of actual danger and in times of genuine peace and security.

Sixth, to dramatize our argument, we offer a case study and cautionary tale of how threat inflation occurs and its larger political consequences: namely, the response to the tragedy of September 11. Public statements and policy decisions made by President George W. Bush and his administration set the tone, agenda, and political incentives of our contemporary fear-mongering but also wasted opportunities in a disproportionate response to a relatively minor and manageable threat.

Finally, we lay out recommendations for reversing this unbalanced perspective and approach to foreign policy that will answer the question of what a U.S. domestic and global policy—properly informed by a more accurate understanding of the world—should look like.

This book is not meant to be a comprehensive treatment of threat inflation or the final word about the nature and degree of foreign threats facing the United States and its citizens. As has been true for the past 240 years, the degree to which foreign dangers threaten

America and its citizens has changed dramatically over time and will continue to evolve in ways that nobody can predict today. Nonetheless, it is quantitatively true that the current global environment is one of relatively few foreign threats, particularly in comparison to other great powers and to America's historical experience. The fixation of American foreign policy and national security should not be what former president John Quincy Adams spoke of nearly two hundred years ago: namely, the impulse to look "abroad in search of monsters to destroy." Rather, it must be to remain focused on ensuring that today's hopeful present is America's brighter future.

A Safer and Freer World

I think, what we need to do is to remind people that the earth is a
very dangerous place these days.

— *White House press secretary Sean Spicer, February 7, 2017*

February 16, 2012, was, from all appearances, an unremarkable
day. The political world was focused on the upcoming Republican
presidential primary in Michigan, in which the frontrunner, Mitt
Romney, was facing a spirited challenge from former Pennsylvania
senator Rick Santorum. Journalists were mourning the loss of the
New York Times reporter Anthony Shadid, who had died on a reporting trip to Syria. New Yorkers obsessed over the Knicks' budding su-
perstar point guard, Jeremy Lin; the *Simpsons* marked its five
hundredth episode; and Chinese President Xi Jinping was in Iowa
hoping, as the *Washington Post* put it, "to emphasize the idea of an
enduring U.S.-Chinese friendship."[1]

Yet, on Capitol Hill, the most senior officer in the world's most
powerful military, chairman of the Joint Chiefs of Staff Gen. Martin
Dempsey, saw something else altogether: danger. Testifying before
the House Appropriations Defense Subcommittee on budget
sequestration—the congressional mandate passed in 2011 that
required all federal agencies, including the Pentagon, to automatically

cut their budgets by 5 to 10 percent in the following decade—
Dempsey warned, "in my personal military judgment, formed over
thirty-eight years, we are living in the most dangerous time in my
lifetime, right now."[2] This is a surprising statement. After all, Martin
Dempsey was born in March 1952, during the tail end of the Korean
War—which killed more than two million people, including 36,574
Americans. When he attended elementary school, the Cuban Missile
Crisis brought the world closer to nuclear holocaust than at any other
point during the Cold War. By the time he enlisted in the army in
1974, the Vietnam War had been going on for several years and before
it ended would take the lives of more than three million people, including 58,220 Americans. As Dempsey rose through the military
ranks, he witnessed the strategic nuclear arms buildup of the 1980s,
when the United States and the Soviet Union had tens of thousands of
nuclear-armed missiles pointed at each other. Later, on September 11,
2001, the most lethal terrorist attack in American history took the
lives of nearly three thousand people. While all of these events directly
affected Americans, there were plenty of other dangerous moments in
Dempsey's lifetime, such as the Biafra separatist civil war in Nigeria
that killed two hundred thousand, the Angolan civil war in which one
million people died, the Khmer Rouge's genocide in Cambodia that
took the lives of approximately a quarter of that nation's eight million
people, the Iran-Iraq War during the 1980s that killed more than one
million people, and the internationalized civil war in Congo that has
led to three million war-related deaths since the mid-1990s.[3] Yet, if
Dempsey is to be taken literally, none of those moments compared to
the dangers facing the world on the morning of February 16, 2012.

What made Dempsey's statement particularly odd was an observation he made one year later testifying before Congress: "I will
personally attest to the fact that [the world is] more dangerous

than it's ever been"—in other words, since the earth was fully formed 4.6 billion years ago.[4] Though Dempsey's comments were clearly hyperbolic—and easily disprovable—they garnered little attention. In a political environment dominated by habitual threat inflation, they barely stand out. Indeed, two years after Dempsey's testimony, the director of national intelligence, James Clapper, told Congress, "looking back over my more than half a century in intelligence, I have not experienced a time when we have been beset by more crises and threats around the globe." Remarkably, he had made virtually the same statement—word for word—a year earlier when testifying before Congress.[5]

In January 2015, army chief of staff Gen. Raymond Odierno told the Senate Armed Services Committee, "today the global environment is the most uncertain I have seen in my thirty-six years of service."[6] This assertion was especially well received by the committee's chairman, Sen. John McCain, who only days before had proclaimed, "we are probably in the most serious period of turmoil in our lifetime."[7] In November 2017, Air Force Lt. Gen. Steve Kwast went further back in time proclaiming, "There's no question that this generation . . . is living in the most dangerous time since the Civil War for the Republic."[8]

There are specific bureaucratic and political reasons for such apocalyptic descriptions of the global environment (the more vivid the threat, the more likely Congress will be to maintain military and intelligence-community funding). Such views, however, are mimicked across the national security community. Indeed, in the elite world of foreign policy punditry (and national politics), the notion of grave, growing, and irreversible dangers facing the United States is the default (and unchanging) position. So we should not be surprised that most Americans think the world is getting more and more dangerous.[9] In the immediate aftermath of the bombing of a subway train and airport terminal in Brussels in March 2016, MSNBC news anchor Brian Williams asked Senator McCain if the world was on the verge of World War III. McCain unsurprisingly said yes.[10] Sen. Lindsay Graham, then in the running for the Republican nomination for president, echoed these fears, claiming, "there is a sickness in the world that has to be dealt with, and the civilized world must come together to confront it."[11] Quite simply, this is the lingua franca of the Threat-Industrial Complex.

There is one problem: this image of the world is completely wrong. In virtually no element of our national discourse are Americans provided with a more inaccurate depiction of the world than when it comes to matters of war, peace, and freedom. Americans live in a world that is safer and freer than ever before in human history—and it is not even close. To state this is not to be insensitive to those who are suffering real harms or being denied their personal freedoms. It doesn't mean one is naïve to the potential of current global challenges—some of which are neither illusory nor false—to become serious threats in the future. But facts are facts, and the transformation in the human experience over the past two to three decades is the most consequential global trend in security affairs in any of our lifetimes—and it is largely unknown to the wider public.

A Safer World

The data supporting the proposition that the world is safer than ever are so overwhelming that they can barely be disputed. For example, interstate war, or war between states, was the defining characteristic of international relations for centuries. Today, such wars have largely disappeared. Since 2012, there have been just two interstate wars: one between Sudan and South Sudan in 2012 and one between India and Pakistan in 2014 and 2015 that led to fewer than one hundred fatalities in total over both years.[12] In the seven years before 2010, there was one major interstate conflict—started by the United States in Iraq in March 2003.[13]

How about great-power conflict? These protracted and bloody wars—such as the Thirty Years' War, World War I, and World War II—have been historically the most devastating and consequential conflicts. They've repeatedly led to massive death tolls of soldiers and civilians, forced transfers of millions of people, and the redrawing of national boundaries to the benefit of the victors. As the historian Timothy Snyder has documented in *Bloodlands: Europe between Hitler and Stalin*, 10.5 million civilians (Germans, Poles, Belarusians, Ukrainians, and Jews from various countries) were killed by Germany and the Soviet Union between 1939 and 1945.[14] Put another way by the eminent British historian Max Hastings, approximately twenty-seven thousand people lost their lives every single day of that conflict.[15] That means that during World War II, between a given Monday and Thursday, there would have been as many deaths as there were battle-related deaths in all of 2016.[16] Despite the December 2015 claim by Chris Christie that the United States was "already in World War III," the world has not seen such a total global conflict in more than seven decades.[17]

All of this might sound like apostasy when you consider the daily fare on cable news segments, in social media feeds, and in the nation's newspapers and magazines. Foreign reporting in these outlets has been dominated in recent years by North Korea's nuclear weapons development, stories of terrorist attacks in Iraq and western Europe, a bloody civil war in Syria that has killed an estimated five hundred thousand people, the barbaric cruelty of the Islamic State, Russia's meddling in its near abroad, and China's campaign of building military facilities on disputed territories in the South China Sea.[18]

For those whose lives are directly affected, these crises are serious matters. But alarmist coverage of these global hot spots has deluded Americans into believing that the world is a chronically violent place. It's not. In fact, modern war is not only a rare occurrence, but when it does happen, it tends to be less violent and of shorter duration. On average, conflicts kill about 80 percent fewer people now than in the 1950s, when wars in Korea, Southeast Asia, and sub-Saharan Africa took millions of lives.[19] The vastly greater harm today is the displacement of civilians caught up in the fighting between combatants. By June 2018, sixty-eight million people around the world had been forced from their homes.[20]

To the credit of the United Nations, international organizations, and nongovernmental groups, the breadth and depth of understanding about the underlying dynamics and drivers of conflict have expanded dramatically, and there now exist far more tools for preventing and mitigating such armed violence. Not surprisingly, conflict gets more attention than does the successful use of international and regional conflict-prevention methods to prevent wars from occurring in the first place. The wars that never occurred between Israel and Iran, Peru and Ecuador, Russia and its Baltic neighbors, and Turkey and Russia after the shooting down of a Russian fighter in 2016 receive precious little attention.

Despite routine alarms of mounting tensions between China and its neighbors over territorial disputes in the East and South China Seas, conflict there has been avoided. This is true of the overwhelming number of maritime and land disputes, which a majority of countries have with their neighbors. Additionally, of the 430 bilateral maritime boundaries in the world, most are not defined by formal agreements between affected states. Unfortunately, peace, even between bitter adversaries, is not an "event" worth recognizing, much less celebrating; the dominant media narrative is that of an ever-threatening world.[21]

The current era of relative peace and stability has also contributed to a notable decline in the prevalence of state-directed mass killings of civilians.[22] During the Cold War, approximately one in seven countries experienced a state-sponsored mass killing. This number increased to nearly 25 percent immediately after the Berlin Wall came down and declined to between 5 and 10 percent by the 2010s.[23] In fact, far fewer people have been killed in war in the past quarter century than in any other quarter century over the past six hundred years. In 1800, one out of every two thousand people on earth—civilians and combatants—died from a combat-related death; in 1900, it was one in every twenty thousand; by 2016, it was one in every one hundred thousand.[24]

The overall decline in global conflict has had extraordinary ripple effects. William Tecumseh Sherman famously declared in 1879 that "war is hell," but his words barely capture the full costs of warfare and armed violence. As one would expect, warfare significantly limits life expectancy. The Syrian civil war, for example, reduced life spans there from 79.5 years before 2011 to 55.7 in 2015, an extraordinary twenty-year decline in just a four-year period.[25] Children living in conflict-affected poor countries are twice as likely to die before their fifth birthday as are children in other poor countries, and warfare diminishes educational opportunities at all levels as well as overall quality of life. For example, children who grow up in conflict-affected countries are less likely to be literate and far less likely to be enrolled in primary school.[26]

Beyond the immediate human costs, wars do untold physical and environmental damage. In 2016, a time of relative peace and stability, all of the world's armed conflicts combined cost the global economy an estimated $14.3 trillion. That is nearly 12.5 percent of global GDP.[27] The relationship between conflict and economic distress is self-perpetuating—just as war drains government coffers, economic slowdowns also increase the likelihood of the outbreak and recurrence of conflict. Finally, conflict-prone countries are far less democratic, and, in fact, the presence of an autocratic government increases the risk of a civil war starting within that government's territory.[28] As noted previously, this matters because civil wars—including those like Syria's that became "internationalized" with external support—are virtually the only type of armed conflicts that still occur in the world today.

Ironically, Americans tend to see the world as far more dangerous than it is precisely *because* the world is safer. Conflicts that were once far more routine have become more unusual and thus receive greater (and more vivid) media attention. This bolsters the impression that we live in a world of constant conflict when compared to recent history. Yet it is often forgotten exactly how bloody the final years of the Cold War were, particularly in comparison to today. The Cold War is mistakenly remembered as an era of relative quiet in which Washington and Moscow co-managed global affairs. For example, in February 2016, Clapper said the reason there were more threats than at any point in his seventy-three-year lifetime was the disappearance of the superpower rivalry between the United States and Soviet Union. "Virtually all other threats were sort of subsumed in that basic bipolar contest that went on for decades and was characterized by stability," said Clapper.[29]

Yet, in the decade preceding the end of the Cold War in 1991, there were more than two million battle-related deaths around the world. In the ten years immediately after, there were 651,000, and in the past ten years, there were even fewer: 402,000.[30] While the Cold War saw a bipolar (albeit unimaginably costly) peace between two nuclear-armed superpowers, it does not mean the rest of the world enjoyed peace and safety. There were significant internationalized wars, genocides and mass killings, and lengthy and bloody civil wars dotting the globe, from Indonesia and Afghanistan to Vietnam, Nigeria, and throughout Central America.

There is also the inconvenient fact that the United States and Soviet Union possessed nearly seventy thousand nuclear weapons, many perched on intercontinental missiles pointed directly at each other. The two adversaries also had tactical nuclear weapons deployed in twelve countries—many poorly secured or with the authority to use them resting with local military commanders.[31] In the event of a full-scale superpower conflict, human life as we know it would have likely ceased to exist. Since Americans misremember what happened during the Cold War—and forget how real the threat of nuclear conflict was—they are far more prone to accept claims that the world is less stable and safe today.

One more reason Americans perceive the world to be so dangerous is that the overwhelming foreign policy focus of government leaders, Congress, and the media is on the Middle East and North Africa (MENA). Chronic political instability, proxy wars, and occasional interstate wars have long come to dominate the region. Indeed in 2017 alone, eight of nineteen MENA countries experienced intrastate conflicts (noninternational conflicts that resulted in twenty-five or more battlefield deaths).[32] That is the exception, not the rule, in comparison to every other part of the world. Though the MENA region gets oversized media attention, it constitutes less than 5 percent of the world's population and is not representative of the overwhelming majority of the planet's seven and a half billion residents. Painting a picture of the world solely using the chaotic and violent imagery from the Middle East severely distorts one's image of global affairs.

More Freedom

The world is not merely safer than ever before; it has also become demonstrably freer over the past quarter century. Just as the Cold War is misremembered for being an era of relative peace and stability, it is often forgotten that the world then was defined far more by authoritarianism and totalitarianism than by democracy. In most corners of the globe, political freedom represented an aspirational, seemingly unachievable, goal. Today, even in the face of troubling reversals and assaults on democracy, a greater percentage of people are freer than before. They enjoy personal, political, and economic self-determination that would have been unimaginable to most people living outside the United States and western Europe just thirty years ago.

In November 1989, as the Berlin Wall was being dismantled, there were just 69 electoral democracies in the world, or 41 percent of 167 countries in total. Today, according to the Freedom House Index, that number is 116 (out of 196 countries), or 59 percent.[33]

In the 1980s, Latin America was mired in economic stagnation, social injustice, persistent conflict (both civil wars and cross-border conflicts), and above all, an almost complete lack of democratic governance. In Chile in 1973, a democratic election was overturned by a military coup, leading to dictatorship, widespread human rights abuses, and a full-fledged economic crisis. In Argentina, a military junta invaded the Falkland Islands in 1982, sparking a pointless war with the United Kingdom. Throughout the late '70s and '80s, Central America became a hotbed of human rights abuses, civilian massacres, and economic deprivation, fueled by superpower competition between Washington and Moscow. Today, while economic and political progress across the region has been uneven and backsliding is evident, all of Latin America—with the exception of Venezuela and Cuba—is today designated as "free" or "partly free" by Freedom House.

Thirty years ago in Europe, half the continent was under the thumb of totalitarian leaders, basic freedoms were restricted, and barbed-wire-topped walls prevented citizens from traveling outside their borders. With the exception of Belarus and Russia, every country in western and eastern Europe is today considered a free or partly free democracy. In the Far East, South Korea, Mongolia, and Taiwan—countries once (wrongly) considered by Western academics as culturally inappropriate for political liberalization—have become full-fledged democracies. Even in sub-Saharan Africa, which has experienced a decline or stagnation in democratization since 2005, the majority of people live in free or partly free countries.[34] Once again, it is the Middle East that remains outside the global shift toward greater political freedom, with only Tunisia and Israel being considered free countries and a handful ranked as partly free.[35] These gains have also led to greater political stability as there has been a marked decline in the number of coup attempts across the globe over the past three decades.[36]

The Polity IV project, a widely respected data source of global governance trends, assigns "polity scores" to states to quantify their governing authority on a scale of −10 to +10. It does this by coding democratic and autocratic traits, such as political participation, competitiveness of political leadership positions, and constraints on the chief of state. A polity score of +10 would be a full democracy, such as Sweden, while a −10 would be a severe autocracy, such as North Korea.[37] In 1989, the average score for all governments was −0.5, the equivalent of an Afghanistan governance score by the latest rankings. By 2016, it had moved all the way to +4.3.[38] Meanwhile, today a country with a score of −0.5 would be somewhere between Afghanistan and the Central African Republic. Moreover, when changes in polity scores from 1949 to 2014 are tracked against changes in "human rights scores" over the same period, a hopeful trend is apparent: as countries become more democratic, their respect for human rights also increases.[39]

Democratic progress, however, remains fragile, and according to Freedom House—which tracks relative democratic rankings—global freedom has declined for the past twelve years. In aspiring great and midlevel powers such as China, Russia, and Turkey, there has been a disturbing uptick in autocratic behaviors. In all three countries, there's been the silencing and even murder of independent journalists, the overregulation and harassment of civil society organizations, consolidation of political rule by authoritarian leaders, and more centralized control of security forces. Notable and troubling declines are also evident in the Philippines, Poland, Hungary, and Nicaragua. Moreover, confidence in elected officials in strongly democratic countries—including the United States and in western Europe—has notably fallen in recent years as populist, nativist, and xenophobic political movements have made inroads.[40] The extraordinary democratic progress made in the years after the fall of the Berlin Wall is now moving in the opposite direction.

Struggles for more entrenched democratization and personal freedoms are constantly contested, messy, and even bloody affairs—and many young democracies go through extended periods of political turmoil. Those who hold power generally seek to exercise it with the fewest possible restraints, and those restraints are growing. Indeed, if there is one area where the path of human progress could potentially be slowed or even reversed, it is on the expansion of political freedom. The growing disinterest among U.S. policy makers toward the issue—and the cultivation of authoritarian leaders by President Donald Trump—will undoubtedly make this situation worse.

Yet the path of progress over the past thirty years cannot be denied. Quite simply, the world is far more democratic and free today than it was during the height of the Cold War.

Why Does This Matter for America?

While fewer armed conflicts and increased political freedom is good news for the vast majority of the world's seven and a half billion people, it is also great news for America. If there is one relatively iron-clad rule of international affairs, it is that democracies tend to have happier, healthier, and better-educated citizens. They almost never go to war with other democracies, much less even threaten each other; and they are also far less likely to find themselves in conflict with non-democratic governments.[41]

A world that is relatively freer and thus less conflict-prone is one that is indisputably better for the United States. It means the U.S. homeland is less likely to be threatened or attacked by great powers with conventional or nuclear weapons. It means treaty allies are not at war, and as a result, the U.S. military is not required to come to their defense. Indeed, in 2015, only five armed conflicts (all internal) took place in countries that are U.S. treaty allies: Philippines (two of them), Colombia, Thailand, and Turkey.[42] It means that fewer countries host or sponsor transnational terrorist groups dedicated to attacking the United States, its citizens, or its overseas diplomatic facilities. It means there are fewer disruptions to global flows of trade, tourism, and energy supplies that benefit the U.S. economy and American jobs. It means fewer people grow up in societies where hopelessness, resentment, and alienation make them susceptible to the appeals of violent extremists. Finally, it means governments are more likely to cooperate on transnational challenges such as fighting climate change, preventing the spread of infectious diseases, lowering the barriers to global trade and furthering human development.[43]

Since terrorism dominates contemporary foreign policy debates, Americans might immediately ask, "What about 9/11?" Understandably, the September 11, 2001, attacks are deeply imprinted into our national consciousness and will remain an inflection point for the division of historical eras, similar to the "Cold War" and "post-Cold War" eras. Yet it is important to understand just how tragically lucky al-Qaeda was on 9/11 and why the attacks were such an anomaly. U.S. homeland security policies, intelligence cooperation, and commercial aviation security were hugely deficient, and this combined negligence made America needlessly vulnerable. As we will detail later, the United States is vastly safer today from such a mass-casualty terror attack.

There are still terrorist groups seeking to kill Americans on American soil, yet they have been overwhelmingly unsuccessful in their efforts to do so. Since 9/11, 103 Americans have been killed within the United States by jihadist terrorists or affiliated terrorist actors, which is almost the same number of Americans killed in hate-crime attacks since 2002.[44] Since 9/11, 402 U.S. citizens have died in terrorist incidents while living abroad, but nearly 75 percent of them died working as diplomats, contractors, aid workers, or journalists in Iraq, Syria, Pakistan, and Afghanistan—the very places where the United States started wars and continues to conduct air strikes to destroy terrorist safe havens.[45] It is tragic but unsurprising that individuals bravely serving in places where conflict is occurring face severely heightened risks to their personal safety, but that does not mean Americans should feel at increased risk of being killed by terrorists.[46]

Indeed, at the same time that Americans have become safer from terrorism, such attacks have increased globally. In 2002, there were fewer than 200 terror incidents worldwide, which killed a total of 725 people; in 2017, there were 8,584 incidents, which took the lives of 18,753 people, one-quarter of whom were the perpetrators.[47] Yet seventy percent of all these fatalities occurred in just five countries: Afghanistan, Iraq, Nigeria, Somalia, and Syria. The perpetrators are relatively weak, nonstate actors using violence to achieve their political objectives, while the victims are overwhelmingly civilians (who themselves are overwhelmingly Muslims) caught between government security forces that cannot protect them and terrorist armies willing to kill them. Even in these five countries, however, there have been notable improvements, especially within Pakistan, which has experienced a decline in civilian deaths from terrorism every year between 2012 and 2017, with 3,007 deaths in 2012 and 540 in 2017.[48]

Contrary to General Dempsey's apocalyptic warnings, the world that existed on February 16, 2012, was far less dangerous than at any point since he had been alive—and it remains so today. In the years after the end of the Cold War, many foreign policy analysts predicted a very different world—a "coming chaos" of continuous ethnic conflicts and genocidal civil wars.[49] The political scientist Samuel Huntington warned of a potential "clash of civilizations," while John Mearsheimer wrote ominously in the pages of the *Atlantic* that we would soon miss the Cold War.[50] The journalist Robert Kaplan predicted that the post-Cold War years would be defined by "anarchy" and regional wars sparked by ancient, tribal hatreds. U.S. senator Daniel Patrick Moynihan warned that renewed ethnic tensions could turn the planet into a "pandaemonium."[51] Contrary to this drumbeat of doomsaying, globalization failed to produce the xenophobia and unchecked ethnic and racial hatreds that were confidently predicted.[52] If anything, the end of the Cold War led to a period of expanded global commerce, communications, and travel, as well as vastly higher living standards for the majority of people on earth.

Global and regional cooperation, not competition, is the defining characteristic of international politics today. That includes national governments, corporations, industry associations, nongovernmental organizations, and individual citizens. As we demonstrate in the following chapter, the world is not just safer and freer; it is a far better place to live now than at pretty much any point in the history of the human race.

Healthier, Wealthier, Better Educated, and More Interconnected

When you look at all the measures of well-being in the world, if you had a choice of when to be born and you didn't know ahead of time who you were going to be—what nationality, whether you were male or female, what religion—but you had said, "When in human history would be the best time to be born?" the time would be now.

—*President Barack Obama, September 7, 2016*

In 2013, a Swedish research firm wanted to know what the residents of the world's most powerful and influential nation knew about the world outside its borders.[1] What it found out is not pretty. That its survey showed the American people lacked detailed knowledge about global affairs was unsurprising. More interesting, however, is the way Americans are wrong. Eighty-three percent believed that less than half of the world's children had been vaccinated for measles. In fact, 85 percent of kids have received this life-saving vaccine.[2] Americans underestimated the number of adults with basic literacy skills (a majority guessed 60 percent; it is actually 80 percent). Most telling, however, was the response to a question about the proportion of people in the world living in extreme poverty. Two-thirds said the global poverty rate had "almost doubled," 29 percent said it has "remained more or less the same," and a mere 5 percent picked what was then the correct answer—that it has been cut in half.

This survey is an incomplete snapshot, but it is backed up by other data. When Americans were polled in the fall of 2017 about their perceptions of the world, just 16 percent agreed that "the world is getting better," while nearly four times as many (63 percent) thought it was getting worse.[3] A 2016 poll found that 92 percent of Americans believed that extreme poverty has either increased or stayed the same over the past two decades.[4]

In short, Americans think the world is a pretty lousy place. That means they are missing the most important international story of any of our lifetimes—namely, that it has never been a better time to be a human being than right now.

Today, the seven and a half billion people who reside on our planet live longer lives; are better educated; have greater access to health care, sanitation, and food; and are far less likely to live in extreme poverty. These improvements, most of which have occurred over the previous two to three decades, have reduced the potential for military conflict, created social and economic opportunities for women and girls that previously never existed, and improved the happiness and quality of life for billions of people. Indeed, these are the fastest and most extraordinary advances in human progress in the history of the species.

Recognizing and celebrating this unprecedented improvement in the human experience does not mean that global development work has reached its conclusion. Neither does it diminish the obstacles facing those who continue to lack access to health services or live in countries where poverty eradication has stalled, which increasingly includes the United States. There are still hundreds of millions of people around the world who remain in dire need. However, to overlook positive social trend lines ignores the unquestioned successes of global development endeavors and further cements the pessimistic view that little can be done to improve the lives of others. If recent history teaches us anything, it is that the opposite is true— the power to enhance people's lives for the better is overwhelmingly within our grasp.

These vast improvements in the health and well-being of people outside the United States—and the increased global interconnectivity among governments, markets, and people—matters a great deal for ordinary Americans. The United States has global interests that range from protecting treaty allies and preventing nuclear proliferation to expanding export markets. Those interests are far better secured when children across the world are in school learning, women are able to work and have greater control of their bodies and their lives, and people's time on earth is longer, happier, and more fulfilling. All of these factors are strongly correlated with greater political stability and lesser chances for conflict. Fewer states at war means reduced regional tensions that may otherwise compel a government to obtain weapons of mass destruction and more stable and prosperous economies to purchase American goods and services. When the world is a better place for more people, it is also a better place for the United States.

How the World Became Far Better for Far More People

Why has the world become such a wealthier, healthier, freer, and less violent place? It is no coincidence that it began to occur at the same time that the Cold War was winding down. As communism was cast into the ashbin of history, once-closed-off countries adopted policies that made them more economically dynamic and interdependent. At the same time, new information technologies became increasingly ubiquitous—even in some of the world's poorest coun-tries. Take the experience of China. Beginning in the early 1990s, Chi-nese leaders opened their country to foreign investment and global trade. Economic growth became a national priority, and while the reigning Communist Party stubbornly clung to one-party rule, it be-gan to loosen the political, economic, and social restrictions that had impeded the country's development. Similar efforts at moving to a more-market-based economy began in India, the world's second-most-populous country. Between 1990 and 2016, GDP per capita in-creased by $7,800 in China and $1,350 in India.[5]

The success of the world's two most populous nations in raising living standards has been a critical driver of global social and eco-nomic change. But the advances in the human condition over the past several decades have hardly been restricted to these two nations. In practically every country on earth, there have been significant and notable improvements in reducing poverty, extending life expectan-cies, and improving health outcomes.

To chart that growth, a good place to start is the Millennium Development Goals (MDGs). The MDGs are an initiative that will be familiar to few Americans outside the world of global develop-ment. Indeed, even for most foreign policy professionals, the MDGs are not well understood or appreciated. But this landmark commitment—agreed to unanimously by all 193 countries in Septem-ber 2000—has been translated into eight sweeping goals that have transformed the developing world and changed the lives of hundreds of millions of people for the better. Moreover, the MDGs offer a com-pelling lesson of how the international community can continue to work together for the common global good—which will be essen-tial as world leaders face the growing and potentially calamitous threat of climate change.

When the MDGs were initially proposed, development trend lines were already moving in a more positive direction, but their global adoption brought more sustained political focus and consolidated numerous governmental and nongovernmental resources. By definition, the creation of strategic goals only occurs when leaders and states agree that they want to accelerate progress. The MDGs represented concrete and actionable goals that every country in the world supported. Moreover, they created metrics that allow us to assess the trajectory of human development—and the results speak for themselves.

The first and most essential MDG was aimed at eradicating extreme poverty and hunger—and for good reason. Reducing poverty, besides making life better, opens up innumerable economic opportunities: more food, more leisure, longer lives, and perhaps, above all else, lowers economic anxiety and stress. It means children in developing countries are more likely to live past their fifth birthday. It means they go to school, rather than toil in fields or factories. And it means they will have access to health care that will ensure they will not be felled by preventable diseases and illnesses. Mothers who have confidence that their children will not just survive into adolescence and adulthood but have an opportunity for success will get pregnant less often. With fewer kids to care for, women are more likely to enter the workforce, which increases overall household wealth. Higher income means that even the smallest luxuries of life—which people in the developed world take for granted, such as taking a vacation, buying a toy, or getting an ice cream cone as a treat for our children—suddenly become available. Quite simply, a life not lived in poverty means far greater happiness.[6]

Since 1990, the reduction in global poverty rates has been astounding. Over the past twenty-eight years, the number of people in the developing world living on less than $1.25 a day (a traditional definition for extreme poverty) has been reduced by one billion.[7] Back then, approximately half the developing world was mired in such crippling poverty; today, it is fewer than one in ten, and it continues to drop year after year, with further reductions challenging but likely.[8]

China accounts for much of this decline, having seen its extreme poverty rate drop by 60 percent in just eighteen years. This means that by 2017 more than eight hundred million Chinese citizens had been lifted out of economic deprivation.[9] But China's evolution has been replicated in countries across the globe. Iran's poverty rate has gone from 17.6 percent in 1986 to under 1 percent in 2014.[10] El Salvador's fell from 36 percent in 1989 to 1.9 percent in 2015, and Ethiopia went from 92 percent in 1981 to under 30 percent today.[11] The underlying cause for these rapid improvements has been the end of conflict: bloody civil wars in El Salvador and Ethiopia and, for Iran, the end to a brutal eight-year struggle with Iraq. It is yet another reminder that fewer wars and greater peace and stability bring enormous residual benefits.

In other places, however, the story is simpler: countries liberalized their economies and removed trade barriers that prevented them from selling their products overseas. They attracted new investment and new businesses with the advantage of lower labor costs. They sent workers overseas to send back remittances to family members, and at home, they strengthened the social safety net to help give those who were mired in poverty a helping hand. And perhaps above all, as more countries became democratic, it put pressure on political leaders to keep the good economic times going—or face the potential prospect of losing their own jobs. We can see positive results from Brazil, where the poverty rate dropped from 20 percent in 1990 to just 4.3 percent in 2015.[12] In Namibia, it went from 69 percent in 1993 to 27 percent in 2015,[13] and in Bangladesh, it dropped from 44 percent in 1990 to 24.3

percent in 2016.[14] While these countries still face serious social and economic challenges, their success in reducing poverty is staggering.

As for hunger, the trend lines are similarly positive. In 1990, about one in five people in the developing world suffered from undernourishment. Since then, that number has been cut in half.[15]

At one time, famine was one of the world's worst killers. In the 1960s alone, it took the lives of more than eighteen million people. Biafra, Bangladesh, North Korea, and Ethiopia had all been witness to famines that killed more than a million in each country. China is estimated to have lost thirty million people during the 1950s and '60s in a famine caused, in part, by horribly misguided government policies. By contrast, from 2010 through 2016, the number of people killed in famine was around a quarter of a million—a tragedy, of course, but also an indication of how far the world has come in preventing such deaths.[16]

The MDGs also established benchmarks for universal primary education and promoted greater gender equality by ensuring that young girls had the same opportunity to go to school as young boys. The benefits of such a strategy are self-evident: a better-educated populace means that more people can read and write. When more people are literate, that translates into a workforce that is more highly skilled and innovative, less unequal, and more productive. But the benefits of education are particularly important when it comes to young women. Girls who are enrolled in school at a young age are more likely to get married later in life. They have fewer children and thus lower levels of poverty. They are at reduced danger of the most common and acute diseases that have long ravaged the developing world. And girls who are given the chance to attend school along with their male peers are more likely to grow up to be women who are socially and personally empowered to take control of their own destiny. Ask any development expert about the best way to lift up a developing economy, and virtually all of them will give you the same answer: make sure girls are going to school.[17]

Increasingly that is exactly what is happening. Primary-education enrollment rates in the developing world have jumped from 83 percent in 2000 to 91 percent today.[18] That might seem like a relatively small rise, but, in fact, it means that more than forty million more children spend their day in a classroom today than did fifteen years ago. In 1990, in sub-Saharan Africa, only 45 percent of the population received a basic education; today, 80 percent do.[19] The jump in South Asia and Southeast Asia has gone from 75 percent to 95 percent; and in the Middle East and North Africa, from 68 percent to 95 percent.[20]

Today, the global literacy rate stands at 91 percent among young people and 86 percent for adults; in 1990, just 61 percent of the world could read or write.[21] For young girls, the story is even more positive. In South Asia, in 1990, the girls' literacy rate was 49 percent, and an average of 74 girls compared to 100 boys were in primary school; today, the rate is 85 percent, and the enrollment ratio stands at 103 girls for every 100 boys.[22] Across all developing countries, girls are less likely than boys to repeat grades or drop out of school. This has helped to promote steady advances in female labor-force participation (for both formal and informal work).[23] Today, a previously unimaginable percentage of young boys and girls around the world are being educated. This both improves lives and, once again, makes the world a safer place, since countries with higher education levels are less likely to find themselves mired in armed conflict.[24]

Two MDGs were aimed at decreasing child mortality and improving maternal health. This has led to notable increases in vaccination rates that have reduced the number of children felled by preventable diseases by more than seven million. This decline has helped cut the under-five child mortality rate in half since 1990. That means that every year, 272,000 children who two or three decades ago would have died are alive today.[25] Here, enhanced access to education has had an enormous impact, since increases in education levels for women strongly correlate with reduced levels of childhood mortality.[26] In the same period, maternal mortality rates have dropped globally by 45 percent, with the sharpest decline occurring from 2000 to 2005.[27] This means that in 2017, more than 136,000 mothers who would have died a couple of decades ago are alive and able to help raise their children. Finally, the increased availability of family planning options cut the number of unintended pregnancies around the world by 44 percent between 1990 and 2014.[28]

An MDG focused on combating HIV/AIDS, malaria, and other infectious diseases has been similarly transformative. Since 2000, new HIV infections have dropped 45 percent around the world, and more than thirteen million AIDS-related deaths have been averted.[29] Additionally, tuberculosis prevention and treatment saved an estimated fifty-three million lives, increased measles immunizations prevented more than twenty million deaths between 2000 and 2016, and polio has largely been eradicated. There were just eleven active cases of the disease as of July 2018.[30] An oral polio vaccine—delivered with just two drops—and the necessary funding to make it widely available had, as of 2014, saved the lives of more than 650,000 people over the previous twenty-five years.[31] In March 2018, South Sudan announced that it had eradicated guinea worm, a parasitic illness that causes agonizing and incapacitating pain. In 1986, the disease afflicted three and a half million people in the developing world. In 2017, the number had fallen to thirty, and by May 2018, there were just three reported cases.[32] According to the Carter Center, which has been at the forefront of the guinea-worm eradication effort, close to eighty million cases of the illness have been averted over the past thirty years.[33]

Improved access to safe drinking water and basic sanitation has been another target of the MDGs. The expanded international commitment to these issues has helped more than a fifth of the current global population (1.3 billion people) gain access to sanitation since 2000.[34] In addition to saving the lives of 340,000 children who used to die from diarrhea because they were exposed to dirty water, improved sanitation also keeps children in school instead of sick at home. Even better, children with access to clean drinking water are in better shape physically, cognitively, and even socially.[35]

Nutritional advances have come so quickly and been so significant that public health officials now express concern over what is known as the "double burden of malnutrition," in which developing countries are simultaneously experiencing health perils generally associated with being overweight as well as those from undernourishment. Amazingly, obesity now poses greater harm globally than lack of adequate nutrition does, a phenomenon that would have been unimaginable even a quarter century ago.[36]

What is perhaps most remarkable about all this sweeping progress is that it was achieved at the same time that the planet's population grew by one and a half billion people, and global life expectancy increased by more than five full years since the MDGs were announced in 2000.[37]

Yet for all of the success of the MDGs (and also the full panoply of public health and human development changes), they are rarely mentioned in current foreign policy debates. Long-term positive trends go largely unreported, with the focus instead, almost exclusively, on "hard" security issues, such as coercive "redlines," nuclear weapons, terrorism, and drone strikes. Highlighting polio eradication, for example, does not drive internet clicks, justify a larger Pentagon budget, or motivate voters to support a more interventionist foreign policy. In the United States, good news about the world has little political salience, and it is simply not deemed newsworthy. The development scholar Laura Freschi pithily captured why this phenomenon matters. She observed in 2010 that more Americans believed that their president was a Muslim than had heard of the improvements in quality of life on our planet.[38]

Global Interconnectivity

While the global development community deserves enormous credit for many of the advances chronicled above, they drafted off of historic geopolitical changes. When the Cold War ended, the most resonant image was the fall of the Berlin Wall on November 9, 1989. The pictures of Germans chipping away at the barrier that had separated them for thirty-eight years—and the pictures of supposed enemies joyfully embracing—were poignant reminders of the universal desire for freedom. From that moment forward, hundreds of millions of people around the world—from Jakarta to Johannesburg and Managua to Minsk—began choosing their own leaders, holding them accountable, and voicing their opinions without the government interference they endured while living under dictatorship.

Yet, in the nearly thirty years since that epoch-making event, it is the economic bonds built between peoples and countries that have played the leading role in changing the human experience for the better. Communism, by its very nature, was an overwhelmingly closed economic system that purposely avoided commercial and business ties with capitalist nations. Even countries outside the Soviet and Chinese orbits often pursued economic policies that protected failing native industries; suppressed talented entrepreneurs, investment, economic innovation, and development; and, more generally, shut the door to the outside world.

But with the breakup of the Soviet Union and the gradual shift in China toward an export-driven economic strategy, all of that began to change. China transitioned along with its regional neighbors—Japan and South Korea and then Taiwan, Singapore, and Hong Kong. Even in noncommunist countries like India and Brazil, the end of the Cold War ushered out protectionist policies in favor of those seeking foreign investment, encouraging entrepreneurship, and creating new and vibrant trade links. Tariffs went down, and subsidies were slowly eased out, as countries worked to fashion themselves into more attractive investment destinations for global businesses.

The results are overwhelming. Foreign direct investment in the developing world has gone from $26 billion a year in 1990 to $653 billion in 2017, while private capital flows went from $91 billion to $1.2 trillion during the same time.[39]

Emerging economies are today deeply reliant on international trade not only as a means of development and job creation but also for attracting new capital investments and technical expertise. The result is stronger and more diversified economies, higher productivity, significant improvements in the welfare of women, and of course, reduced poverty.[40]

Recent trends, such as a decline in G-20 imports and new trade restrictions, suggest that this economic openness has slowed—the consequences of which have been hundreds of billions of dollars in lost global GDP.[41] In addition, while the process of globalization has contributed to higher living standards, it can contribute to greater income inequality and has given impetus to nativist and anti-immigrant movements in Europe and the United States. These are issues of serious concern, and if they go unaddressed in Western democracies, it could undermine the economic progress made over the past quarter century. Nonetheless, it is undoubtedly true that far more people have benefited from globalization than have been harmed.[42]

From the perspective of global security, the benefits are even more clear-cut because when a country trades with other states, it significantly diminishes the likelihood of conflict. Doubling a country's international commerce can reduce its risk of interstate violence by up to 30 percent, while countries with no regional trade ties are more than twice as likely as their highly integrated neighbors to experience a civil war.[43] Similarly, when a country experiences an increase in foreign direct investment, it significantly improves the welfare of women and reduces the likelihood that the country will participate in an armed conflict.[44] Being an active participant in today's globalized economy does not eliminate the possibility of a country going to war, as is evinced by America's ongoing military operations in Afghanistan, Iraq, and Syria. However, it is a fact that countries with increased economic interconnectivity are less likely to find themselves mired in conflict.

The Smartphone Story

The foregoing numbers, while impressive, do not fully do justice to the impact of economic integration over the past few decades. Visualizing the spectrum of changes that global interdependence has wrought is as simple as reaching into your pocket and pulling out your phone. That device that you use to talk to and text with your friends and family, get news, watch soccer or basketball clips, find out what the president of the United States just tweeted, or play *Words with Friends* offers one of the best possible explanations for how the world has become more connected, wealthier, and safer—and why it is likely to stay that way.

Since there are many smartphones, let's pick the one that is perhaps most ubiquitous: Apple's iPhone. Since its introduction in 2007, the iPhone has improved productivity, sped up communications, and allowed for more people to live and work remotely from their employers, customers, or clients. The iPhone is sold in more than 130 countries—a symbolic example of how the removal of trade barriers has spurred the rapid adoption of transformative technologies in both rich and poor countries. Some 725 million smartphones were sold in 2012, increasing to more than 1.5 billion by 2016, of which more than 600 million went to emerging-market customers from China, India, Brazil, and Indonesia.[45] Additionally, while mobile internet usage in Western countries is increasing fourfold annually, it is rising twenty-seven-fold in developing countries. There are 5.2 billion smartphone subscriptions globally, with 8.5 billion projected by 2023—and most of them will be in the developing world.[46] In many countries, there are actually more cell phones than people. In places like Afghanistan, one of the poorest countries in the world, the landscape is defined by omnipresent cell towers that now provide mobile services to more than 80 percent of the population.[47]

The iPhone contains components that have been developed and manufactured in multiple countries, which exemplifies how patent protections, increased foreign investment, and globalized supply chains have spread economic development across the globe. Take, for example, the iPhone X, which was released in fall 2017. Its accelerometer comes from the German firm Bosch, the display screen from the South Korea–based giant Samsung, the electronic compass from the Japanese firm Alps Electronic Company, and various radio-frequency components from Skyworks Solutions, a company located in a suburb of Boston, Massachusetts.[48] The iPhone X was assembled at a Taiwanese-owned Foxconn plant in southern China, which is emblematic of the inflow of low-wage manufacturing jobs that have taken the world's most populous nation from impoverishment to becoming among the most dynamic and steadily growing economies in the world.

The iPhone and the internet access it provides have further empowered hundreds of millions of people in developing nations. From Tunisia to Egypt's Tahrir Square and in multiple elections in fledgling democracies, ordinary citizens have used their cell phones to safeguard votes against electoral fraud and organize activists and pro-democracy demonstrators. Mobile technology and social media apps have made it possible for citizens to compile damning information about their governments, report abuses to news outlets outside their communities, and more easily publicize those abuses on a variety of social media platforms. This has even, ironically, become a problem for Apple itself. In 2012, after workers at the company's Foxconn factories in China documented and publicized poor working conditions there, Apple agreed to independent audits of the facilities by the Fair Labor Association. Here in America, cell-phone cameras have served as an invaluable tool for documenting and holding local police officers accountable for police shootings and gave critical impetus to the Black Lives Matter movement.[49]

Governments have also occasionally used mobile technology to expand democratic participation. In 2014, Libya's election commission worked with the firm Reboot to digitize the country's voter registration system, making it possible for voters (including diaspora Libyan citizens) to register for upcoming parliamentary elections on their phones. Considering that mobile penetration in Libya stood at nearly 150 percent, it was a move that made more sense than asking Libyans to register in person. More than 1.1 million citizens living in Libya and thirteen other countries were successfully signed up, and the system is still being used today to manage voter rolls. Libya remains fractured along ethnic and geographic lines, but the digital voting infrastructure remains in place if political leaders choose to reuse it in future elections.

Communication technologies are, of course, a double-edged sword, and governments have leveraged internet and mobile-phone penetration to spy on, influence, track, and harass their citizens. Journalists, activists, opposition-party leaders, and others have found their phones unknowingly implanted with spyware—often with the assistance of Western cybersecurity firms—that allows security services to monitor political opponents. Governments have also, at times, blocked or limited access to social media networks on the whims of political leaders. Yet technologically savvy and creative citizens are constantly developing workarounds to such spying—with encrypted communications, like Telegram and WhatsApp, as well as virtual private networks and other digital solutions that are not widely publicized. Government authorities have tried to control the flow of information and communications for centuries, and one should be under no illusion that this will not continue for the foreseeable future. Yet never before have so many people been more empowered to learn, connect, and collaborate in real time for relatively little cost.

Moreover, one does not need a cutting-edge smartphone to take advantage of the mobile revolution. Basic mobile phones are increasingly essential in those places where citizens do not have access to brick-and-mortar banks or any credit history. Mobile banking is benefiting hundreds of millions of new individuals each year by allowing them to document and save money, safely transfer funds, and pay down loans.[50] In Kenya, 96 percent of households use mobile phones and mobile money, mostly through a text-message-based payment system called M-PESA.[51] Researchers found that mobile banking makes it easier for breadwinners to provide for their families or for friends and family to send emergency funds immediately to each other when facing a health crisis. Between 2008 and 2014, more than 194,000 households were lifted out of poverty and 185,000 women were induced to enter the business world as a direct result of the societal shift provided by M-PESA.[52]

Similarly, smartphones are empowering a wide range of entrepreneurs in all sectors, from small business owners to farmers. For example, a free mobile app called MandiTrades allows farmers in India to receive real-time market information to help manage their crops, upload information about their produce right from the field, and finally connect with markets for sales.[53] In India, where one of the biggest challenges to cell-phone proliferation is getting the devices in the hands of women, wider access to smartphones will make it easier for women to find and apply for jobs outside the home and, as a result, increase their participation in the workforce.

Finally, that iPhone on which you play *Candy Crush Saga* and *Fortnite* is also saving lives. In Mozambique, for example, a free app alerts patients with HIV or tuberculosis when to take their medicine and reminds them of upcoming appointments.[54] Other programs send text messages and voice mails to new and expectant mothers, with basic advice on nutrition, health, and immunization schedules. In Bangladesh, the Mobile Alliance for Maternal Action has reached more than five hundred thousand pregnant women and new moms.[55] In Pakistan, targeted calls from provincial educational officials and local school council members increased the school enrollment rates for young girls by 12 percent.[56] More broadly, in classrooms around the developing world, tablets and cell phones are increasingly replacing books and notepads, as students can now download reading assignments directly, helping to improve literacy and promote reading.

There are hundreds, if not thousands, more stories that speak to the direct positive impact that mobile technology has had on global public health, the promotion of democracy, the improvement of educational outcomes, and the expansion of economic growth. But there is one behind-the-scenes component that makes all of this possible. What, for example, protects the patents used to develop the iPhone? The answer: international treaties (starting with the Paris Convention for the Protection of Industrial Property of 1884) that uphold patent rights and bolster international organizations (namely, the Patent Cooperation Treaty), which ensures that Apple's intellectual property rights are protected. What makes it possible for you to get on a plane, fly to China, and use a phone as if you were in your home country? Answer: several international agreements (starting with the International Convention for the Protection of Submarine Telegraph Cables, also of 1884) and industry groups (particularly the International Cable Protection Committee), which govern and share best practices for laying and maintaining undersea cables. This might seem minor, but keep in mind that these three hundred transoceanic cables stretching six hundred thousand miles are responsible for 95 percent of the world's internet, phone, and data traffic.

This overlapping web of reciprocal agreements and international understandings is unknown to all but a few Americans. But the ability to connect people, ideas, and markets from every corner of the earth is the direct result of an international system that is specifically constructed to further global cooperation. That iPhone in your hand tells the story of an interdependent and interconnected world that would have been unimaginable just a generation ago.

Why should Americans care that the world has become a far better place for far more people than ever before? Because a world that is more prosperous, healthier, better educated, and closely connected is a less chaotic and violent place—and more likely to stay that way.[57] Countries that are more democratic are also more politically stable and more open to trade and foreign investment that is likely to benefit American workers and consumers.[58]

Yet, despite all of these remarkable gains, there is significant work to be done. Eight hundred million people still live in extreme poverty, 160 million children under age five do not get enough to eat, and 61 million are not attending school. Only half of the 36.7 million who are living with HIV in developing regions receive antiviral treatments, and 884 million people still lack adequate drinking water.[59] These numbers are sobering, and they demand greater resources and a more concerted effort on the part of the international community.[60] But the fact that sizable problems remain cannot take away from the sustained progress that has been made.

Domestic politics, in part, explain why Americans remain unaware of these tremendous changes. Stating that the world is actually a pretty safe and much-better place to live is somehow a taboo, a sign of naïveté, or deeply insensitive in light of the real harms experienced by Americans. Yet politicians should recognize and celebrate the positive accomplishments that have improved the lives of so many people, and U.S. citizens should come to expect this from their elected leaders. All too rarely have U.S. "national interests" included advancing the health, well-being, and economic opportunities of humanity. But the top foreign policy priority for whoever sits in the Oval Office or controls Congress should be precisely that—not just because it is the right thing do but also because it makes America safer.

That Which Harms Us

At what point shall we expect the approach of danger? By what means shall we fortify against it? Shall we expect some transatlantic military giant to step the Ocean and crush us at a blow? Never! All the armies of Europe, Asia, and Africa combined, with all the treasure of the earth (our own excepted) in their military chest; with a Buonaparte for a commander, could not by force, take a drink from the Ohio, or make a track on the Blue Ridge, in a trial of a thousand years. At what point then is the approach of danger to be expected? I answer, if it ever reach us, it must spring up amongst us. It cannot come from abroad. If destruction be our lot, we must ourselves be its author and finisher. As a nation of freemen, we must live through all time, or die by suicide.

—*Abraham Lincoln, Lyceum Address, January 27, 1838*

Master Sgt. Mike Landsberry served tours in Kuwait and Afghanistan as a member of the Air National Guard. At home in Nevada, he worked as a high school math teacher and sports coach. Chris Kyle was a Navy SEAL sniper and decorated Iraq War veteran who had 160 confirmed kills of Iraqi insurgents—the most in U.S. military history. When Kyle returned home, he set up an organization to help troubled vets and wrote a best-selling memoir, *American Sniper*, which was adapted into an Oscar-nominated film, directed by Clint Eastwood.

Patrick Zamarripa enlisted in the Navy less than one month before 9/11 and saw combat during three tours in Iraq. When he left the service, he joined the Dallas Police Department. What did all three of these men have in common? They survived fighting the war on terrorism in Iraq and Afghanistan—but they could not survive America's deadly gun culture.

When a young student came to school armed with a Ruger nine-millimeter semiautomatic handgun that had been stored in his family's unlocked kitchen cupboard, Landsberry leapt into action. Relying on his military training, he tried to calm the young gunman and disarm him. But the twelve-year-old boy, who claimed he had been a victim of bullying, could not be reasoned with: he shot and killed Landsberry before shooting himself in the head in front of his classmates.[1]

Kyle, along with his friend Chris Littlefield, was trying to help a tormented former Marine corporal, Eddie Ray Routh, who suffered from posttraumatic stress disorder. Kyle and Littlefield brought him to a gun range, but Routh turned his weapon on the two men.[2] Zamarripa, who had recently begun an assignment as a bike officer in downtown Dallas, was killed when a gunman opened fire at the end of a peaceful Black Lives Matter protest. They are just three of the more than thirty-eight thousand Americans who die every year from gun homicides, accidents, or suicides.

The tragic and senseless deaths of these men highlight one of the great ironies in the way Americans think about threats and, in turn, national security. American politicians and a news media that adheres to an "if it bleeds, it leads" mind-set focus inordinately on violence that is random and rare and that can be blamed on "others," such as jihadists or terrorists. Far less attention is paid to nonterrorist acts of violence and systemic harms that occur on a daily basis in the United States—and cause far greater suffering. Even less attention is paid to the silent killers: noncommunicable diseases such as heart disease, respiratory illnesses, cancer, and diabetes that take hundreds of thousands of lives every year and are largely preventable.

Today the dominant "national security" narrative emphasizes the number of ships in the Navy and soldiers in the Army, as well as the perceived seriousness of overseas threats. The actual dangers all around us, which not only put our lives at risk but undermine our basic standard of living, barely register.

In 1983, the eminent international relations scholar Richard Ullman made the persuasive—and all too rarely heard—argument that discussions of national security would be more useful if they addressed "human security." Ullman argued that the greatest challenges to national security are twofold: those actions that threaten "drastically and over relatively brief span[s] of time to degrade the quality of life for the inhabitants of the state" and those that dramatically "narrow" the range of policy choices available to the government or state to private nongovernment entities (persons, groups, corporations)."[3] Limiting policy choices and undermining quality of life may not seem like pressing national security issues, but they go to the heart of how national power is built and retained. A country in which its citizens see their wages go down, their health get worse, their children receive a subpar education, and the infrastructure around them crumble can hardly feel secure—no matter how effective its armed forces may be or how many nuclear-tipped missiles it deploys.

Ullman's notion of an expansive view of national security is not merely the navel-gazing of an Ivory Tower–ensconced academic. It reflects the sentiments of the architects of America's post–World War II hegemony. Defense secretary James Forrestal, who is generally credited with coining the expression "national security," made clear that the term should take into account "our whole potential for war, our mines, industry, manpower, research, and all the activities that go into normal civilian life." He argued that the best weapon the United States had against communism was its economic leadership, and "the only way in which a durable peace can be created is by world-wide restoration of economic activity and international trade."[4]

The Eisenhower administration adopted this view, incorporating virtually every element of national power—from scientific research and transportation to education and military technology—into discussions of national security. Investments in these areas, from the National Highway System and the National Defense Education Act to the National Science Foundation and the Advanced Research Projects Agency (ARPA, later renamed DARPA for "Defense"), laid the foundation for America's technological and economic dominance over the Soviet Union during the Cold War. Indeed, DARPA is credited with funding and supporting the precursor to the internet.

Since then, America's political leaders have continued to make a fundamental link between economic power and national security as well as the quality of life for the American people. George H. W. Bush's National Security Strategy in 1993 noted, "Our national security requirements must be viewed in the context of our overall national well-being."[5] President Obama's 2010 National Security Strategy took a similar position: "Our national security begins at home. What takes place within our borders has always been the source of our strength, and this is even truer in an age of interconnection."[6] However, these words have rarely been translated into concrete action. Instead, it is the military inputs of national power rather than investments at home that receive predominant attention.

Thinking about national security in a broader manner would transform how we talk about foreign policy. It would mean prioritizing the physical protection of the American people, which would include their immediate safety, their health outcomes, their social and economic opportunities, and to quote the nation's founding document, their "pursuit of happiness." To do so would also mean focusing on the primarily domestic, human-induced behaviors or negligence that needlessly kill and injure millions of Americans each year. Indeed, the greatest threat to Americans does not originate in the Middle East or the South China Sea or the Hindu Kush but rather in communities and neighborhoods across the United States.

Near-Term Harms

The most pressing risk that Americans face has nothing to do with radical Islamic terrorism, allegedly "existential" threats from Russia or China, or even America's standing in the world. Rather, it is something that is overwhelmingly under their control: how they take care of themselves.

There are four specific behaviors that put Americans in the greatest danger: smoking, drinking, unhealthy diets, and lack of exercise. These risk factors directly increase the chances of being diagnosed with and dying from a noncommunicable disease (NCD), which includes cancers, respiratory illnesses, diabetes, and cardiovascular diseases. In all, NCDs take 2.3 million lives every year (and account for 90 percent of all deaths within the United States).[7] This preventable carnage costs the country $330 billion each year in health expenditures and lost productivity and makes life for the afflicted progressively worse.[8] These illnesses restrict normal daily activities, keep people home-bound, and make workers far less productive. They send health care costs skyrocketing and heighten anxiety and depression, particularly among family members and even the unborn, as NCDs alter the genes passed on to future generations as children of parents with NCDs are more likely to suffer from the diseases as well.

The striking tragedy of NCDs is that, unlike communicable diseases such as polio and many cancers, chronic diseases are essentially self-inflicted. The behavior and lifestyle choices that Americans make on a daily basis determine how vulnerable they will be to these illnesses.

When surveyed, Americans believe that they make about fifteen food and beverage choices every day, but in reality, it is more than two hundred.[9] When those choices include large portions of red meat, salt, and fat, it contributes to heart disease, cancer, and strokes. Or consider simply what people drink with each meal. Sugary beverages—such as soda, energy drinks, or sweetened iced tea—contribute directly to cardiovascular diseases (heart attacks and strokes), cancers, and diabetes that are estimated to kill over twenty-five thousand Americans every year.[10] Recent studies even suggest a link between such drinks and dementia.[11]

While every country with access to unhealthy foods, alcohol, and tobacco is confronted by the challenge of NCDs, the problem is particularly acute in the United States. According to a comprehensive 2013 report by the Institute of Medicine and the National Research Council, ominously titled *Shorter Lives, Poorer Health,* the United States—compared to other developed countries—ranks near the bottom on a host of health metrics.[12] These include infant mortality rates and low birth weight, as well as diabetes, heart disease, and chronic lung disease. More recent studies have found that children in the United States are three times more likely to be born dangerously premature and 76 percent more likely to die in the first year of life than are kids in other developed nations. For those who make it past the first year of life, they are 57 percent more likely to die before they reach the age of twenty. These declining health outcomes mean that since 1961, more than six hundred thousand American children have needlessly died.[13]

A big part of the problem—and there is really no nice way to say this—is that America needs to go on a diet.

Today, around 40 percent of Americans are considered obese.[14] That is more than double the average of all Organization for Economic Co-operation and Development (OECD) countries—the thirty-five-member club of advanced, democratic nations. Among children, the obesity rate stands at 18.5 percent—a 34 percent increase from just fifteen years earlier.[15] In all, more than two-thirds of American adults—and 31 percent of children—are overweight.[16] This problem has gotten steadily worse. In 1990, not one state in America had an obesity rate above 15 percent. By 2016, not one state had a rate below 22 percent, forty-six states were above 25 percent, and twenty-five states had a rate higher than 30 percent.[17] This rapid increase in the size of Americans has also led to a corresponding rise in the prevalence of hypertension, diabetes, and heart disease. It is small wonder that in 2016 life expectancy in the United States (78.6 years) declined for the second consecutive year—the first time that happened in the United States since a particularly virulent flu epidemic in 1962–1963.[18]

The consequences of America having a population so severely overweight go far beyond mortality. Obesity-related medical costs in the United States are estimated to run as high as $315 billion a year.[19] Obese children miss more days of school and have lower grade point averages than do their peers who are not overweight.[20] Obese workers are less productive, are more likely to be absent from work, and produce an estimated $70 billion annual drain on the economy.[21] They make less money, have greater economic anxiety and higher health care costs, and are also more likely to suffer from depression.[22] Not surprisingly, being overweight is the leading medical reason that otherwise-eligible recruits are turned away from military service, as one in four young adults are deemed ineligible.[23] Retired generals and admirals have in recent years described this epidemic as a national security priority, because it shrinks the pool of potential soldiers and sailors.[24] But this is a good example of how America's national security discussions tend to miss the forest for the trees. A smaller pool of military recruits is problematic, but it pales in comparison to the far more consequential health and economic implications—and the vast societal costs—of a national population that is so overweight. Indeed, if there is one thing that Washington could do to make Americans safer, extend their lives, reduce their anxiety, and improve the nation's economic performance, it would be to encourage and incentivize them to eat healthier.

Along the same lines, drug interdiction has been considered a national security issue for nearly four decades. President George H. W. Bush's 1990 National Security Strategy stated that the "international traffic in illicit drugs constitutes a major threat to our national security and to the security of other nations."[25] Less focus, however, has been given to the national security implications of drug use in America.

In recent years, America's problem with drugs has become a national catastrophe. In 2016, more than seventy-two thousand Americans died from a drug overdose—far more than the number of American soldiers killed in Vietnam and approximately twenty-four times the number of people killed on 9/11. Drugs now kill nearly as many Americans as guns and cars combined and are the third biggest killer in the United States.[26] The major reason for this startling increase in mortality rates is the increasing popularity and prescription of opioids and highly addictive prescription pharmaceuticals like hydrocodone and oxycodone. Indeed, two-thirds of overdose fatalities in 2016, or forty-two thousand deaths, were from opioids. That represents a 28 percent increase from just the previous year. As addicts get hooked, they begin to seek out bigger and better highs, and that means drugs like heroin and synthetic opioids like fentanyl, the latter of which killed twenty thousand Americans in 2016—a 540 percent increase in just three years.[27] One 2015 White House estimate put the economic costs of America's opioid crisis at $504 billion, or 2.8 percent of GDP—and the situation has worsened since.[28] Moreover, like NCDs, drug addiction alters the genes that are passed down to a user's sons and daughters. This matters because scientists estimate that genetic factors account for as much as 50 percent of a person's vulnerability to addiction.[29]

As this carnage has unfolded, annual federal drug-control spending has grown by 16 percent from 2013 to 2018, even as the Obama administration shifted the federal government's focus toward treatment and prevention and away from law enforcement and interdiction.[30] This suggests that despite the ever-worsening dangers of drug use—and the heightened media attention to the issue—the country has not adequately grasped its severity or fully adopted an agenda of prevention and recovery.

Beyond food, drink, and drugs, the most significant near-term harm to Americans—and one that is exceptional compared to other developed nations—comes from guns. The direct human costs of America's loose gun laws and the easy availability of weapons are staggering. In the past decade, more Americans have died in their homes and communities from gun violence than all the Americans who died fighting fascism in World War II.[31] More American civilians have died from gunfire since 1968 (1.5 million), than were killed in every war fought by the United States since 1775 (1.01 million).[32] While firearm deaths have fallen nationally—along with all major violent crimes over the past quarter century—38,658 Americans are killed and more than 80,000 are injured every year by guns.[33] The societal acceptance of guns, along with the ease with which Americans can purchase and carry them, means that one American is killed every fifteen minutes by a firearm. Here again, America is an inauspicious global leader. Of all the children killed by gunfire in developed countries between 1961 and 2010, 91 percent of them lived in the United States.[34]

Americans are painfully familiar with the mass shootings at Columbine, Sandy Hook, Orlando, and Parkland, as well as gang-related violence in Chicago. But the majority of gun deaths occur when Americans turn a weapon on themselves. Suicides in America have increased by 47 percent over the past fifteen years to nearly forty-five thousand a year in 2016, with almost half the result of a firearm.[35] Many of these deaths are easily avoidable. Suicide attempts are frequently not actual attempts to end one's life but instead are a proverbial cry for help. Indeed, when a person tries to take his or her own life by poisoning or drug overdose, the effort is fatal only about 2 percent of the time. When a gun is used, the fatality rate rises to 85 percent. Moreover, suicide is generally an impulsive decision. A majority of attempts take place almost immediately after someone has decided to take his or her life—and the chances that these attempts will end in tragedy are exponentially heightened by the presence of a firearm. Indeed, more than 90 percent of those who survive a suicide attempt will not try to harm themselves in the future.[36] Not surprisingly, a 2014 *Annals of Internal Medicine* study found that people with access to guns are more than three times more likely to kill themselves than those who do not have access to guns.[37]

What about the argument often promoted by the National Rifle Association (NRA) and gun advocates that firearms "protect" Americans from criminals and terrorists?[38] In reality, the opposite is true. Rather than serving as protection from "bad guys," having a gun at home doubles the chances that somebody connected to the gun owner will be killed—either by suicide, homicide, or accident. Most of the eleven thousand gun homicides that occur each year in the United States are committed by a family member, acquaintance, or friend, not a rampaging stranger.[39] The FBI has deemed only between two and three hundred of these shootings to have been "justifiable homicides."[40]

Then there are the most needless and negligent gun deaths, such as the two-year-old who found his mother's handgun in her purse and accidentally shot her to death while they were shopping at a Walmart in Idaho, or the eleven-year-old who was killed by her two-year-old brother after he picked up a .357-caliber handgun in their Philadelphia home, or the four toddlers who shot and killed themselves in the span of one week in April 2016. From 2015 to 2017, a child died every other day from an accidental shooting.[41] Even more remarkably—and this could truly only happen in America—in 2015 and 2016 at least one toddler every single week fired a gun that killed or wounded someone.[42] In fact, a toddler with a gun killed more Americans in 2015 than were killed in terrorist incidents. Every single one of these deaths was preventable and is the direct result of an adult leaving a loaded gun where a curious child can find it, rather than in a locked vault or with tamper-proof trigger locks.[43]

Beyond the senseless loss of life and the emotional devastation that comes from gun violence, there are the tremendous and underappreciated socioeconomic costs. A joint investigation by the economist Ted Miller and journalists from *Mother Jones* in 2015 estimated the annual price tag of gun violence in America to be at least $229 billion in medical costs, lost economic productivity, and diminished quality of life in the communities where violence occurs. The cumulative human and economic toll posed by firearms is a form of armed violence that is originating at home, not from terrorists abroad. There are precautionary approaches that could reduce this carnage, but pro-gun advocates and a national security mind-set that is seemingly inured to this constant drumbeat of violence and focuses instead, almost exclusively, on foreign threats have repeatedly stymied them.

Finally, there is a vast category of accidental deaths in the United States that, with minimal investment, could easily be prevented. More than thirty-five hundred people unintentionally drown each year in bathtubs, lakes, and pools, the latter of which mostly can be prevented with swimming lessons, four-sided fences, and adult supervision.[44] Eighty die from carbon monoxide poisoning, also preventable with twenty-dollar CO monitors and having heating systems annually checked by a technician, which costs about seventy-five dollars.[45] Around thirty people die every year from being crushed to death by televisions or furniture (80 percent of whom are under eight years old).[46] These are tragedies that can be easily prevented simply by anchoring flat-screen TVs and large pieces of furniture to walls, which is relatively inexpensive to do.[47] The number of deaths from these causes may seem small, but less than twenty people were killed by terrorism in the United States in 2017—and yet the United States spends billions every year to keep Americans safe from such attacks.[48]

Systemic Harms and Diminished Opportunities

Of course, when politicians and pundits talk about the risks from terrorism, their concerns generally run deeper than just lives lost. They claim that America's very way of life, its freedoms, and its liberties will be at risk if the terrorists have their way. In a 2017 speech, White House Chief of Staff John Kelly claimed, "We are under attack every single day . . . from people who hate us, hate our freedoms, hate our laws, hate our values, hate the way we simply live our lives."[49] His boss, President Trump, has gone even further. After a terrorist attack in Egypt in

May 2017, he declared, "Terrorists are engaged in a war against civilization—it is up to all who value life to confront & defeat this evil."[50]

But if that frame is applied to domestic threats that are not terrorism related, Americans' quality of life, political freedoms, economic opportunities, and social mobility are constantly being undercut by structural inequalities and systematic harms that receive far less attention.

These reduced opportunities directly impact America's actual national security and the country's ability to project power and influence globally. A great power like the United States that cannot ensure a safe environment for its citizens, severely underinvests in critical infrastructure, has a poorly educated citizenry compared to other advanced countries, fails to encourage economic growth and social mobility, and is wracked by partisanship and policy paralysis is one less capable of supporting international institutions, deterring interstate wars, and above all, competing effectively in global markets. In addition, the image of domestic political unrest and politicians trafficking in xenophobia diminishes the United States as a democratic, pluralistic example for the rest of the world. The foundation of U.S. power is the strength and well-being of its environment, education system, economy, and political institutions. When these are allowed to deteriorate, Americans suffer at home, and U.S. influence is undermined overseas. It is impossible to talk about national security today without talking about these domestic sources of American power—and they are increasingly rotting.[51]

Infrastructure

In the summer of 2015, national attention was drawn to Flint, Michigan, as city residents turned on their water faucets and were greeted by streams of brownish, smelly water. The failure to properly

treat the city's drinking water with the corrosion-inhibiting com-
pound orthophosphate had caused lead from aging pipes to contami-
nate the city's water supply. Further tests showed that lead levels in
many of the city's homes were far above normal for clean drinking
water. In some cases, the amount of lead in Flint homes was more
than twice what the Environmental Protection Agency (EPA) consid-
ers to be "toxic waste."[52] Civil and criminal lawsuits were filed, and a
federal investigation and congressional inquiry were launched. The
Flint situation, though an extreme example, is emblematic of a much-
larger public health problem: water is being delivered to millions of
homes across the United States via lead pipes. As a result, there is the
distinct possibility of multiple Flint-like crises. In fact, according to
data compiled by the EPA, forty-one states have unacceptable lead
levels in their drinking water.[53]

Inadequate infrastructure also takes an estimated $27 billion toll
on American businesses every year—which gets passed along to consumers in the form of higher prices for everyday goods.[54] Then there is
the direct human cost. When pavement conditions are allowed to
deteriorate and when streets crack and potholes form, Americans are
more likely to die in car crashes.[55] Here again, the United States dangerously lags behind its wealthy counterparts: 40 percent more Americans die when they get in a traffic accident than their European
counterparts do.[56]

America's rail and subway transit badly trails that of other developed nations. The Northeast corridor, which has a GDP equivalent to
the fifth-largest economy in the world and is responsible for one
out of every five jobs in the United States, still lacks consistent high-
speed rail service. Much of the essential equipment that keeps this vital transit artery functioning—including the key rail tunnels that
connect New York and New Jersey—is more than a century old and

in constant danger of breakdown. In three of the major metropolitan centers in the Northeast—Boston, New York, and Washington, DC—the subway systems are chronically delayed, which weakens economic productivity and increases anxiety and frustration among commuters. Indeed, New York City has been judged to have the "worst on-time performance of any major rapid transit system in the world."[57]

America's waterways are badly deteriorating too. Poorly functioning locks and dams cause needless hours of delay for farmers and manufacturers taking their products to market. On a one-hundred-mile passage of the Ohio River, more than 150 million tons of soybeans, wheat, scrap metal, and other assorted items travel through 1920s-era infrastructure, which adds on more than $640 million in additional transportation costs.[58] According to a report by the American Society of Civil Engineers, by the year 2020, 70 percent of dams in the United States will be more than fifty years old, and more than two thousand dams are considered "high-hazard" and in need of repair. The cost of repairing all these aging dams could run as high as $60 billion.[59]

It is not as if the policy steps required to roll back this decay and rebuild critical infrastructure are unknown. There is widespread bipartisan agreement that Congress and local governments should fund new building and repairs by issuing bonds; and with long-term interest rates at historically low levels, it has never been cheaper to make these necessary investments. The longer the United States waits to make these improvements, the greater economic dislocation it will lead to today and the more expensive repair costs will be down the road. In the interim, Americans will suffer, and U.S. economic performance will be further weakened relative to other advanced countries. While America's economic rivals move forward with the kind of infrastructure ventures that are essential in a modern twenty-first-century economy, the United States will find itself falling further and further behind. A country unwilling and unable to sustain the foundational elements of national economic power cannot remain an economic powerhouse forever.

Education

It is hard to think of a more important driver of economic competitiveness than a well-educated workforce. Indeed, there is a rule of thumb among economists that a one-year increase in any country's average level of schooling corresponds with a 3 to 4 percent increase in long-term economic growth.[60] Yet, here again, America trails the rest of the developing world—and badly so. America's second-class schools, particularly primary and secondary, are inadequately educating the next generation of young people, who will struggle to compete with workers in other developed countries. Indeed, in global rankings last done in 2015, compared to thirty-four other advanced OECD countries, the United States was twentieth in reading skills, nineteenth in science, and thirty-first in math.[61] According to the National Assessment of Educational Progress, in 2015 average math scores for fourth and eighth graders declined for the first time in twenty-five years. The study found that just a quarter of twelfth graders were proficient or advanced in math. Only 22 percent of the same students reached the same level in science.[62] This record of failure is happening at the same time that America's federal, state, and local governments spend more money per student than practically any other country in the world.[63]

America's poor educational outcomes are also influenced by its high (and increasing) rate of income inequality and low rate of social mobility. In 2014, only 30 percent of twenty-five- to sixty-four-year-olds had attained a higher level of education than their parents had, which is a key indicator of upward mobility. This rate is one of the lowest levels among OECD countries.[64] One particularly alarming OECD survey found that when it comes to literacy, math, and technical skills, "American adults lag well behind their counterparts in most other developed countries in the mathematical and technical skills needed for a modern workplace." Young adults ranked worse in the survey, though even middle-aged Americans are "barely better than middle of the pack in skills."[65] Cumulatively, this indicates that Americans preparing to enter the workforce are not receiving the kind of education or learning the type of skills that will ensure they have greater economic success than their parents did. One of the core principles of the "American Dream" has long been that children will do better economically than their parents. Today in America that is no longer true.

Economic Inequality and Social Mobility

These troubling education numbers have a dangerous ripple effect on the quality of life for millions of people. Americans who cannot find good-paying jobs to care for their families and who have little prospect for social mobility are at greater risk of being afflicted by a host of social ills. They are more likely to live in unstable homes, to suffer from depression and anxiety, and to fall victim to drug and alcohol addiction. It is no exaggeration to say that this lack of opportunity is killing Americans.

In 2016, Princeton University economists Angus Deaton and Anne Case began studying the death rates of forty-five- to fifty-four-year-old groups in the developed world. They made a harrowing discovery: while such rates were falling for nearly all other groups, they unexpectedly rose for white men and women living in the United States. The most marked increases were experienced by those who had a high school education or less, and the causes of death spoke to a larger sense of hopelessness: drug overdoses, suicide, and chronic liver diseases and cirrhosis tied to alcoholism. Had the white mortality rate continued declining at the same pace that it had during the 1980s, nearly half a million deaths would have been avoided between 1999 and 2013. As Deaton and Case observed, "This figure is comparable to the number of deaths caused by the AIDS epidemic in America."[66]

While the cause of this turn of events is hotly debated, it hardly seems coincidental that this unfolding horror is happening at the same time that the social safety net has frayed, obesity rates have increased, wage growth has stagnated, and the nation's schools have underperformed. Many Americans, it seems, have lost faith in the idea that they can move up the rungs of the country's economic ladder.

A 2016 McKinsey Global Institute report offered compelling evidence that these perceptions are well founded. The report found that between 2005 and 2014, real incomes in the United States stagnated or fell for 81 percent of all households.[67] The United States has one of the highest national poverty rates in the world and the second-highest child poverty rate among OECD countries, and by some estimates, approximately half of all Americans between the ages of twenty-five and sixty will find themselves at some point living at or below the poverty line. Even as the U.S. economy has steadily grown since 2000, wage growth has not kept up, and household income has declined. Jobs in low-wage, low-skill occupations are plentiful, while those in middle-wage business have shrunk. Part of this is a result of automation and certainly also the de-unionization of the American workforce, which has made it harder for workers to fight for higher wages and better benefits.[68]

Whatever the reasons, it should hardly come as a surprise that a 2017 poll found that more than half of adults believed that the next generation of Americans would be worse off financially.[69]

Ironically, while it is middle-aged whites who have seen the most dramatic shift in death rates, black and Hispanic households are in far worse shape. According to a 2017 analysis of Federal Reserve data, the median wealth for white families in 2016 was $171,000, compared to $20,600 for Hispanics and just $17,100 for blacks.[70] After the Great Recession, this racial disparity only became more severe: while median wealth of white households increased by 2.4 percent from 2010 to 2013, that of black and Hispanic households fell 33.7 percent and 14.3 percent, respectively.[71]

Not surprisingly, America lags behind other developed countries in social mobility. A 2014 study that measured the probability of somebody ascending from the bottom fifth income level to the top fifth over his or her lifetime found that a Danish child is 35 percent more likely to do so than an American child and that a Canadian child is 55 percent more likely. The authors note accurately and depressingly, "the chances of achieving the 'American Dream' are considerably higher for children in Denmark and Canada than those in the United States."[72]

For people at the top of the economic ladder, however, things have been quite different. Since the 1970s, wealthy Americans have become increasingly richer, more secure, and more disconnected from the vast majority of Americans. In 2014, the top 1 percent of all households—slightly more than one million homes—earned 20.2 percent of all the income earned in America, which is the highest percentage since the Great Depression.[73] To put it more starkly, the top 1 percent earns twenty-five times more than the bottom 99 percent.[74] In modern America, the rich are getting richer, the middle class is treading water, and the poor have little hope of fully escaping poverty.

While Americans seem largely inured to the extraordinary want in their own country, others are taking notice. In the fall of 2017, Philip Alston, the United Nations special rapporteur on extreme poverty and human rights, spent two weeks touring the United States and in a harrowing report concluded that "the United States is one of the world's richest, most powerful and technologically innovative countries; but neither its wealth nor its power nor its technology is being harnessed to address the situation in which forty million people continue to live in poverty."[75]

Political Paralysis

All this data might beg an obvious question: what does this have to do with national security? The answer is that there is a growing body of economic research that suggests widening income gaps negatively affect economic performance and productivity, which are the foundations of national power. Economists at the International Monetary Fund have found that in countries with greater income inequality, that inequality is "robustly associated" with longer growth spells.[76] In other words, the less inequality, the more likely a country is to sustain its economic growth. But one does not need a raft of statistics to see the dangers of an ever-widening chasm between the rich and poor and ever-diminishing opportunities for advancement. When workers lose hope that they can get to a place of economic security and get out of the cycle of living paycheck to paycheck, it is inevitable that their morale will suffer and Americans will be more likely to make poor economic decisions—or be too afraid to start a new business and become entrepreneurs.

As was evident in the 2016 campaign and the election of President Donald Trump, "economic anxiety" can lead Americans to embrace political scapegoating and demagoguery that further frays the nation's already-tattered social fabric. An economic system that puts so much power into the hands of so few and a political system that allows the wealthiest Americans to have the greatest access to political leaders also ensure that those groups' interests will receive the greatest focus and attention in the halls of government.

Of course, there is no requirement that the federal government should be so uninterested in the myriad signs of national decline. Yet it is hardly debatable that many of the domestic threats, risks, and systemic harms just documented have been allowed to worsen simply because of the apathy and negligence of America's elected leaders. In an increasingly polarized political environment where compromise has become associated with capitulation, political gridlock is one of the biggest reasons for Americans to be concerned about their country's decline. With the Republican Party wedded to an ideological position that rejects nearly any federal initiative to improve educational outcomes, guarantee health care access, or strengthen the social safety net—and indeed prefers to slash such programs—there is little near-term hope for tackling these challenges. The 2017 passage of a massive $1.5 trillion tax cut that delivers disproportionate benefits to the nation's wealthiest citizens and substantially increases the nation's budget deficit will make it that much harder to tackle the country's numerous domestic challenges. The most likely outcome from the vats of red ink projected to result from the legislation will be calls for spending cuts, particularly for social insurance programs like Social Security, Medicare, and Medicaid that represent a large percentage of federal spending.

Washington's political paralysis and toxic partisanship themselves also pose a more direct national security challenge to Americans. Research shows that political instability inhibits cross-border flows into the developing world, scaring off investors and tourists alike. According to the Political Conflict Index (PCI), which was developed by the Federal Reserve Bank of Philadelphia, for years there was little change in political disagreement between Republicans and Democrats. Suddenly, in 2010, partisan conflict increased more than 50 percent, spiking during a federal government shutdown at the end of 2013. This post-2010 increase in political discord, say PCI researchers, resulted in a 25 percent decrease in foreign direct investment into the United States.[77]

Gridlock also hits Americans in their pocketbooks. In October 2013, when Congress failed to meet a deadline to pass spending legislation, the government shut down for seventeen days, resulting in a 0.3 percent dip in GDP growth and the loss of 120,000 private-sector jobs.[78] The shutdown came after two years of congressionally created fiscal crises that undermined consumer confidence and cost the economy almost a million jobs.[79] By way of comparison, the attacks on the World Trade Center cost New York City 146,100 jobs.[80] In other words, deep ideological divisions in Washington, DC, have wrought far greater economic damage than the terrorist attacks on 9/11 did.

It's Not All Bad . . .

All of this sounds pretty bad, right? But not all hope should be lost: if Congress and state legislatures wanted to adequately address national security challenges at home, the roadmap to doing so is readily available. We know how commonsense prevention works and have repeatedly seen that when proper attention is paid and resources allocated, millions of lives can be saved. Heart disease, for example, may still be the leading cause of death in the United States, but it kills far fewer Americans (1.6 for every 1,000 Americans today) than it did at its peak (5 per 1,000 in 1969).[81] While the reasons for this life-saving decline are complex, it is generally understood that better treatments, the adoption of preventive tools including public education campaigns, and the collapse of smoking rates have each played key roles.[82]

Tobacco is the most statistically significant risk factor for an NCD and has prematurely killed twenty-one million Americans in the past half century. It remains the leading preventable cause of death within the United States (and throughout the world).[83] Yet smoking in the United States has fallen by more than half since 1980—from 33 percent of adults then to just 15 percent in 2016.[84] This did not happen by chance but instead is the result of simple and relatively inexpensive smoking prevention and cessation programs.

For example, when cities and states began raising the price of cigarettes by putting new taxes on each pack, it contributed to a significant drop-off in smoking rates.[85] According to one recent study, a one-dollar price hike on cigarettes was associated with a 20 percent increase in people quitting smoking and a 35 percent reduction in the average number of cigarettes smoked each day by the heaviest smokers. Other studies find that creating smoke-free buildings, banning smoking in restaurants and bars, and public education programs warning about the significant dangers of tobacco usage have a modest impact as well.[86]

The result is a virtual collapse in the number of respiratory and cancer deaths from smoking. This has single-handedly saved more than eight million Americans' lives since 1964—or 167,000 people per year. The quality of life for countless others who have quit smoking has been dramatically improved. No longer are they poisoning family members with secondhand smoke, and their health care costs have almost certainly declined.[87] The success in reducing smoking rates shows that when a public health challenge is prioritized, the impact can be dramatic—and often at a minimal cost.

Similar progress has also been made in reducing automobile deaths, the number of which has fallen dramatically in the past forty years. Seat-belt laws, mandated air bags, vehicle designs that prioritize safety, and reduced drunk-driving rates have saved countless lives. Since 1975, the number of people killed in car accidents has fallen by half, from 20.6 deaths per 100,000 then to 11.6 per 100,000 in 2016.[88]

Nonetheless, thirty-seven thousand people are killed every year in car accidents.[89] Many of these fatalities are the result of poorly maintained roads or human error, such as texting and drowsiness, and could easily be prevented. In fact, half of drivers and passengers killed on America's roads die because they were not wearing a seat belt.[90] Vehicle deaths could be further reduced with more comprehensive public policy efforts, such as New York City's "Vision Zero" campaign, which has set a goal of no traffic deaths or serious injuries. This initiative is focused on emphasizing safety over convenience when building roads and intersections, heightening public awareness, and imposing stricter punishments for drunk drivers or speeders. This effort could not be timelier, considering that almost six thousand pedestrians are killed every year on America's roads—and that number has actually increased an astounding 46 percent since 2009.[91]

The greatest hope for reducing these deaths, however, is coming from car companies that are developing technologies that can drastically reduce road accidents. This includes sensors that can detect when a car is drifting from its lane and automatically correcting the car's route, as well as those that can identify an oncoming obstacle, alert the driver, and automatically brake if the driver does not react in time. With the ongoing development of driverless cars, we may even reach a point in our lifetimes when vehicular deaths are practically eliminated.[92]

Other efforts could be made to immediately prevent needless deaths caused by human misjudgments or mistakes. Every year, for example, medical errors—such as misdiagnosis, overtreatment, or acquired infections in hospitals—kill as many as 250,000 Americans.[93] While this figure is not without controversy, due to the difficulty in attributing deaths to such errors, even more conservative estimates of error-associated deaths top 175,000—an astonishingly high number that gets little public attention.[94] Hospitals, which should be the safest environments possible, threaten everyone who enters them for treatment. Take one unfortunate patient in Saint Vincent Hospital, outside Boston, who had a perfectly healthy kidney removed because of a patient identification error.[95] Significantly reducing this leading cause of death for Americans would come at a fraction of the cost that the government currently spends to fight terrorism. Commonsense measures like checking patients' full names and birth dates, avoiding diagnostic errors, assuring better hygiene through widespread use of disinfectants, and administering correct medications could save tens of thousands of lives.[96] According to a 2016 *Journal of the American Medical Association* study, 32,000 deaths could be prevented every year simply by encouraging male physicians to adhere to the same clinical guidelines and evidence-based practices as their female counterparts.[97] Yet, the past two years, congressional Republicans have tried to repeal the Affordable Care Act (also known as Obamacare), even though this legislation had reduced the number of "hospital-acquired conditions" by 21 percent, saving more than 125,000 lives.[98]

The goal of this book is to change how Americans think about the world and to fully appreciate the consequences of foreign-threat inflation. Doing so requires broadening the very conception of "national security" by acknowledging that Americans face far more lethal and preventable threats at home. Those dangers diminish not just Americans' mortality but also their quality of life, opportunities for achievement, and economic productivity. These attributes represent the very foundations of national power, and when they are allowed to weaken, America itself is weakened. The threats, systemic harms, and reduced opportunities documented in this chapter could be far more effectively addressed—and more cheaply—than America's open-ended seventeen-year (and counting) war on terrorism. What is lacking is the national recognition that these domestic threats are indeed national security threats and as such deserve the political attention and resources to counter them.

The Grand American Tradition of
Threat Inflation

This war is different than the other wars we've been in. If we leave, they will follow us here.

—*President George W. Bush, defending the Iraq surge, October 2006*

In March 1947, less than two years after the bloodiest conflict in human history, President Harry Truman faced a herculean political task—convincing Americans to go back on a war footing. Tensions between the United States, its Western allies, and the Soviet Union were rising. Soviet support for communist rebels in Turkey and Greece had become a rising flashpoint between the two sides. The British government, which had been picking up the bill for economic and military aid to both governments, informed the U.S. State Department that it could no longer shoulder the responsibility and needed the United States to step in. In effect, the torch of global hegemony—and anticommunism—was being passed from the British Empire to the United States.

Truman wanted $400 million ($4.4 billion in today's dollars) from Congress to assist the two countries and prevent the "collapse of free institutions and loss of independence" in the face of Soviet interference. Americans, however, were exhausted by war, and Congress had little appetite for sinking more resources into overseas entanglements. The chairman of the Senate Foreign Relations Committee, Sen. Arthur Vandenberg, reportedly gave Truman the best advice he could muster for how to win Americans' support: "scare hell out of the country."[1] The president willingly complied.

Appearing before a joint session of Congress, Truman told the American people, "nearly every nation must choose between alternative ways of life": Soviet-sponsored communism or U.S.-backed freedom. To counter potential communist gains in southeastern Europe, Truman evoked the specter of an inevitable spread of communism to all corners of the globe. In what soon would be labeled the "Truman Doctrine," the president offered a groundbreaking and all-encompassing vision for U.S. foreign policy that would, in time, come to form the foundation of postwar American politics. "It must be the policy of the United States," said Truman, "to support free peoples who are resisting attempted subjugation by armed minorities or by outside pressures."[2]

To sell this radical peacetime change in America's role in the world, Truman took dramatic license. He argued that "totalitarian regimes imposed upon free peoples, by direct or indirect aggression, undermine the foundations of international peace, and hence the security of the United States. The free peoples of the world look to us for support in maintaining their freedoms. If we falter in our leadership, we may endanger the peace of the world. And we shall surely endanger the welfare of this nation."[3] Rather than talk about U.S.-Soviet rivalry in geopolitical terms, Truman turned the superpower conflict into an ideological and existential one.

Truman's stark speech, combined with an expansive public relations effort, worked. Public opinion polling showed that a majority of citizens supported the spending request. Vandenberg quickly shepherded it through Congress, where it passed by one hundred votes in the House and forty-four in the Senate.[4] Even after signing the legislation, Truman continued defending it as essential to protecting the American homeland, telling a *New York Times* columnist, "If Russia gets Greece and Turkey, then they would get Italy and France and the iron curtain would extend all the way to Western Ireland. In that event we would have to come home and prepare for war."[5]

The Political Tradition of American Vulnerability

Truman's speech had enormous long-term consequences for U.S. foreign policy and American politics. It created a narrative of fear that defined post–World War II America. From the "missile gap" of the late 1950s to claims made during the Vietnam War that if the communists won in Southeast Asia, then America should "throw in the towel in the area and pull back our defenses to San Francisco," to campaign ads in 1984 warning of Soviet bears in American forests, threat inflation became an essential tool for selling an internationalist—and interventionist—foreign policy to the American people. After the Soviet Union disappeared, however, threat inflation did not fade away. It found new targets and narratives, most pungently in the Bush administration's evoking of the terrifying image of mushroom clouds over American cities to justify the war in Iraq.[6]

Many of the foreign threats detailed in this chapter were not, at the time, illusory or fabricated by government officials, military leaders, or media commentators. Throughout much of the Cold War, the threat of superpower conflict was real, and Soviet gains had the potential to undermine America's political and economic interests. What was deceptive, however, were the depictions of urgency and potential severity that these threats allegedly represented. During the Cold War and long after, threats to America never seemed to decrease in likelihood or consequence. Instead, Americans and their way of life only became more at risk and more susceptible to intimidation by overseas dangers. The players might have changed—from communists and terrorists to undocumented immigrants and gang members today—but the game remained the same.

This habitual foreign-threat inflation is a combination of the political and the parochial. For Republicans, saying that the world is a bubbling cauldron of potential hazards played to the party's traditional political advantage on national security issues—one that dates back to the earliest years of the Cold War. (Ironically, before Pearl Harbor, Republicans were seen as the party of isolationism and the most strident opponents of U.S. military involvement in World War II.)

For Democrats, put on the defensive by communist gains in the late 1940s and early 1950s while a Democrat slept in the White House, adopting alarmist rhetoric was protection against relentless Republican attacks of "weakness" on national security issues. Playing down fears by either party would lead to accusations of insufficient "toughness" in confronting potential dangers—and even greater risks if one of those threats ended up being tragically realized. Adopting the position that America can never let down its guard became the safest and thus default political stance of both political parties—and a surefire way to build support for military action and/or increased defense spending.[7]

But this bipartisan practice is about more than just electoral politics. For any president intent on maintaining an internationalist foreign policy, it is essential to convince Americans that without the country's web of security alliances, trade agreements, participation in multilateral arrangements, and vast power-projection capabilities, the U.S. homeland would be vulnerable to foreign aggression and influence. After all, a democratic country, surrounded by peaceful neighbors and two oceans, that devotes as much attention and money to national security as the United States does during peacetime is unnatural in the history of global affairs. Perhaps if Washington explicitly ran a global empire that regularly seized territory and plundered natural resources, it would be easier to explain. But American leaders are primarily focused on maintaining an international system that furthers the nation's interests in ways that are often difficult to quantify.

While "maintaining the international system" might persuade policy wonks, for ordinary Americans this mantra does not quite have the same power. Suggesting that anything less than an active U.S. global presence will imperil their security is an easier lift. As the United States expanded its global role, the definition of its national interests expanded along with it—so much so that events in far-flung corners of the world that most Americans had never heard of were increasingly depicted to be as important to national security as protecting the homeland from attack. Whether or not one believes that it is essential for America to maintain an outsized international role, one thing is certain: without threat inflation, the case for American internationalism and a $600 billion military budget is that much harder to make.[8]

Other groups in what we call the Threat-Industrial Complex— from defense contractors and think tankers to military officials and the media—push an agenda of fearmongering, but the incessant exaggeration of foreign threats to America begins at the top, from the president to Congress and further down the spectrum of political power. Indeed, the entire infrastructure of America's national security state—both inside and outside government—is geared toward overseas activism and maintaining a hair-trigger defense against potential threats.

Threat inflation in U.S. foreign policy discourse is not new, nor is it a post-World War II phenomenon.[9] In 1898, the sinking of the USS *Maine* in Havana harbor, which was likely caused by an onboard coal fire, was employed as a pretext by President William McKinley—and a frenzied print media—for the Spanish-American War. "Remember the Maine, to Hell with Spain!" was the national rallying cry.[10] Yet foreign-threat inflation since World War II has been vastly more consequential, due to the global scope of U.S. interests. That every president since has willingly embraced it is evidence of how routine and politically effective it can be.

Truman and the Early Cold War

Truman's speech to Congress in 1947 recast U.S. foreign policy as an ideological competition between communism and the West. But it did not directly presage the twilight struggle between the United States and the Soviet Union that unfurled over the next forty years. Truman had used fear-based arguments to build support for containing communism in Europe, but the United States still trod on the international stage with a relatively light peacetime footprint. A series of events in the summer and fall of 1949 and then a year later in the summer of 1950 changed the political stakes and pushed Truman in a more militarized direction.

First came the Soviet Union's first-ever nuclear weapons test in August 1949. The nationalist government in China fell to communist rebels weeks later. The former event raised the specter of a potentially existential threat to the U.S. homeland; the latter suggested that the United States was increasingly on the defensive in the face of communist gains. At home, those who were close to the Chinese nationalist leadership excoriated Democrats for being the party responsible for "losing China" to the Reds.

But it was the Soviet-backed North Korean soldiers streaming across the thirty-eighth parallel into South Korea in the summer of 1950 that served as the final straw. Even though Korea fell outside the original focus of U.S. containment policy—the European theater—Truman quickly decided on a military response and dispatched U.S. troops to the Korean peninsula. In the wake of the "who lost China" debate and the Soviet Union's detonation of the bomb on his watch, Truman understood the huge political risks of appearing flat-footed in the face of clear communist provocation.[11] "Free nations have learned the fateful lesson of the 1930s," he told the American people in a radio address on July 19, 1950. "That lesson is that aggression must be met firmly. Appeasement leads only to further aggression and ultimately to war."[12]

Three years after sounding the alarm about the fate of western Europe, Truman warned that events in Asia could also have a ripple effect on U.S. interests elsewhere. "The fact that communist forces have invaded Korea is a warning that there may be similar acts of aggression in other parts of the world," he said. "The free nations must be on their guard, more than ever before, against this kind of sneak attack. It is obvious that we must increase our military strength and preparedness immediately. We know that the cost of freedom is high. But we are determined to preserve our freedom—no matter what the cost."[13] Truman called for higher taxes, steps to "prevent inflation," and an "increase [in] the production of goods needed for national defense." He told the American people, "We must plan to enlarge our defense production, not just for the immediate future but for the next several years." From 1950 to 1953, military spending nearly tripled, from 5 percent of GDP to 14.2 percent.[14]

By portraying any communist gains as direct threats to the United States, Truman made it more difficult for him or any other president to resist the urge to respond to future Soviet or communist provocations. If "totalitarian regimes . . . undermine the foundations of international peace, and hence the security of the United States," as he said at the time, how could the United States justify anything less than a strong response to communist aggression?

Truman's choice to defend South Korea was defensible, but it was his next decision that proved disastrous—allowing the U.S. commander in Korea, Douglas MacArthur, to take U.S. troops across the previous border between North and South Korea in an effort to destroy the North Korean army and unify the peninsula. This action, which brought U.S. troops up to the Yalu River, sparked a Chinese counteroffensive that ensured the war dragged on for nearly three more years at a loss of more than thirty-six thousand American lives and an estimated two and a half million Koreans. Truman's support for MacArthur's dangerous offensive had been informed less by a desire to unify Koreans and more by the political fear that to settle for partial victory in the Korean peninsula would open him up to charges of weakness in fighting communism. As was so often the case during the Cold War, raising the specter of international threats had a boomerang effect.

Yet Truman's tough stance on Korea did him and the Democrats little good. During midterm congressional elections in 1950, Republicans branded them "appeasers" and "soft on communism." In California, Rep. Richard Nixon famously labeled his opponent in the state's Senate race, Helen Gahagan Douglas, the "Pink Lady"—all the way down to her "pink underwear." She lost by nearly twenty points on Election Day. Across the country, prominent Democrats, including the Senate majority leader Scott Lucas and others in Utah, Maryland, and Washington, also were turned out of office.

Truman was not untouched by the fallout from Korea. His presidency was so discredited that by 1952 he had little political choice but not to seek reelection. The eventual Democratic nominee that year, Adlai Stevenson, was swamped by his opponent, Gen. Dwight D. Eisenhower, who had pledged to go to Korea and end the war. The lesson that should have been taken from Korea was that fighting an endless war with high American casualties would spark a political backlash. The conclusion drawn by Democrats was the opposite: only vigilance against the Soviet threat could protect them from Republican charges of being soft on "communism."

That mind-set received a boost from Wisconsin's junior senator, Joseph McCarthy. In February 1950, he famously declared in Wheeling, West Virginia, that the State Department was "infested with communists" and that he even had a list of these "card-carrying" members. The McCarthy-led witch hunts of the early 1950s had a profound and lasting political effect. Seemingly no charge made by McCarthy and his Republican allies failed to be given prominence by an increasingly rabid, anticommunist news media. It hardly mattered that the United States enjoyed an enormous military advantage against the Soviet Union or that communist "infiltration" in the United States—insofar as it existed—was the furthest thing from an existential threat to America. Both Democrats and Republicans came to learn that no political benefit could be gained from playing down the Red threat or, even worse, appearing soft on communism.

Other factors also played an increasingly critical role. As Fredrik Logevall and Craig Campbell note in their seminal Cold War history, *America's Cold War: The Politics of Insecurity*, a bipartisan infrastructure developed, with one clear goal—to sustain a national consensus of tough-minded anticommunism. "Many more powerful interests stood to benefit from a vigorous prosecution of the Cold War and from increased military spending—the armed forces themselves, civilian officials associated with defense issues, arms industrialists, labor unions associated with weapons industries, universities and businesses that benefited from military research. Few organizations—at least few powerful ones—had reason to fight such a rise."[15]

Rather than fight this new consensus, the political incentives swung in a different direction.

Eisenhower and Missile Gaps

In the fall of 1957, an internal review of U.S. nuclear weapons policy gave Democrats the chance to turn the tables on Republicans. The Gaither Report, as it became known, claimed that U.S. civil defenses were wholly unprepared for nuclear war and that the Soviet Union was gaining a wide advantage over the United States in nuclear missiles and warheads.[16] By December 1957, the "secret" report, egged on by leaked comments from intelligence analysts, particularly Air Force officials looking to increase congressional attention for their budget, sparked a public debate about the Soviets' apparent advantage and put Republicans on the defensive.[17]

The Eisenhower administration was pilloried—and not just by Democrats—as Republican hawks went after the president as well. There was one problem: the data were completely wrong. There was no missile gap. During the 1960 presidential campaign, the CIA estimated that the Soviets had 90 intercontinental ballistic missiles, while the United States had 108, with 30 more being deployed to Turkey. Later estimates concluded that the actual number of Soviet missiles was *three*.[18]

The entire episode, however, provided a rich irony. Eisenhower had focused throughout his presidency on increasing America's nuclear capabilities and, in turn, cutting spending on conventional forces. In his view, a buildup of tactical nuclear weapons and strategic bombers would be enough to deter superpower conflict and fulfill his goal of keeping government spending in check. Now he was being lambasted for allegedly leaving the United States vulnerable to nuclear attack. Eisenhower, however, was not blameless. In 1953, he had initiated a public relations effort of speeches and public service announcements ironically known as "Project Candor," which aimed to scare Americans into recognizing the dangers of a Soviet nuclear attack in order to make them more supportive of his nuke buildup.[19]

Sen. John F. Kennedy, the Democratic nominee for president in 1960, took the purported missile gap and ran with it. He argued that Eisenhower and Vice President Richard Nixon—Kennedy's opponent—had left America vulnerable. He called for increased defense spending and new vigilance in confronting the Soviets. It was an effective message, and it would not be left on the campaign trail. Kennedy famously declared in his inaugural address that America must be willing to "pay any price, bear any burden, meet any hardship, support any friend, oppose any foe to assure the survival and the success of liberty."[20]

Kennedy's tough talk had a profound impact on national security policy. After he took office—and the CIA informed him conclusively that no missile gap actually existed—Kennedy could hardly argue against funding for ultimately unnecessary long-range nuclear missiles. By December 1961, White House officials believed that 450 additional strategic missiles would be needed but recommended that the president ask Congress for 600. Secretary of defense Robert McNamara agreed but argued that the White House should actually request 950, because it was "the smallest number he could imagine asking Congress for and, in his words, 'not get murdered.' "[21] McNamara eventually asked, and Congress authorized, 1,000 strategic missiles.

By 1967, McNamara publicly acknowledged that the size of the force was excessive, stating, "current numerical superiority over the

Soviet Union in reliable, accurate and effective warheads is both greater than we had originally planned and in fact more than we require." Yet that same year, the number of strategic-delivery nuclear vehicles in the U.S. arsenal peaked at 2,268.[22] Fearmongering on the missile gap helped get Kennedy elected, but America was ultimately stuck with the price tag.

LBJ and the Vietnam Escalation

At the same time that Kennedy and Congress were vastly increasing spending on unnecessary nuclear weapons that made Americans no safer, his administration was facing a far-bigger set of questions about Vietnam. Kennedy's tough anticommunist rhetoric during the campaign and in his inaugural address placed him in a difficult political spot. He could either escalate U.S. involvement in Vietnam or face the political repercussions of allowing South Vietnam to fall to the communists. Tragically, he did not live long enough to decide. To the nation's great loss, Kennedy's assassination on November 22, 1963, brought Lyndon Baines Johnson to the Oval Office—a man for whom the political aspects of anticommunism came to define his decision-making on Vietnam.

Having seen firsthand the political backlash over the "who lost China" debate as a Senate leader, Johnson was convinced that if he "lost" in Vietnam—and it fell to the communists—the political catastrophe would doom his ambitious Great Society agenda. At no point did Johnson seriously consider leveling with the American people about Vietnam and making the case that a communist takeover there would not seriously threaten the United States. Nor did he consider the possibility that he could withstand the political firestorm that would come from failing to man the barricades in Southeast Asia.

Convinced that he had little political choice but to escalate in Vietnam, he fell back on fearmongering as the best tool for making the case to the American people.

Less than a year after taking to the campaign trail and confidently telling the American people that "American boys would not be sent 8,000 miles away to do what Asian boys should be doing for themselves," Johnson announced in July 1965 that he would be sending fifty thousand combat troops to Vietnam. "Why must young Americans, born into a land exultant with hope and with golden promise, toil and suffer and sometimes die in such a remote and distant place?" he asked Americans at a hastily convened midday press conference.[23] "The answer, like the war itself, is not an easy one," said Johnson, but in what would be a familiar refrain in the Cold War years, he reminded Americans of the supposed "lesson" from World War II: "retreat does not bring safety and weakness does not bring peace." According to the president, "We learned from Hitler at Munich that success only feeds the appetite of aggression. The battle would be renewed in one country and then another country, bringing with it perhaps even larger and crueler conflict."[24]

Johnson warned that the communists' goal in Vietnam, like Hitler's goal in Europe, was not just to conquer South Vietnam but "to defeat American power, and to extend the Asiatic dominion of Communism." If America restrained its commitment to the war, "then no nation can ever again have the same confidence in American promise, or in American protection. In each land the forces of independence would be considerably weakened," Johnson said. And it was not just the Far East at risk, as "an Asia so threatened by Communist domination would certainly imperil the security of the United States itself."[25] Johnson continued to employ this rhetoric throughout the conflict, claiming in February 1966 that stopping the Communists in South

Vietnam was vital, because if they were allowed to win there, it would "become easier and more appetizing for them to take over other countries in other parts of the world."[26] Johnson's warning was dire: "We will have to fight again someplace else—at what cost no one knows."[27]

In the fall of 1967, as support for Johnson's Vietnam policy declined, the president stuck to his guns. In a speech in his home state of Texas, he tied North Vietnamese aggression to the peace and security of the United States and "the entire world of which we in America are a very vital part."[28] He borrowed the words of Eisenhower and Kennedy and statements from Asian leaders on the risks of communist victory in Vietnam (though he failed to mention that many of these leaders were rejecting U.S. entreaties to send more troops to the war effort). He admitted that he could not be sure "that a Southeast Asia dominated by Communist power would bring a third world war much closer to terrible reality," but he had his suspicions. "All that we have learned in this tragic century," he said, "strongly suggests to me that it would be so." He made his case that the risks of not continuing the fight were simply too grave to tolerate: "As President of the United States, I am not prepared to gamble. . . . I am not prepared to risk the security—indeed, the survival—of this American Nation on mere hope and wishful thinking. I am convinced that by seeing this struggle through now, we are greatly reducing the chances of a much larger war—perhaps a nuclear war. I would rather stand in Vietnam, in our time, and by meeting this danger now, and facing up to it, thereby reduce the danger for our children and for our grandchildren."[29] Thirty-five years later, President George W. Bush used eerily similar language in making the case for preemptive war against Iraq: "We cannot defend America and our friends by hoping for the best," he told graduating cadets at the U.S. military academy at West Point. "If we wait for threats to fully materialize, we will have waited too long."[30]

In both conflicts, the costs of direct military action would out-weigh the price of inaction. By the time the U.S. war in Vietnam ended, 58,220 U.S. service members had given their lives.[31] Estimates of Southeast Asian fatalities—Vietnamese, Cambodian, and Laotian combatants and civilians—range from 3.1 to 4.8 million.[32] Casualties from U.S. munitions and in particular cluster bombs that remained after troops departed have taken another 220,000 lives in the years since the war ended. Potentially millions more bear the scars from defoliants like Agent Orange used by the U.S military during the conflict.[33]

The 2.8 million tons of bombs that the United States dropped on neighboring Cambodia—more than the United States dropped during World War II—helped to grow the Khmer Rouge movement, which eventually took power in 1975 and initiated a genocide that killed more than two million Cambodians in less than four years.[34] But perhaps the cruelest irony of two decades of U.S. involvement in the region is that Cambodia was the only other Far East country to be ruled by commu-nists after the fall of South Vietnam. The oft-stated threat of a domino effect in Asia—and the increased potential for global conflict and im-periled U.S. security—simply never materialized.

Nixon and the Temporary Détente

While the Vietnam War represented a moral and political disaster for the United States, one unseen benefit emerged from the conflict: a tamping down of Cold War rhetoric. President Richard Nixon, who succeeded Johnson in 1969, was an unlikely embodiment of this ten-dency. Throughout his political career, Nixon was one of the loudest and most assertive public figures stirring up the fears of Americans toward foreign threats. As president, he moved in a different direction. He eased relations with the Soviet Union through the policy of détente and most famously, in 1972, traveled to China to reestablish relations with the world's most populous communist state. Under Nixon, the United States began to step away from its all-encompassing global role of confronting communism everywhere (outside of the Soviet Union) and instead sought to share this burden with its allies.

Yet Nixon's transformation into a fear assuager was incomplete. At home, he depicted antiwar protesters as a threat to domestic security and asked for the help of America's "silent majority" in repelling them. Seeking a breakthrough in peace talks with the North Vietnamese, he publicly authorized the deployment of U.S. troops across the border into Cambodia in an effort to cut off supply lines to Vietcong insurgents in South Vietnam. In announcing the move, Nixon said he would not allow "the world's most powerful nation" to act "like a pitiful, helpless giant."[35]

Nixon only had to go so far in the direction of threat inflation, however. His earlier stridency about communist threats gave him the leeway to reach out to Moscow and Beijing without paying a significant political price at home. Indeed, Nixon planned his trip to China in February 1972 and a trip that same year to the Soviet Union to burnish his foreign policy bona fides in the run-up to the fall election. Ramping down the national security rhetoric—and reaching out to once sworn enemies—was a winning political strategy. It would have been impossible if not for Nixon's two-decade career as one of America's foremost red-baiters.[36]

Nixon's presidency was a brief, rare period of threat deflation in American history. Normalizing relations with communist China, while helping ensure Nixon's reelection, fundamentally roiled Republican politics, particularly for his successor, Gerald Ford. Ford largely followed Nixon's lead on détente during his two years in office, which included an arms-control treaty (SALT II) and the Helsinki Accords with the Soviet Union. But doing so produced harsh pushback from foreign policy hawks who demanded greater vigilance against the communist threat.

Under pressure from these strident voices—in and out of government—the director of central intelligence, George H. W. Bush, commissioned a so-called Team B review of Soviet military capabilities that bore striking similarities to the Gaither committee of 1957. The report, led by the Harvard University history professor Richard Pipes and staffed with anti-Soviet hard-liners, determined that the CIA had underestimated Soviet military strength. The Team B report claimed that CIA estimates were based on actual capabilities rather than likely intentions and that there was no chance the Soviets would change their motivations or behavior in the future. The results were leaked to multiple news outlets and, for more than a decade, served as talking points for proponents of an arms race with the Soviets. Of the Team B's ten members, six later held senior positions in the Reagan administration, while another was a presidential campaign adviser.[37]

The hawks fundamentally undermined Ford's efforts to continue Nixon's moderate approach. "I never backed away from détente as a means for achieving a more stable relationship with our Communist adversaries," Ford later noted, "but the situation that developed in connection with the presidential primaries and the fight at the convention made it necessary to deemphasize détente."[38] That fight came directly from the former California governor Ronald Reagan, who launched a spirited challenge to Ford from his political right. Reagan accused Ford and Henry Kissinger (who had stayed on as secretary of state and had become a bête noire to conservatives) of turning the United States into a "number two . . . military power in a world where it is dangerous—if not fatal—to be second best."[39]

In the face of Reagan's challenge, Ford's aides urged the president to "posture himself as sufficiently hardline that no major candidate can run to the right of him on defense and foreign policy."[40] The president jettisoned his moderate vice president, Nelson Rockefeller, for the more hawkish and conservative Kansas senator Bob Dole. He shelved efforts for further arms-control agreements with the Soviets, moved away from a focus on détente, and talked more like a foreign policy hard-liner. He blasted Democrats for proposing billions of dollars in defense cuts, which he claimed would weaken the United States vis-à-vis the Soviet Union. His secretary of defense, Donald Rumsfeld, warned that any further reduction in Pentagon spending would "inject greater instability into the world."[41]

While Ford barely outlasted Reagan in the Republican primaries, he could not get past his Democratic challenger, Jimmy Carter. Regardless, the foreign policy battle lines had been drawn for the Republican Party. Nixon's efforts to tone down the aggressive foreign policy rhetoric that had led to disaster in Vietnam did not survive long within the party.

The Carter Doctrine's Lasting Legacy

Jimmy Carter, unlike his Democratic predecessors, showed little inclination to act like a foreign policy hawk. In a commencement speech at Notre Dame University in May 1977, he decried the "inordinate fear of communism" that had led the United States to "embrace any dictator who joined in our fear."[42] Carter sought to deemphasize superpower conflict by making human rights a core foreign policy concern—even if this meant upsetting relationships with America's anti-Soviet allies. What made the issue so politically palatable for Carter is that it appealed to Democrats, who had opposed the

Vietnam War, and was endorsed by Republicans, who saw human rights as a way to draw clear moral demarcations between the capitalist and communist worlds.

Unfortunately, Carter's efforts were upended by the intricacies of both international and domestic politics. While troubled by the human rights record of Iran and its shah, Mohammad Reza Pahlavi, Carter found it difficult to separate the United States from its primary ally in the Persian Gulf. In Nicaragua, he cut off support for the nation's strongman, Anastasio Somoza, only to see him overthrown in 1979 and a communist government take power. Carter pushed forward with the Panama Canal Treaty, which would return the strategically and economically vital waterway to Panama in 1999. Conservatives narrowly failed to kill the agreement in the U.S. Senate, but the treaty's passage further emboldened them to push back on Carter's more conciliatory approach to foreign policy.

Carter was already on the defensive, and the seizure of the U.S. Embassy in Tehran in the fall of 1979—and a tough primary fight against Sen. Ted Kennedy followed by a likely reelection campaign against Reagan looming—placed Carter in a tough political spot. When the Soviet Union invaded its southern neighbor, Afghanistan, in December 1979, Carter used the opportunity to ratchet up Cold War tensions. He named the cross-border invasion "the most serious threat to peace since World War II" and called for substantial defense-spending increases over the next five years. Secretly he authorized arms transfers to mujahedin rebels fighting the Soviet invaders.[43]

But the Carter policy that was to have the most enduring and costly impact on U.S. foreign policy was captured weeks later in one paragraph of the 1980 State of the Union Address: "An attempt by any outside force to gain control of the Persian Gulf region will be regarded as an assault on the vital interests of the United States of

America, and such an assault will be repelled by any means necessary, including military force."[44] The "Carter Doctrine," motivated by politics and fears that the Soviet Red Army, now ensconced in Afghanistan, would roll through post-revolution Iran and control its oil-rich Khuzestan Province, located on the Persian Gulf, mirrored Truman's widening of U.S. security interests after the North Korean invasion of South Korea in 1950. In both cases, the presidential argument relied on the untested supposition that failing to broaden the way the U.S. defined its vital interests would put the country at risk.

Carter's expansion of the U.S. defense umbrella had disastrous long-term consequences. The rhetorical pledge created an entire government bureaucracy—U.S. Central Command (CENTCOM)—and political incentives to retain a permanent U.S. military presence in the region. As Carter's number-two Pentagon official, Robert Komer, declared at the time, "The viability of this military policy depends critically on our access to facilities in the area," adding, "we do not seek permanent garrisons."[45] Access to these ports, bases, and airstrips required the permission of Gulf states, all of which were led by autocratic regimes with poor human rights records. In exchange for this approval, these countries received billions of dollars in foreign aid, advanced weapons, and tacit acceptance of their dreadful human rights policies. Over time, jihadist terrorist groups would use U.S. support for Gulf leaders as an effective propaganda and recruitment tool for terrorists, including al-Qaeda.

The ever-enlarging American military footprint in the Middle East, ironically and tragically, placed U.S. soldiers at far greater risk: 241 Americans were killed in the Beirut attack in 1983 (detailed shortly), 37 on the USS *Stark* in 1987, 19 during the bombing of the Khobar Towers in Saudi Arabia in 1996, and 17 serving aboard the USS *Cole* in 2000. Of course, there are also the Gulf War in 1990 and the Iraq War from 2003 to 2011. There are also the billions of dollars spent enforcing no-fly zones in the years between. In all, more than 7,500 U.S. troops have died stabilizing the continuously unstable CENTCOM region since Carter's sweeping declaration. Even though the United States has decreased its reliance on oil exports over the past decade (particularly from the Gulf), 55,000 U.S. troops and 43,000 military contractors remained stationed throughout the Middle East in 2018.[46]

Just as Truman's description of the Soviet threat laid the foundation for intervention in Vietnam twenty years later, Carter's elevation of the strategic vitality of the Persian Gulf set the stage for the Iraq War two decades later. Like Truman and Korea, Carter's move brought him little political benefit. Ronald Reagan, who during the 1980 presidential campaign compared him to the former British prime minister Neville Chamberlain, crushed Carter in his bid for reelection. Carter's efforts to outhawk the hawks failed spectacularly.[47]

Reagan, Rollback, and the Evil Empire

When Ronald Reagan took the oath of office in 1981, détente appeared to be all but over. The harsh Cold War rhetoric of the 1950s and '60s returned to American politics. Reagan, who had been a rabid anticommunist for most of his adult life, stayed that course as president. He regularly portrayed the Soviet Union and communism in general as a threat to U.S. national security. He famously labeled the country an "evil empire" and said the anticommunist fight was "a struggle between right and wrong and good and evil." He warned that Americans who opposed his nuclear weapons expansion policies "would place the United States in a position of military and moral inferiority" to the Soviets.[48] Even though CIA estimates showed the Soviet economy in free fall and trailing far behind the United States and even as the Soviet Union's population grew increasingly discontent, Reagan insisted that Soviet leaders sought "world conquest—world communizing" and a "one-world Communist state"—as if such goals were actually attainable.[49]

Reagan's tough language bolstered one of his top legislative priorities: massively expanding the Pentagon's budget. Military expenditures jumped by $200 billion, a 56 percent increase, from 1980 to 1985, as Congress agreed to Reagan's request for more B-1 bombers, research and development money for stealth bombers, new cruise and intercontinental nuclear weapons, a six-hundred-ship "blue water" Navy, and increased monies for stockpile maintenance. It represented the biggest jump in peacetime military spending in American history.[50]

While there was some evidence that Reagan and some of his advisers viewed this spending spree as a way to bankrupt the Soviet Union, the language from Reagan-administration officials left little ambiguity as to why it was needed: America's national security was at stake.[51] Throughout 1981, as Reagan mobilized public support and congressional approval for increased defense spending, he talked regularly of a "margin of safety" that had been eroded by the Carter administration. He asserted that this margin could only be restored with the "long-range buildup of our Armed Forces."[52] In his first State of the Union Address, he made clear that any "imbalance" in defense between the United States and the Soviet Union represented "a threat to our national security."[53] In pushing for new strategic nuclear forces, he warned that a "window of vulnerability is opening, one that would jeopardize not just our hopes for serious productive arms negotiations, but our hopes for peace and freedom."[54] As Reagan spoke, both countries had enough nuclear warheads to destroy each other many times over: 24,104 for the United States and 30,655 for the Soviets.[55] At the same time, Reagan proposed deploying new nuclear weapons in the territory of NATO allies to target the Soviet Union. The move sparked a furious backlash in Europe and bolstered the growing nuclear-freeze movement in the United States.[56]

Reagan's focus on the potential for nuclear war—as well as heightened tensions between the United States and the Soviet Union—had a profound impact on Americans. In November 1983, ABC broadcast the infamous television movie *The Day After*, which depicted in horrifying detail the consequences of a U.S.-Soviet nuclear exchange. Watched by more than one hundred million Americans, it captured the fearful sentiments of many who imagined a *Day After*–type war in the not-too-distant future.[57] In response to a November 1985 poll, more than a quarter of Americans (26 percent) said that they thought nuclear war with the Soviet Union was likely "in the next few years."[58]

A year earlier, Reagan was caught on an open microphone joking about having signed legislation that "will outlaw Russia forever": "We begin bombing in five minutes."[59] Reagan's push for the so-called Star Wars, or Strategic Defense Initiative (SDI), missile-defense program suggested to many (particularly the Soviets) that the United States was thinking about ways to win a nuclear war. For the first time since the Cuban Missile Crisis, the potential for nuclear conflict seemed to be not so far-fetched—and it was a view held not just by ordinary Americans but also by noted international analysts.[60]

Not content with simply building up America's nuclear capabilities, Reagan enacted a policy known as "rollback," which sought to "reverse the expansion of Soviet control and military presence around the world."[61] In 1983, he issued National Security Decision Directive 75, which called on America "to support effectively those Third World states that are willing to resist Soviet pressures or oppose Soviet initiatives hostile to the United States, or are special targets of Soviet policy."[62] This guidance effectively committed the country to a foreign policy of compelling a change in Soviet behavior, rather than simply deterring Moscow.

This strategic decision resulted in a host of harmful and harebrained military and covert operations. In 1982, Reagan, against the unanimous advice of the Joint Chiefs of Staff, authorized the deployment of U.S. troops to war-torn Lebanon. While the force was nominally part of a peacekeeping effort, the larger goal was to check Soviet influence in the now "vital" Middle East. The mission was seen as a limited one, and Reagan claimed that the American force would not engage in combat operations.[63] However, in October 1983, after the deaths of five Marines in three separate incidents, Reagan authorized the USS *New Jersey* to shell local militias as well as Syrian forces. Less than a week later, Hezbollah-linked militants (with ties to Syria) drove a truck bomb containing more than twenty thousand pounds of TNT into the Marine barracks at the Beirut International Airport, killing 220 Marines and 21 other service members. Not long after, U.S. troops withdrew from the embattled country.[64]

Closer to home, Reagan made support for the Contras, pro-American rebels in Nicaragua fighting the Soviet-backed Sandinista regime, a key element of his foreign policy agenda. Adopting the threat-mongering rhetoric that he used to describe the Soviet Union, he publicly warned that their defeat "would mean consolidation of a privileged sanctuary for terrorists and subversives just two days' driving time from Harlingen, Texas."[65] In late 1983, Reagan authorized a CIA covert operation to mine three critical harbors in Nicaragua to prevent cotton exports and petroleum imports. Though the mining program was intended to merely "scare off" ships—amounting to what one of the planners referred to as "a loud fart"—the explosives ended up damaging ships flagged by the Soviet Union, Japan, and the

Netherlands and ultimately backfired by pushing the Sandinista government closer into the Soviet orbit. After the mining, the Soviets replaced Mexico and Europe as the chief oil supplier to Nicaragua.[66]

When Congress passed legislation restricting U.S support for the Contras, Reagan's National Security Council responded with innovative and illegal approaches to funding the group. In 1984, staffers created dummy companies to arrange for private contributions to be used to illegally purchase weapons for the rebels.[67] In 1985, they funneled the proceeds to the group from an ill-fated arms-for-hostages scheme with Iran.[68] The Iran-Contra scandal, which led to a joint congressional investigation, an independent prosecutor, and criminal convictions for several officials involved, dominated Reagan's second term and tarnished his presidency.

While some administration decisions to confront communism were justified on moral and strategic grounds, such as support for mujahedin rebels in Afghanistan waging a bloody war against Soviet invaders (Reagan dubbed them "freedom fighters"), others were harder to defend.[69] In 1986, the Reagan administration refused to go along with sweeping economic sanctions against South Africa's apartheid regime. Officials claimed that the South African government should not be weakened in the fight against the allegedly pro-Soviet African National Congress. It put the White House in the isolated position of supporting a regime that was condemned by nearly every other nation in the world. In response to federal inaction, twenty-six states and ninety cities went so far as to enact their own sanctions on South Africa.[70] In the fight for freedom and democracy, American policy makers put opposition to communism ahead of all else. Eventually Congress overrode Reagan's veto of sanctions legislation, increasing international pressure on South Africa and ushering in the end of apartheid rule.

Yet, ironically given all Reagan's alarmist talk, there were important and notable limits to his hawkish tone. He only once used U.S. ground troops to intervene militarily—the 1983 invasion of Grenada. In the early 1980s—just a few years after the end of the Vietnam War—domestic political support for military interventions was in short supply.[71]

Reagan's second-term foreign policy, surprisingly, would be defined by a ratcheting down of his early pledges to roll back communist influence globally and of the threats posed by the Soviet Union more generally. This was reflected in the more measured tone of the Reagan administration's final National Security Strategy (NSS). While Reagan's first NSS in 1982 had characterized the Soviet Union as a threat to "U.S. security" directly, by 1988 it had been downgraded to the less specific and less existential threat to U.S. "security interests."[72]

The NSS offered support to the economic and political reforms proposed by the new Soviet premier, Mikhail Gorbachev—a step opposed by many of Reagan's more hawkish advisers. "While recognizing the competitive and predominantly adversarial character of our relationship," the document read, "we shall maintain a dialogue with the Soviet Union in order to seize opportunities for more constructive relations."[73] With the Cold War winding down, it seemed that the time had come to step away from the precipice and shelve the incessant threat inflation in Washington, DC, which had long been used to characterize superpower rivalry.

George H. W. Bush, Clinton, and "The Last Campaign of the Cold War"

While the international climate had dramatically changed by the end of Reagan's presidency, the political benefits of fearmongering remained. In George H. W. Bush's 1988 campaign for the White House, the vice president trotted out the traditional Republican playbook: "arousing fear about the future," wrote the political journalist Sidney Blumenthal, who aptly described this race as "the last campaign of the Cold War."[74] Bush savaged his opponent, Michael Dukakis, for endorsing cuts to the defense budget and opposing "every new weapons system since the slingshot."[75] He said that a win for the Democrats would return America "to the days when the military was as weak as they could be, when the morale was down, and when we were the laughing stock around the world." According to Bush, the "jury [was] still out" on Gorbachev's reforms, but one thing remained clear: "there is nothing [the Soviets] admire so much as strength, and there is nothing for which they have less respect than for weakness, military weakness." In Bush's attack ads, one phrase appeared prominently to characterize Dukakis: "America cannot afford that risk."[76]

As president, Bush utilized the same tone but against a different set of enemies. In December 1989, he sent more than twenty-five thousand U.S. troops into Panama to combat illegal drug trafficking. A year later, he assembled a broad international coalition to dislodge Saddam Hussein's Iraqi forces from Kuwait. To build public support for the war, Bush inflated the threat posed by Hussein, in part by publicly describing him as another Adolf Hitler (or worse) more than ten times.[77] But while Bush's mobilization efforts succeeded and America achieved its military objectives, the political benefits were muted. When the war ended, Bush had a 91 percent approval rating. Within a year, his numbers were well under 50 percent, and his opponent in the 1992 presidential election, Bill Clinton, even used Bush's international expertise and focus on global affairs as a political weapon against him.[78] It was evidence, said Clinton, of Bush's lack of attention to domestic issues. Bush became only the second president since Herbert Hoover in 1928 to lose reelection—and Clinton entered the presidency with little international experience and a skeletal foreign policy agenda. But in the first post–Cold War presidential election, Americans were far less focused on the world outside U.S. borders.

The challenge for policy makers in mobilizing Americans to continue caring about foreign policy was well captured in a February 1992 *New York Times* article that noted that, with the Cold War over and the Soviet Union vanquished, "Americans are facing not just the giddy spectacle of a grand, global political victory" but also "a quandary of historic dimensions, as disorienting as any this nation has ever faced." Quoting John Mack, director of the Center of Psychological Studies in the Nuclear Age at Harvard University, the paper wondered, "How will the nation's leaders cope when 'they can't find a reliable enemy to mobilize the nation any longer?' "[79]

Absent such an "enemy," Clinton faced obstacles throughout his presidency in building domestic support for assertive international moves. In October 1993, the image of slain Army Rangers being dragged through the streets of Mogadishu hastened a quick military withdrawal from a peacekeeping mission in that beleaguered nation. Similar casualty aversion hamstrung U.S.-led efforts to resolve the Yugoslav civil war or to stop genocide in Rwanda. Indeed, even after al-Qaeda's attacks on U.S. embassies in Kenya and Tanzania killed hundreds, including twelve Americans, the bombing of the USS *Cole*, and plots to attack targets on U.S. soil were exposed, Clinton could not marshal public backing for aggressively taking on the still-shadowy terrorist group.

During the 2000 presidential campaign, Clinton's Republican challenger, George W. Bush, called for a humble foreign policy and pledged to step back from the assertive U.S. international role of the Clinton years. If the 1990s had shown anything, it was that after the end of the Cold War, the lack of an obvious adversary made it increasingly difficult to rally Americans around an aggressive and costly peacetime global role. By the time Bush was inaugurated in January 2001, it seemed that, barring an unforeseen, emotive, and focusing event to organize domestic attention, America had perhaps begun to turn its back on the threat inflation that had defined U.S. foreign policy for the previous half century.

The Threat-Industrial Complex

A decade of fear-mongering has brought power and wealth to those who have been the most skillful at hyping the terrorist threat. Fear sells. Fear has convinced the White House and Congress to pour hundreds of billions of dollars—more money than anyone knows what to do with—into counterterrorism and homeland security programs, often with little management or oversight, and often to the detriment of the Americans they are supposed to protect. Fear is hard to question. It is central to the financial well-being of countless federal bureaucrats, contractors, subcontractors, consultants, analysts, and pundits. Fear generates funds.

—*James Risen*

Why does threat inflation work? What is it about humans that allows them to be inordinately susceptible to arguments that so clearly exaggerate and mislead? The answer from two researchers offers disturbing evidence that being inundated with fear-based arguments practically rewires our brains.

Jennifer Merolla and Elizabeth Zechmeister, political science professors, organized separate groups of college students. One watched a ninety-second presentation of government statements and media reports about terror threats. A second was shown a more positive segment describing peace and prosperity at home, modeled on President

Ronald Reagan's uplifting "It's Morning Again in America" advertisements, used during his 1984 reelection campaign.

Unsurprisingly, those who viewed the doom and gloom report were far more concerned about future terrorist attacks and even showed higher levels of anxiety. But the ultimate impact went much deeper. The group also became less trusting, less tolerant, more inclined to endorse authoritarian policies, and less sympathetic toward minorities—even those having nothing to do with the terrorist acts shown in the video.[1]

Today, when it comes to foreign affairs, Americans are disproportionately bombarded by news reports, social media posts, and Hollywood movies focused on the scariest possible depictions of the world. Tales of fiendish terror plots, bloodthirsty jihadists, scheming rival nations, and potential, allegedly complex dangers are routine fare for American news consumers. These messages are coming not just from politicians but also from a vast network of individuals and institutions that peddle the latest threat du jour for often self-interested reasons.

Military leaders regularly inflate threats or warn of the armed forces becoming hollow and unable to maintain its competitive advantage vis-à-vis other countries in order to justify the Pentagon's nearly $700 billion annual budget. "I'd love to see the budget go down," secretary of defense James Mattis told Congress in April 2018, but with "the world that we're looking at out there, I don't think that's going to be the case." In reality, no military leader wants to see his or her budget decrease, which means that the threats facing America are always severe.[2]

Military contractors that are deeply reliant on defense spending and think tankers who increase attention paid to their issues by reporting them in alarmist terms—and ignoring positive global trends—lend a hand as well. The media endorses, and even cultivates, the notion that America faces serious threats because such stories sell newspapers, get more viewers, and lead to more clicks. "If it bleeds it leads" is true not only of local crime reporting but of international coverage too.

Activists, human rights groups, national lobbies, and cybersecurity firms play their part by presenting the issues they work on as potential threats so as to ensure they receive heightened media and policy-maker attention. As Stephen Walt, the noted international relations scholar at Harvard University, succinctly put it a few years ago, "Whether the issue is Cuba, Darfur, the Middle East, Armenia, arms control, trade, population, human rights, climate policy, or what have you, there is bound to be some group pressing Washington to focus more energy and attention on their particular pet issue."[3]

This constellation of actors represents what we call the Threat-Industrial Complex (TIC). It bears direct similarities to the "military-industrial complex" and "its acquisition of unwarranted influence" that President Dwight D. Eisenhower famously warned of in his farewell address in January 1961. Like the group that Eisenhower described then, the TIC is not clandestinely plotting behind closed doors in hidden mountain lairs. It is not a club that its members sign up for or pay yearly dues to. Neither is this far-flung group part of a secret or deliberate conspiracy to shape public perceptions—though it certainly has that effect.[4]

Rather, the TIC shares interests, objectives, and perhaps, above all, an inherent and self-interested pessimism about the global environment. These collective yet uncoordinated efforts have a tremendous influence on the way Americans think about security and their place in the world. From a position of perceived authority (behind a news desk, before a Senate committee, or bedecked in a uniform), members of the TIC disseminate a glass-half-empty perspective on the international environment that inflates foreign risks and overwhelmingly disregards positive—or even less threatening—characterizations of the world. The TIC's breadth has created a virtual national consensus that the world is a dangerous place—and will always remain that way. This creates a strong "existence bias" that not only is rarely challenged by nonexperts but is passively absorbed by them and then subsequently parroted and amplified.[5]

There are few prominent researchers or foreign policy and national security specialists willing to push back on this narrative because the incentive structure almost always leans toward panic. After all, it is hard to get attention or funding for a prominent international issue if one's position is "everything is fine." Members of the TIC, like politicians, understand instinctually that black-and-white proclamations that play on hardwired, primal fears are going to be more potent than nuanced, caveated arguments.

This constant scare-mongering has a profound impact on U.S. national security and foreign policy. People who are scared of overseas threats, who see dangers lurking in the shadows, and who are bombarded with news stories about the latest terrorist attack will be more likely to endorse higher defense spending and back dubious foreign military adventures. They will be more inclined to look positively on expanding intelligence capabilities, even if it means putting their own civil liberties at risk. They will be more willing to support political leaders who tell them they can keep Americans safe against the myriad of threats "out there" and, as our aforementioned researchers found out, even give their backing to undemocratic policies. As a result, alternative domestic and foreign policy choices are given far less consideration, and the ones that are overwhelmingly supported by—and coincidentally consistent with—the TIC's professional and financial interests are lavished with attention, often to the detriment of U.S.

national security interests, both at home and abroad. Quite simply, threat exaggeration and inflation might be bad for America, but it is good for business—and, in turn, good for the Threat-Industrial Complex.

"Saves Lives"

In June 2013, Gen. Keith Alexander, the head of the National Security Agency (NSA), was having a rough month. His agency, which few Americans had even heard of, was rocked by the biggest and arguably the worst leak of classified material in American history.

On June 6, the *Guardian* newspaper published its first blockbuster story from a trove of leaked documents that detailed the agency's vast surveillance capabilities.[6] Soon after, the *Washington Post* followed suit with more details about the NSA's most highly classified programs.[7] The material stolen by a former NSA contractor, Edward Snowden, exposed the NSA's collection of bulk metadata from phone calls made by American citizens and the interception of web-based communications of suspected terrorists, which inadvertently included Americans. Over the next few weeks, a steady stream of stories emerged detailing the broad scope of the NSA's spying programs. The revelations showed that the NSA's targets ranged from jihadist terrorist groups and U.S. rivals, such as China and Russia, to close allies like German chancellor Angela Merkel, the office of UN secretary general Ban Ki-moon, and even the UN Children's Fund (UNICEF). The Snowden leaks also brought attention to the fact that the NSA had actively worked to undermine global encryption standards—increasing the vulnerability of Americans' phones, laptops, and any internet-connected device—in order to make it easier for the agency to conduct cyberhacking and collect information.

For the NSA and Alexander, the leaks were more than just a black eye. They raised serious questions as to whether the post-9/11 buildup of the nation's intelligence capabilities—and the approximate doubling of the intelligence community's budget since 2000—had gone too far.

For most of the NSA's first fifty years, it had been tasked largely with collecting and interpreting signals intelligence, primarily from computers and phones for the defense and intelligence communities. This provided policy makers with intercepted communications that gave them an advantage in negotiating international agreements or dealing with foreign leaders.[8] The NSA's work is largely done in the shadows: tapping transoceanic cables, planting listening devices, or using Navy radars to eavesdrop on rival government and military leaders. In the immediate aftermath of 9/11, the NSA—like every other member of the intelligence community—was recruited for the fight against terrorism. Yet that still represented just a third of what the NSA did on a daily basis. That hardly stopped Alexander, though, from trotting out a familiar playbook in justifying the extraordinary capabilities and legal rationales that the Snowden leaks revealed.

"I much prefer to be here today explaining these programs, than explaining another 9/11 event that we were not able to prevent," read the first line of talking points prepared for NSA officials in the wake of the Snowden leaks.[9] This twenty-five-page guidance sounded quite familiar to what Americans had consistently heard from senior intelligence and military officials over the previous decade: noun + verb + 9/11.

In prepared congressional testimony that October, Alexander continued along this path: "First, how did we get here? How did we end up here? 9/11—2,996 people were killed in 9/11. We all distinctly remember that. What I remember the most was those firemen running up the stairs to save people, to there themselves lose their lives. We had this great picture that was created afterward of a fireman handing a flag off to the military, and I'd say the intelligence community, and the military and the intelligence community said: 'We've got it from here.' " Evoking the horrors that Americans saw at Ground Zero became the agency's go-to public relations strategy—even though most of the leaks had exposed surveillance efforts that had little to do with terrorism. But Alexander's defense of the NSA's most controversial activities went beyond just evoking the worst terrorist attack in American history. He also claimed that, as a result of these programs, fifty-four new attacks had been prevented.[10]

Members of Congress took Alexander's talking point and ran with it. Rep. Mike Rogers, chairman of the House Permanent Select Committee on Intelligence and a key ally of the agency, proclaimed on the House floor that the "fifty-four times [NSA programs] stopped and thwarted terrorist attacks" had saved "real lives" (as opposed to phony ones).[11] Rep. Joe Heck of Nevada claimed that "fifty-four terrorist plots against the US (and counting)" had been stopped by the NSA. Rep. Brad Wenstrup of Ohio took a similar tack, arguing that "the programs in question" had foiled fifty-four attacks, many "targeting Americans on American soil."[12]

The problem with this notable assertion is that it did not stand up to scrutiny. Only thirteen of the fifty-four cases had any connection to terrorism in the United States, and most were not actual plots or attacks but rather potential evidence of material support for terror groups. The New America Foundation later determined that just seventeen of the cases cited could be credited to any NSA surveillance program and had resulted in just one conviction—a San Diego cab driver who transferred $8,500 to al-Shabaab, a terrorist organization in Somalia.[13]

To be sure, NSA surveillance capabilities serve as important and often cost-effective intelligence-gathering tools and a deterrent against potential plots. If terrorists are constantly worried that their communications are being monitored, it makes it that much more challenging to plan and execute a complex and highly lethal attack. But the language of the NSA and its defenders suggested that those programs, which danced on the knife's edge of constitutionality, were essential to stopping those who were intent on striking America again. That was not the case.[14]

Nonetheless, Alexander's public relations offensive had done its job. Congress eventually reined in the NSA's domestic surveillance programs, but the agency avoided major reforms. There would be little discussion of whether the NSA's expanded surveillance mission—and ever-growing list of sophisticated hacking and eavesdropping capabilities—was truly in the country's best interests. Many members of Congress were simply unwilling to put restrictions on an organization that had come to be seen as a key bulwark in the fight against terrorism.

For the NSA, the rhetorical focus on counterterrorism became more pronounced. In 2016, three years after the Snowden leaks and Alexander's terrible month, the agency made a slight, but revealing, modification to its public website. Where the NSA once emphasized its long-standing missions to "protect U.S. national security systems and to produce foreign signals intelligence information," the newly created "What We Do" page listed as its very first bullet point "Saves lives."[15]

Selling the Military's Message

As President Eisenhower prepared to deliver his farewell speech to the American people in the twilight of his presidency, he agonized for months over just the right words to capture his growing concerns over what he would term the military-industrial complex. One passage contained a prescient warning about the incestuous relationship between the military and its industrial partners: "flag and general officers retiring at an early age take positions in [the] war-based industrial complex shaping its decisions and guiding the direction of its tremendous thrust." These words, which were left out of the final version of the speech, proved prophetic.[16]

Eisenhower's decision to omit this passage may have had something to do with the fact that it described a problem that, at the time, was in its infancy. In 1961, few prominent retired military officials were entering the budding defense industry. The former five-star general and head of the Veterans Administration Gen. Omar Bradley ran a watch company. Both Gen. George Marshall and Adm. Chester Nimitz turned down lucrative business opportunities to be, respectively, Red Cross president and a roving goodwill ambassador for the United Nations. Eisenhower himself retired to his farm in Gettysburg, Pennsylvania, to paint, play golf, and raise Angus cattle. Many other former combatants took the path for old soldiers described most famously by Gen. Douglas MacArthur: they faded away.[17]

Today, it is a very different story. Retired military officials increasingly travel through a revolving door, from the billet to the corporate boardroom. They earn high-six-figure salaries for not just their advice but also their ability to influence their former colleagues on behalf of defense and homeland security corporations. One 2010 analysis of 750 retiring three- and four-star officers found that while, from 1994 to 1998, fewer than 50 percent had gone to work as defense consultants or executives, between 2004 through 2008, the number had jumped to eight out of ten.[18] Of course, this revolving door also features civilians: more than half of Obama's top Pentagon nominees came straight from the defense industry, and after his second term, more than half left to take up jobs within that same industry. President Trump's initial top civilian Pentagon appointees were even more immersed, with 82 percent of them coming from defense-contractor positions.[19]

The incestuous relationship between retired military officers and defense contractors should come as little surprise—after all, commitments for defense contracts in 2017 alone totaled $320 billion.[20] Indeed, there is more spending on contracts for the defense industry than for all other federal government agencies—combined.[21]

This total involves more than just the Pentagon's next big weapons system. Health care for service members and their families, much of which is outsourced to the private sector, makes up a significant chunk of the Pentagon's budget. Then there is the role of contractors in military operations. Over the course of the wars in Iraq and Afghanistan, it has been common for half or more of the total military presence in each country to be private contractors. From 2007 to 2016, the Pentagon spent $249 billion on these private-sector actors in the Iraq and Afghanistan theaters of operation.[22]

These hired guns—whose ultimate loyalty is as much to a paycheck as a flag—became the lifeblood of U.S. overseas operations, assisting on everything from security and logistical support to laundry, food services, and transportation. Without this vast army of paid workers, the United States would have likely found it impossible to wage war in Iraq and Afghanistan. Contractors often provide an invaluable service and at a price cheaper than using enlisted soldiers. In today's all-volunteer army, it makes little sense to spend hundreds of thousands of dollars on training, equipping, and providing a lifetime of benefits for soldiers who wash clothes, stock mess halls, or drive trucks. But relying on contractors creates a vested interest on their behalf to ensure that these jobs do not disappear.

Not surprisingly, as the defense budget steadily increased after 9/11—and U.S. overseas military operations dramatically expanded—the lobbying efforts by defense contractors on Capitol Hill ramped up as well. Since 2006, annual spending for defense lobbying has topped more than $115 million.[23] Evidence of this is not difficult to find in Washington, DC. There are the daily briefings that retired generals, employed by defense contractors, give for congressional staffers and journalists. There is the large financial support for defense-friendly research programs at DC-based think tanks; and then there are the wall-to-wall ads that blanket Washington's pristine metro system—in particular the one located at the Pentagon station. Thousands of officers and civilian Department of Defense employees see those metro ads during their commute every day. In comparison, when Eisenhower saw defense-company advertising in journals, he would disgustedly throw them in the Oval Office fireplace.[24]

Sometimes, however, the revolving door goes in the other direction. In 2002, the Defense Department's public relations office came up with a unique strategy for overcoming public resistance to the war with Iraq: bypassing journalists and targeting authoritative "key influentials" who routinely appeared on television news. The "Retired Military Analysts" program ran six years, and seventy-four retired military officers participated. Provided free trips to Guantanamo Bay, Cuba, and Iraq, the members of this august group were given special briefings with secretary of defense Donald Rumsfeld and other top Pentagon officials, as well as with senior policy makers in the White House, Justice Department, and State Department. In total, there were 147 organized events; at least two included classified information. But the benefit of all-expense-paid trips to American war zones did come with a catch: the officers also received detailed talking points that they were expected to use in their upcoming media appearances.[25]

Not coincidentally, this messaging was overwhelmingly supportive of the Iraq War, the use of Guantanamo Bay as an indefinite detention facility, and the utilization of enhanced interrogation
techniques or, as it is more correctly described, torture. The best tool
for convincing Americans that prolonged military conflicts and potential violations of international law were justified was the same
weapon used by Alexander in 2013: fear that not acting would imperil
America's security.[26] When one prominent member of the group, retired Gen. Barry McCaffrey, then an NBC News commentator, became a public critic of the war effort, he stopped being invited to
Rumsfeld's private gatherings and overseas trips.[27] The Pentagon had
effectively—and secretly—outsourced its public relations efforts to
former military officials who traded their independence for access. As
one of the participants, retired Col. Kenneth Allard, put it, the program was "psy-ops on steroids." Another said it was the Pentagon
saying, "We need to stick our hands up your back and move your
mouth for you."[28]

But there was another important reason that so many retired officers were willing to participate: a majority of them simultaneously
worked for or lobbied on behalf of defense firms. Access to Pentagon
officials helped them provide their clients and employers with privileged insights about what senior Pentagon officials were thinking, including what sorts of weapons systems and logistic services they might
be interested in purchasing.[29] A review of the videos and transcripts of
appearances by the participating retired officers between 2002 and
2008 shows that there is never any mention by the news networks on
which they appeared of their links to the private sector.[30] These former senior military officials provided a viewpoint informed by Pentagon messaging efforts. Moreover, they had a financial interest in
promoting such views and the audience they were seeking to influ-

ence was left in the dark about their inherent conflicts of interest. More than four decades after the fact, Eisenhower's fears that retired officers would guide the "war-based industrial complex" was realized—and then some.

Think Tanks on the Take

Huntington Ingalls Industries, the nation's largest military shipbuilding company, with revenues close to $7 billion a year, had a major problem in the fall of 2011: enthusiasm on Capitol Hill for new military spending was waning.

The previous summer, Congress had passed a deficit-reduction measure that—for the first time since the beginning of the war on terrorism—dramatically cut the Pentagon's budget. With the military forced to take a haircut, plans for modernizing the Navy and building the next generation of America's seafaring fighters were in peril. Belt tightening in Washington risked dampening the prospects for building more nuclear-powered aircraft carriers, which had $11 billion price tags and one private-sector builder: Huntington Ingalls Industries. Huntington began to appreciably increase its political contributions, going from $578,000 in 2010 to close to $1 million by 2012.[31]

But convincing lawmakers about the specific importance of aircraft carriers to U.S. national security would take more than campaign contributions. The company needed to make a strong case for expanding the size of the U.S. Navy—and that meant finding a threat. Huntington Ingalls did what has become an increasingly prominent element of lobbying in Washington, DC: it hooked up with a foreign policy think tank.

For decades, Washington-based think tanks represented a repository of careful deliberation and new research and thinking on major policy issues. The organizations were generally nonprofits, and many had been started by philanthropists (such as the Brookings Institution, Century Foundation, and Carnegie Endowment for International Peace). Their focus had long been on influencing and shaping important domestic and international policy issues. But as new think tanks emerged and as the battle for a diminishing supply of outside funding dollars to sustain their missions took form, the influence of the Threat-Industrial Complex became increasingly hard to ignore.

A series of reports by the *New York Times* in 2016 charted the increasingly incestuous ties between the think tank world and the private sector.[32] According to the *Times*, "an examination of 75 think tanks found an array of researchers who had simultaneously worked as registered lobbyists, members of corporate boards or outside consultants in litigation and regulatory disputes." The paper found "dozens of examples of scholars conducting research at think tanks while corporations were paying them to help shape government policy." Some think tanks conferred "'nonresident scholar' status on lobbyists, former government officials, and others who earn their primary living working for private clients" and placed "few restrictions on such outside work."[33]

For a deep-pocketed company like Huntington Ingalls, DC-based think tanks offered an enormous opportunity to validate and promote its pro-shipbuilding message to the nation's defense officials and congressional appropriators. The Hudson Institute, a self-described "pro-sea power" think tank, took $100,000 from Huntington for its newly created Center for American Seapower. More money flowed to the Center for Strategic and Budgetary Assessments (CSBA).[34] Both soon issued reports calling for new nuclear-powered carriers because of an allegedly growing maritime threat from China.

"The People's Republic of China (PRC) has developed powerful forces capable of challenging the U.S. ability to project power, deter and defeat aggression, and operate effectively in the various warfighting domains," read the Hudson Institute paper, titled *Sharpening the Spear: The Carrier, the Joint Force, and High-End Conflict.* Without expanded U.S. naval capabilities, America's "ability to advance its interests and sustain its global leadership" would be imperiled. The report's conclusion was clear: that this "emerging threat environment increases the need for aircraft carriers, and that none of the alternatives to the CVN [nuclear-powered aircraft carriers] offer an equal or better capability and capacity across the range of military options from peacetime presence through major power war."[35]

The release of the report, which omitted Huntington Ingalls' financial contribution, took place at the Rayburn House Office Building and featured remarks by Rep. Randy Forbes, then chairman of the House Armed Services subcommittee responsible for the Navy and whose home district is a major locus of naval operations on the Eastern Seaboard. Subsequent letters to the editor, op-eds, and a social media campaign helped amplify Hudson's conclusions.[36]

A month later, CSBA took up the baton and issued its own report, alarmingly titled *Deploying beyond Their Means: America's Navy and Marine Corps at a Tipping Point.* Funding came from the Navy League of the United States, an organization whose corporate donors included Huntington Ingalls (this contribution also went unmentioned in the report).[37]

Not surprisingly, CSBA drew similar conclusions to that of the Hudson Institute. "Given the growing size of China's submarine fleet and the proliferation of Anti-Access/Area Denial (A2/AD) technology in the region," a reduced U.S. presence could decrease the Navy's capacity "to contain Chinese undersea and airborne power projection."[38]

CSBA warned that a "Looming Presence Crisis" in U.S. naval capabilities could have larger global implications. The Department of

Defense could be forced to "accept declining overseas presence" at a time when "it may want to increase presence around Europe and Africa to counter instability around the Eastern and Southern Mediterranean; Russian hybrid attacks and aggression; and continued violence by the Islamic State."[39]

While the primary role of the Navy in combating the Islamic State is unclear, the paper concluded, "U.S. seapower today plays a role in responding to contingencies, assuring U.S. allies of our continued commitment to their security, and deterring potential adversaries from undermining the global order. U.S. naval forces can often create a positive impact merely by showing up and providing foreign statesmen with a visible reminder of America's maritime superiority."[40] From this perspective, a big Navy was essential in deterring not just specific threats but also amorphous ones, because all potential challengers to American hegemony would be dissuaded from even considering taking on the United States after receiving a visual "reminder" of America's vast naval reach.

Other defense contractors took a more direct approach to shaping and influencing national security debates. The prominent think tank American Enterprise Institute (AEI) hired Roger Zakheim, a former deputy assistant secretary of defense in the Bush administration and general counsel to the House Armed Services Committee, as a "visiting fellow" and expert on military affairs. Left unstated by the think tank was that in his spare time Zakheim was a lobbyist for Northrop Grumman and BAE Systems, two major Pentagon contractors.[41]

In August 2016, Zakheim coauthored an article for the *National Review*, which referenced his fellowship at AEI, warning against the "myth of readiness" in the U.S. military. Instead, according to Zakheim, the United States was dangerously unprepared for future potential conflicts. The "real readiness crisis," the article stated, "is not measured in the fight against ISIS, or in Afghanistan, but in the capacity and capability needed in a more demanding contingency."[42]

"Readiness shortfalls induce a kind of wasting disease that becomes a crisis in a surprising situation like the one that marked the beginning of the Korean War, when the Army's 'Task Force Smith' was overrun by North Korean tanks."[43] The reference to armored vehicles was not coincidental: one of BAE Systems' key objectives was to increase congressional spending on ground-combat vehicles that the company builds.

The piece also expressed concern that "current U.S. systems" and in particular fighter jets like the F-15, F-16, and F/A-18 "no longer provide the technological edge they did when introduced." These aircraft "cannot penetrate modern air defenses of the sort fielded by the Russians, the Chinese, and, in short order, the Iranians, without extensive and expensive support from a variety of electronic warfare aircraft."[44] Not surprisingly, Zakheim's other client, Northrop Grumman, is a key provider of fighter jets to the U.S. military. With the veneer of a respectable, self-described "nonpartisan public policy" research institution, Zakheim was in effect promoting the interests of his lobbying clients.

Despite the routine denunciations of "expertise," in Washington, DC, think tanks and the experts who inhabit them still enjoy a prominent perch. They provide advice to government officials behind closed doors, offer insights in congressional testimony, and publish articles and op-eds in major outlets chock full of policy recommendations. Yet their funders or other financial connections are rarely mentioned, and it is that money that often drives their analysis and the frequently alarmist conclusions they reach. For deep-pocketed funders, an investment in think tank "research" can reap sizable dividends that do more to further their financial security than to further actual national security.

Clicks, Chyrons, and Fearbola

On the fifth anniversary of 9/11, ABC News broadcast a special report looking back on the horrific day, titled "Why Aren't We Safer?" According to the network's nightly news anchor, Charles Gibson, the changes wrought by September 11 had fundamentally transformed even the most routine daily activities. "Now," said Gibson, "putting your child on a school bus or driving across a bridge or just going to the mall—each of these things is a small act of courage. And peril is a part of everyday life."[45] Apparently no one had bothered to tell Gibson that there had not been a successful foreign terrorist attack on U.S. soil in the previous five years.

But such alarmist declarations have become the norm since September 2001. This reflects a long-standing bias in news reporting on foreign affairs and national security toward highlighting threats and a lack of interest or imagination in covering stories on dangers being reduced. Members of the industry acknowledge openly that they overwhelmingly prioritize negativity over progress. For example, in the summer of 2016, *New York* magazine surveyed several prominent journalists to gauge the media's perception of itself. The magazine's own Jonathan Chait, reflecting on the aversion to reporting good news, admitted that "the opposite of a bad story isn't a good story, it's a nonstory."[46] The journalist Jesse Singal chalks up the phenomenon to evolution: "There's a reason that whatever the world's actual trajectory, there will always be disproportionate coverage of threats to health and wellbeing. We are wired to be finely attuned to negativity. Throughout our evolutionary history, it's been beneficial to sense danger quickly. . . . We will always be more likely to share the story online about the earthquake that killed a few hundred people in a distant corner of the world than the one about a small decrease in infant mortality somewhere that reflects a much larger quantity of saved lives."[47] Such overt acknowledgments of threat inflation matter, because even as newspaper subscriptions and broadcast television viewership has declined, most Americans still receive news about the world from mainstream outlets, few of which still invest in foreign news reporting. Newspapers have dramatically cut their overseas bureaus, with only a few elite outlets maintaining offices abroad, but foreign bureaus for cable news stations are also declining.[48] As a result, international stories also account for less and less airtime. For example, in 2013, foreign coverage was just 7 percent of all stories on MSNBC.[49] Limited foreign coverage makes it nearly impossible to offer the context and history needed for positive stories, and so what ends up dominating coverage are one-off tragedies such as earthquakes, hurricanes, and, of course, terrorist attacks—but not all terrorist attacks, mainly just those that occur in western Europe.

The amplification of foreign threats dominates in other, more pernicious ways as well. Consider the questions that news anchors used during the presidential debates in the last presidential election. In total, there were twenty-eight primary debates held between August 2015 and April 2016 and three presidential debates in the fall of 2016. When foreign policy was discussed, it was almost exclusively in terms of international threats. The continent of Africa—where the United States operates fifty-one embassies, spends billions of dollars annually on aid and development, contributes significantly to UN missions, and has focused military attention by launching an entirely new combatant command—was mentioned only in reference to terrorism emanating from its northern states. Climate change went largely unmentioned, as did U.S.-China relations, global development, and foreign aid.

The self-proclaimed Islamic State, on the other hand, received more than five hundred mentions—and that was just in the Democratic and Republican primary debates.[50] The first GOP debate after the San Bernardino terrorist attack in December 2015, perpetrated by a husband and wife sympathetic to the Islamic State, dealt exclusively with the issue of foreign terrorism. There was no mention of domestic terrorism—or even gun violence, which, at that point, had killed more Americans than violent jihadist attacks had since 9/11. To watch these debates, one might conclude that the only region in the world that matters to American foreign policy is the Middle East.[51]

While many news executives would argue that they are simply responding to the foreign policy issues of greatest concern to the American people, the reality is that the same news organizations—with their coverage decisions—are doing more than reflecting the concerns of voters; they are creating them.

One of the most vivid examples of this phenomenon came in the summer of 2014, when a nurse in Texas fell ill from the Ebola virus, transmitted from a Liberian national who had contracted the deadly disease while in West Africa. Quickly, "Fearbola" swept across the country, aided by astonishingly hyperbolic and inaccurate media reporting.

The CNN anchor Ashleigh Banfield wildly speculated, "All ISIS would need to do is send a few of its suicide killers into an Ebola affected zone and then get them onto mass transit." The Fox News contributor Andrea Tantaros warned that travelers arriving to the United States from the region "could get off a flight and seek treatment from a witch doctor who practices Santeria."[52] *Newsweek*, however, captured the brass ring with an article titled "Smuggled

Bushmeat Is Ebola's Backdoor to America."[53] In October of that year, 45 percent of newly panicked Americans expressed concern that they or a member of their family would contract the virus.[54]

In reality, there were just four cases of Ebola in the United States, and only one resulted in death.[55] Yet media coverage contributed to a national hysteria about the disease. A Texas community college sent rejection letters to applicants from Nigeria because that country had a handful of isolated cases of the virus. An elementary school teacher from Maine was forced into twenty-one days of quarantine because she stayed at a hotel located ten miles from the Dallas hospital where the aforementioned Liberian had died. In Mississippi, parents of middle schoolers kept their kids out of class when they found out the principal had recently traveled to Zambia for a funeral. Zambia is approximately two thousand miles from West Africa, about as far as Mississippi is from Peru. Kaci Hickox, a Doctors Without Borders nurse who treated Ebola patients in West Africa, was unlawfully held in a tent located within an unheated parking garage at a hospital in Newark, New Jersey.[56] In each case, decision-makers claimed to be acting out of an abundance of caution, but in reality, they were acting out of an abundance of misplaced fear.

The real story of Ebola was not the threat to Americans but rather the U.S.-led multilateral response to the crisis in West Africa. With three thousand troops and at a total cost of $2.5 billion—only 25 percent of which went to the Pentagon—the United States, in concert with other states, helped to slow the virus's exponential growth in the region. By the time the last U.S. troops departed in March 2015, the World Health Organization reported less than one hundred new cases a week in West Africa, from a high of fifteen hundred a week at the height of the epidemic.[57] On December 23, 2016, the World Health Organization announced that an experimental vaccine had been shown to be highly effective in treating the disease, but by that point, the news media had moved on to other stories. News headlines on the same day of the WHO announcement focused on the story of a Tunisian national who had been shot by police after driving a truck into a Berlin Christmas market.[58]

The TIC's Unusual Suspects

Military leaders, defense contractors, think tankers, and pundits are, not surprisingly, the first groups that come to mind in any discussion of Washington's habitual practice of inflating threats and exaggerating dangers. But there are plenty of other, less obvious groups that do their part to scare Americans. This includes everyone from Hollywood celebrities and human rights activists to cybersecurity firms and your local Cineplex. All, in their own way, contribute to the perception of an international environment seething with potential dangers.

In 2015, as the Iran nuclear deal was being debated in Washington, lobbying groups supportive of Israel—particularly those close to the right-wing government of Benjamin Netanyahu—prepared to mobilize. For the American Israel Political Action Committee (AIPAC) and others, the goal was clear and legitimate: to protect Israel from a nuclear-armed Iran. How these groups, which were opposed to the deal, framed their message will come as little surprise.

AIPAC created Citizens for a Nuclear Free Iran, which ran commercials in twenty-three states claiming that the agreement with Iran would increase the likelihood of both nuclear proliferation and a terrorist group getting nuclear weapons.[59] The implication is not hard to discern: not only would Israel's security be at a risk from a nuclear-armed and Muslim-majority Middle Eastern country, but so too would the United States and its allies.

Indeed, the Anti-Defamation League took exactly this line of argument, claiming, "Iran having a nuclear weapons capability can potentially directly threaten the United States and its inhabitants."[60] In reality, the United States has a massive nuclear deterrent capability, not to mention its overwhelming conventional and cyber military advantage in the region itself.

AIPAC is not the only national lobby that presents threats to the country it represents as ones that also pose dangers to the United States and its allies. Pro-Indian, pro-Taiwanese, pro-Armenian, and pro-Cuban groups have adopted similar tactics, as do lobbying firms hired by foreign governments. As of March 2018, there were 426 such firms or nonprofit groups, which were represented by nearly twenty-five hundred U.S. citizens and foreign individuals who are registered with the Department of Justice to be representatives of foreign principals.[61] Many focus on benign matters—particularly tourism and trade—but some seek greater U.S. security assistance and foreign aid. In some cases, the goal is deeper military intervention, such as the armed opposition in the Syrian civil war, which has hired U.S. public relations firms to make its case to American political leaders.[62] Most famously, during the first Gulf War, the Kuwait government enlisted Hill & Knowlton to spread stories—that turned out to be untrue—of Iraqi soldiers killing hundreds of babies in the nation's hospitals, in order to strengthen the humanitarian case for militarily liberating Kuwait.[63]

While these groups may often have altruistic motives, the objective of many members of the TIC is financial. Take, for example, cybersecurity firms, which have a disproportionate influence on how Americans perceive digital vulnerabilities and the fear of potential attacks. In 2013, allegations surfaced of the Chinese People's Liberation Army hacking into U.S. government and corporate websites. These charges were raised by the cyber firm Mandiant and reported in the

New York Times. In 2016, allegations of Russian hacking of Democratic National Committee servers was discovered by the cybersecurity firm Crowdstrike. Over the years, there have been countless similar stories about cyber vulnerabilities and the potential havoc that a digital breach could wreak on America.[64] While the threat of hacking is real (if overstated), so too is the potential money to be made by firms selling services and software to protect against it.

As a result, media discussions about digital security overwhelmingly reflect this self-interested and glass-half-empty viewpoint. So the next time you read about an alleged hacking of a corporate or government server and see a cybersecurity firm quoted, scan for any disclaimer about that firm's financial motivations to uncover the hack. You will rarely find one.

Then there are former national security officials who transition to private security firms. For example, soon after Richard Clarke stepped down from his role as special adviser to the president on cybersecurity, he sought to turn his government expertise into a money-making opportunity. He quickly became chairman of the Good Harbor consulting group, which specializes as a "trusted advisor on cyber security risk management."[65]

Clarke routinely serves as a source for journalists reporting on cyber-related issues, and not surprisingly, he tends to see dangers lurking around every corner. In 2010, he coauthored a book titled *Cyber War: The Next Threat to National Security and What to Do about It.*[66] The title might seem alarmist, but it is hard to run a company that focuses on minimizing cyber risk if cyber risk does not exist. When promoting the book, Clarke regularly claimed that an effective cyber-attack could cause a national catastrophe. It "could disable trains all over the country," he said. "It could blow up pipelines. It could cause blackouts and damage electrical power grids so that the blackouts would go on for a long time. It could wipe out and confuse financial records. . . . It could do things like disrupt traffic in urban areas by knocking out control computers. It could, in nefarious ways, do things like wipe out medical records."[67] No such attack had ever occurred at the time Clarke made the statement—and in the seven years since, there has been no such occurrence remotely similar to the apocalyptic scenario he described.

Clarke was not alone in cashing in after he left government. Keith Alexander, the former NSA director, went from threat-mongering about terrorism in the public sector to threat-mongering about cyber in the private sector. Within two months of his retirement from the NSA, he formed IronNet Cybersecurity, which offers advice to financial corporations for as much as $1 million a month.[68] Upon starting the company, he testified before Congress, "I believe that those that want to do us harm can do that in one swipe. . . . If that happens, the cost to our nation could be measured in the trillions." He later told a technology reporter, "cyber and terrorism are interrelated."[69] For Alexander, it was the perfect merging of his former job as head of the NSA with his current consulting business.

Such doomsaying is repeated and promoted by media outlets at the expense of scholars like Thomas Rid, who detailed in his book *Cyber War Will Not Take Place* that many of the direr warnings about cyberhacking are wholly implausible. Or there is the security researcher Chris Thomas, who with his database, Cyber Squirrel 1, provides a helpful corrective to digital-threat inflation. Thomas compiles news stories of disruptive attacks against critical infrastructure systems, primarily those within the United States. As of June 2018, there were 2,436 documented attacks but thankfully just three by humans—two power outages in the Ukraine and the U.S.-led Stuxnet attack of Iran's nuclear program.[70] That is far fewer than the disruptions caused by squirrels (1,182) and even jellyfish (13), which in 2013 actually shut down a nuclear reactor in Sweden.

In Hollywood, filmmakers play a role in exaggerating and inflating dangers to the American people. Whereas in the post-Watergate era, American moviemakers took a more skeptical view of the U.S. military and U.S. foreign policy, the years after 9/11 saw a shift in the other direction: moviemakers promoted threats, often in concert with the agencies that Hollywood once demonized. The first and perhaps most insidious example is the Fox show *24*, which premiered in November 2001—just two months after 9/11. The show depicted an immediate and existential terrorist threat facing the United States, capable of causing catastrophic harm if not stopped within twenty-four hours. Most controversially, it showed—and normalized—the use of torture by its lead character, Jack Bauer, in literally ticking-time-bomb situations. In all, *24* portrayed acts of torture sixty-seven times during its first five seasons, and torture depictions on prime-time network television grew by more than 500 percent from 2000 to 2003.[71]

In a bizarre and disturbing example of life imitating art, during a 2007 Republican primary debate, Rep. Tom Tancredo said, "You say that nuclear devices have gone off in the United States, more are planned, and we're wondering about whether waterboarding would be a bad thing to do? I'm looking for Jack Bauer at that time, let me tell you."[72] But it was not just political rhetoric. Concern over the fact that soldiers in Iraq were emulating interrogation tactics depicted in *24* led the dean of the Military Academy at West Point and three veteran interrogators to fly to Los Angeles and personally urge the producers of *24* to stop "promot[ing] unethical and illegal behavior" on the show.[73]

In 2012, *Zero Dark Thirty* won the Oscar for best picture and best original screenplay. The movie, which featured direct input from CIA officials, took a page from the *24* playbook by highlighting the use of torture techniques and openly implying that such tactics played a crucial role in helping the CIA locate and kill Osama bin Laden. This, however, was not true. In fact, Sen. Dianne Feinstein, then the chairman of the Senate Select Committee on Intelligence, and Sen. John McCain, then the ranking member of the Senate Armed Services Committee, rebuked the movie's producers and called the film "grossly inaccurate and misleading in its suggestion that torture resulted in information that led to the location of [O]sama bin Laden."[74]

The involvement of the CIA in *Zero Dark Thirty* is not unusual. The agency has long maintained an Entertainment Industry Liaison office and has collaborated on such films as *The Sum of All Fears*, which featured a wildly improbable depiction of nuclear terrorism; *The Recruit*, which is essentially a two-hour recruitment advertisement for the CIA; and television shows such as *Alias* and a CBS series that ran from 2001 to 2003, *The Agency*.[75] The series producer of *The Agency*, Michael Frost Beckner, noted that CIA advisers suggested integrating agency drone strikes in Pakistan into a story line, *before* the CIA began attacks there, in June 2004. Beckner acknowledged, "The Hellfire missile thing, they suggested that. I didn't come up with this stuff. I think they were doing a public opinion poll by virtue of giving me some good ideas."[76] According to John Rizzo, the agency's acting general counsel or deputy general counsel for eight years after 9/11, Hollywood productions have routinely allowed CIA operatives to pose as members of film crews for movies filmed in foreign countries, and star actors have served as assets for specific projects.[77]

A suite of offices at 10880 Wilshire Boulevard in West Beverly Hills is home to liaison offices of the Army, Navy, Air Force, and Marine Corps. Each service branch offers advice and even actual military equipment for movies, music videos, and video games—but only after the armed services have determined that they are comfortable with the content. As the Pentagon's technical adviser to the 1994 thriller *Clear and Present Danger*, Army Maj. David Georgi, said of the production, "If things were being changed, if they were shooting scenes in different ways, I'd say, 'Well, I'm taking my tanks and my troops and my location, and I'm going home.' "[78]

The Pentagon and the CIA—in concert with Hollywood—dole out access to projects that inflate threats and promote their missions, thus shaping American perceptions about the world. The story lines they endorse are overwhelmingly tilted toward playing up foreign dangers and promoting the indispensability of their own organizations in combating them.

Ironically, the tools utilized by members of the TIC are so effective in drawing attention and raising national concerns that they are imitated by groups that literally are trying to save the world. Humanitarian relief organizations, human rights activists, and even environmentalists will frequently portray their pet causes in the most alarmist and selective manner. It is hard to be overly critical of such efforts because the ultimate goals of such groups are primarily well meaning. However, by highlighting bad news at the expense of much more prevalent good news, they are yet again giving Americans a misleading characterization of the world.

Take, for example, the Belgian beer giant Stella Artois, which in 2017 began a massive, multiyear advertising campaign featuring the actor Matt Damon, a longtime champion of improving access to clean drinking water. In one commercial, Damon approaches a tower of spinning Stella-branded glasses, pauses, and despairingly tells the camera, "A glass of water—it's one of the simplest things for some of us, but for many, it's the most complicated." The Stella Artois logo on the gold-rimmed glasses then changes to a cartoon of a woman balancing a bucket on her head while walking down a dirt road. Damon explains how his organization is pairing with the beer company to provide access to clean water and to end the "global water crisis." The name of the campaign? "Buy a Lady a Drink." Unmentioned in this ad is that potable drinking water has become readily available to 90 percent of the world's population today.[79] Diseases associated with lack of clean water have collapsed: most prominently, guinea worm—an often painful and debilitating disease caused by drinking water contaminated by water fleas. In 1990, there were six hundred thousand cases of guinea worm worldwide. By May 2018, the number had fallen to three.[80] It is not that those who lack clean drinking today do not need help, but the notion that consumers need to enable a beer company to solve "the global water crisis" is deeply misleading.

Or consider the Doomsday Clock, a tool put out by the *Bulletin of Atomic Scientists* to raise awareness about the dangers of nuclear weapons. But the clock's setting (which has always been incredibly close to midnight) is completely subjective. In fact, when the clock was introduced in 1947, it was set at seven minutes to midnight because, according to the artist who created it, "it looked good to my eye."[81] Yet, even as the threat of nuclear war has dissipated with the end of the Cold War, the Doomsday Clock has actually moved closer to Armageddon. In January 2018, it was set to two minutes away, which is the closest it has ever been. The clock's boosters do not even try to hide their intent. According to Lawrence Krauss, who is a member of the *Bulletin*'s Science and Security Board, "For one day a year, there are thousands of newspaper stories about the deep, existential threats that humanity faces."[82] Of course, in reality, while the threat of nuclear war exists, it is a smaller danger than it was in the 1960s and 1980s—and one might argue that the clock, rather than raising awareness, is raising fears of a nuclear conflict, which can increase popular support for a risky, destabilizing, and uncertain preemptive military attacks to alleviate the threat.

Us

The final and most essential participant of the Threat-Industrial Complex is all of us. As humans, we are hardwired to care first and foremost about our survival, passing on our inherited genetic traits, and ensuring the safety of our children and grandchildren. Threatening information or imagery imprints far deeper on the brain and is more readily recalled than nonthreatening information is. As the Nobel laureate and leading scholar in the field of human judgment Daniel Kahneman describes this phenomenon, "Organisms that treat threats as more urgent than opportunities have a better chance to survive and reproduce."[83] More colloquially, President Richard Nixon vocalized what many politicians intuitively know and practice: "People react to fear, not love. They don't teach that in Sunday school, but it's true."[84]

In short, fear trumps facts, and to a disproportionate degree, that simple truism drives America's foreign policy and national security debates. Whether it is Condoleezza Rice evoking the image of mushroom clouds over American cities to justify the Iraq War or Richard Clarke and Keith Alexander raising fears of cyberterrorism or even a TV talking head fearmongering over the threat of a rising China to promote military sales, we are all susceptible to manipulation and exaggeration based on perceived danger. The fact that these dangers pose, at worst, minimal danger to actual Americans is all too rarely considered or discussed.

One does not need to be a politician to understand this very human vulnerability—and how to use that knowledge to promote not America's interests but rather one's own.

An Alternative Post-9/11 History

Terrific dangers and troubles that we once called "foreign" now constantly live among us. If American lives must end, and American treasure be spilled, in countries that we barely know, then that is the price that change has demanded of conviction and of our enduring covenant.

—*President Lyndon B. Johnson, January 20, 1965*

Philadelphia is passionate about its sports teams. The city's fan bases are regularly ranked among the most loyal in all of sports, and Philadelphians are so fanatical that the National Football League's Eagles briefly put a courtroom in the team's stadium to deal with unruly fans. When the team won its first Super Bowl in 2018, fans celebrated by tearing down Philadelphia's light posts, flipping cars, and setting fires in the streets.[1] This is a city whose fans once famously heckled and threw snowballs at Santa Claus. So on September 20, 2001, the 19,117 fans at a Philadelphia Flyers game did something quite in character for the City of Brotherly Love: they booed. Why they did so is the surprising part.

That night, nine days after September 11, President George W. Bush spoke to a joint session of Congress, and during the second intermission of an exhibition game between the Flyers and the rival

New York Rangers, Bush's remarks were played in the arena. As the players returned to the ice, the big-screen operator at the team's home stadium, First Union Center, turned off the speech in preparation for the third period. Under a torrent of boos, the speech was quickly turned back on, and for the next thirty-three minutes, the fans and players watched in silence. Afterward, both teams shook hands. The remainder of the game was canceled and declared a 2–2 tie.[2]

It might have been the first time in the city's history that fans chose to hear the words of a politician over rooting for their team.

This unusual display of "country before team" is an important reminder that presidents maintain a powerful bully pulpit, particularly when it comes to explaining global events to the American people. In total, eighty-two million citizens watched President Bush that evening—the largest-ever audience for a presidential address. The speech was delivered at the recommendation of the Speaker of the House, Dennis Hastert, who suggested to Bush that he needed to address the nation after the catastrophe, just as President Franklin Roosevelt had done after Pearl Harbor. Like Roosevelt's famous declaration that December 7, 1941, would be a date that lived in "infamy," Bush's speech had a seismic impact on the nation. His remarks that night turned out to be among the most consequential—and, in time, most calamitous—of the twenty-first century and served as a powerful framing event for all Americans in understanding the post-9/11 world.[3]

On September 20, 2001, Americans were still grieving for those who had been killed. They were scared, unsure of what had happened and what might come next. As the fire at Ground Zero continued to burn and the search for bodies had only just begun, they looked to their president for answers.[4] Bush followed firmly in the footsteps of Harry Truman, Lyndon Johnson, and countless other politicians—he scared the hell out of them. "Our war on terror begins with al-Qaeda, but it does not end there. It will not end until every terrorist group of global reach has been found, stopped, and defeated," Bush defiantly declared. He announced the start of a global war on terrorism and prophetically promised a "lengthy campaign." Bush claimed that "freedom and fear are at war," and like Truman, he cast the struggle against jihadist terrorists who lived in caves in Afghanistan as an existential fight between good and evil. "The advance of human freedom, the great achievement of our time and the great hope of every time, now depends on us," he declared. "Our nation, this generation, will lift the dark threat of violence from our people and our future. We will rally the world to this cause by our efforts, by our courage. We will not tire, we will not falter, and we will not fail."[5] After the speech, Bush told his chief speechwriter, "I have never felt more comfortable in my life."[6]

Bush's speech had its desired effect. U.S. media outlets were sympathetic to Bush's call for a strong military response, and the public was primed to lend support. According to one study, 83 percent of those who viewed the president's speech to Congress felt it made them "more confident in this country's ability to deal with this crisis." They were also "significantly more likely than those who did not watch it to support Bush's handling of the crisis, the use of force against Afghanistan, and the use of force against other states that may have supported al-Qaeda."[7]

Four months later, in January 2002, Bush delivered his first State of the Union Address as a wartime president. He told the nation of a North Korea, Iraq, and Iran "axis of evil" that threatened the United States, even though none of those countries had any connection, even indirectly, to the 9/11 attacks. He also raised the specter of terrorists getting their hands on weapons of mass destruction and declared, "the United States of America will not permit the world's most dangerous regimes to threaten us with the world's most destructive weapons."[8]

In May 2002, Bush again took to the bully pulpit in a commencement speech at the U.S. Military Academy at West Point. There he told the graduating cadets, "the gravest danger to freedom lies at the perilous crossroads of radicalism and technology." He offered a new doctrine of preemptive war that called for the United States to "take the battle to the enemy, disrupt his plans, and confront the worst threats before they emerge."[9]

That fall, Bush married all of these themes together as he marshaled public support for invading Iraq to protect the United States, both from the menace of that country's alleged stockpiles of weapons of mass destruction and from Saddam Hussein's purported connection to al-Qaeda-affiliated terrorists. In March 2003, the United States invaded Iraq and initiated a war that lasted nearly eight years, took the lives of forty-six hundred Americans, and reached at least $1 trillion in direct costs.

This history ought to be well-known to the American people. The global war on terror, the wars in Afghanistan and Iraq—and then Libya and Syria—the drone strikes that became ubiquitous under the next two presidents, and a newfound domestic vigilance to "see something" and "say something" defined the first decade and a half of twenty-first-century America.

But imagine for a moment that a different speech had been broadcast that evening to the Flyers fans in Philadelphia. Bush could still have urged Americans to grieve those who were lost on 9/11 and pledged vengeance against those who directly attacked the United States. But what if he had also reminded his audience that the threat posed by terrorist groups like al-Qaeda was serious but manageable?

Imagine if Bush had proclaimed, "The one thing the terrorists want more than anything else is for this great nation to overreact to this terrible act of violence. They want us to play into their hands, as

Osama bin Laden himself has stated. America is stronger than that, and the world is overwhelmingly on our side. We will patch up the nation's wounds, punish those who are responsible, and strengthen our defenses to ensure that this never happens again. But above all, we will act smartly and with restraint, secure in the knowledge that the international community and peace-loving people everywhere—are overwhelmingly on the side of the United States." If Bush had delivered these words, America—and the world—would likely be a very different and much safer, healthier, and more prosperous place today.

The strategic mistakes made in the prosecution of the war on terror and invasion of Iraq have been examined and reexamined, and there is no need to fully rehash them here. Less scrutinized, however, are the indirect costs of the conflicts and, in particular, the tremendous opportunity costs. Money and attention spent on fighting phantom threats in the Middle East could have been better utilized not only to keep citizens safe from the domestic threats and systemic risks that actually harm them but also to further promote U.S. national security interests abroad.

In this chapter, we envision a plausible alternative post-9/11 history and detail the small but crucial steps that the Bush administration did right (implementing policies that better protected the U.S. homeland at little cost). We also look at the great many things that it got wrong (initiating the occupation of Afghanistan after the toppling of the Taliban and invading and occupying Iraq). The response to 9/11 offers perhaps the most enduring lesson about the catastrophic consequences—and lost opportunities—that come from foreign-threat inflation.

The Smart Response to 9/11

One of the great ironies of 9/11 is that the initial response to the worst terrorist attack on American soil was smart, modest, and appropriate. Though the attacks seemed to be a transformative event in the nation's history, it was neither a "strategic surprise" nor a "failure of imagination," as the 9/11 Commission later determined. Before 9/11, political leaders were well aware of the growing problem of transnational terrorism, including the weaponization of civilian airliners.[10] Scholars and experts had repeatedly warned about the threat from al-Qaeda and had called for commonsense and inexpensive counterterrorism and homeland security policies, such as better airport security, improved information sharing between intelligence and law enforcement agencies, and stronger border security.[11]

A tragic combination of political inertia, disinterest, and bureaucratic turf protection had made the United States needlessly vulnerable. But policy makers learned from their mistakes. Much of the negligence and policy shortcomings that predated 9/11 were addressed through new laws and regulations, increased government spending, and an expansion of America's homeland security and intelligence infrastructure.[12] These improvements ranged from the obvious and immediate to the complex and ongoing.

For example, prior to 9/11, the Federal Aviation Administration (FAA) mandated that aircrews keep cockpit doors closed and locked while in flight, but this regulation had never been rigorously observed. The 9/11 Commission could never determine exactly how hijackers accessed the cockpits of the four planes seized that day, whether they took the keys from flight attendants, forced them to open the door, or somehow lured a pilot outside.[13] Had the cockpit doors remained closed, the airliners would never have been turned into flying missiles. The Transportation Security Administration (TSA), which was created in the wake of 9/11, updated the requirements for cockpit security, replacing flimsy doors and simple latches with hardened, bulletproof doors that had electronic locking devices. Congress provided $97 million to defray the costs for airlines—a negligible price relative to the outsized impact on airline security.[14]

The 9/11 Commission also proposed legislation to "set standards for the issuance of birth certificates and sources of identification, such as driver's licenses."[15] This led to the Real ID Act of 2005, which required states to include certain information on licenses (such as full legal name, date of birth, and signature), demand more identification material, and ensure that licenses are more securely produced. Since the implementation of the act, about 90 percent of driver's licenses comply with these new standards and are now far more difficult to forge.[16] This means that the airlines and the TSA have a far better chance of accurately detecting individuals attempting to evade no-fly lists or at least ensuring that they receive secondary screening.

The most consequential homeland security improvement originated in the 9/11 Commission's recommendation that intelligence agencies better share intelligence information and "break down stovepipes" that had previously prevented such cooperation. For example, when the CIA learned in January 2000 that an individual with al-Qaeda connections, Khalid al-Mihdhar, had been issued a U.S. visa, it kept that information from the FBI and the State Department. Two months later, when it received evidence that another al-Qaeda member, Nawaf al-Hazmi, also had a U.S. visa and had purchased a plane ticket to Los Angeles, it again failed to inform the FBI.[17] Both men were among the nineteen 9/11 hijackers.

Improved information sharing was addressed with the 2004 Intelligence Reform and Terrorism Prevention Act, which established the Director of National Intelligence (DNI) to ensure better cooperation among intelligence agencies. The act also established the National Counterterrorism Center (NCTC), which is the government's analytical hub for all intelligence related to foreign terrorism. Today, the

FBI and CIA better share intelligence about potential terror plots, and there is a central clearinghouse for all terror-related information.[18]

This focus, not surprisingly, led to a doubling in federal counterterrorism spending after 9/11.[19] While still disproportionate to the terrorist threat actually facing the United States, it is a relatively small fraction of taxpayer dollars, particularly in comparison to the trillions spent invading, occupying, and rebuilding Iraq and Afghanistan.[20]

These post-9/11 measures have made Americans vastly safer from terrorism today. If the homeland security apparatus currently in place had existed on September 11, 2001, it is highly unlikely that Americans would have any reason to remember that date.[21]

But preventing terrorist attacks is about more than dollars and cents. One of most important factors in keeping the United States safe from Islamic terrorism is the significant challenge in recruiting of Muslim Americans to the jihadist cause. Despite the Islamophobic sentiments expressed by some politicians and media figures, Muslims in America overwhelmingly reject terrorist violence (few, for example, have joined the Islamic State caliphate in Syria and Iraq, particularly compared to Muslim populations in western Europe).[22] Many Muslim Americans have worked with law enforcement in identifying individuals vulnerable to recruitment by extremist groups or potential perpetrators of lone-wolf attacks. Indeed, the decision by President Bush to show solidarity with the American Muslim community—including visiting a mosque in Washington, DC, not long after the attacks—helped to prevent the kind of radicalization that is all too familiar to European authorities.[23]

The Immediate Costs of Threat Inflation: $3.8 Trillion

While the Bush administration and Congress made several smart homeland security choices after 9/11, their decisions overseas tell a different story. The so-called global war on terrorism became the dominant, and at times exclusive, frame for Bush's post-9/11 foreign policy. In the days and weeks after the attacks, Bush was greeted each morning with the Threat Matrix, a collection of potential terrorist attacks that included even the most unlikely and least verifiable threats amassed by the intelligence community. The director of central intelligence George Tenet later wrote that it was impossible to read what crossed his desk "and be anything other than scared to death."[24] The theater of post-9/11 security measures affected policy makers as well. According to Condoleezza Rice, then the national security adviser, "large, menacing men swathed in black and armed with assault rifles and shotguns suddenly showed up everywhere" around the White House; "it had a huge impact on our psyches."[25]

With the Bush administration already committed to an aggressive policy of preventive war against states that allegedly harbored or assisted terrorists, there would be little political or media pushback in inflating the terrorist threat. "The people who did this act on America, and who may be planning further acts, are evil people," Bush said just two weeks after 9/11. "They don't represent an ideology. They don't represent a legitimate political group of people. They're flat evil. That's all they can think about, is evil."[26] Two weeks later, he declared even more directly, "Our war is against evil."[27]

Counterterrorism quickly became the defining language of official Washington, a catch-all justification for presidential priorities, from a new volunteerism initiative to a push for increased domestic energy production. "We will prevail in the war, and we will defeat this recession," Bush said in his 2002 State of the Union Address, as he conflated the war abroad with his economic policies at home. Fear that a congressional inquiry into the events of 9/11 would weaken America's fight against the terrorists was even used as a rationale to shut it down.[28]

Fighting terrorism also became the basis on which America's bilateral and multilateral relations were judged. "Either you are with us, or you are with the terrorists" was the binary choice that Bush presented to all other 191 countries in his speech to Congress.[29]

Viewing the world through such a lens led to policies that significantly undermined America's reputation and credibility. In January 2002, the United States began dispatching terrorist suspects from Afghanistan and Pakistan to a detention center at the Guantanamo Bay Naval Base in Cuba. They were housed there without Geneva Convention protections and under a new and dubious legal designation: "enemy combatant."[30] The first twenty prisoners to arrive were stripped naked, placed in diapers and orange jumpsuits, blindfolded, and shackled to the floor of a military transport aircraft, because "these are people that would gnaw through hydraulic lines in the back of a C-17 to bring it down," according to Gen. Richard Myers, then chairman of the Joint Chiefs of Staff.[31] In the years after these prisoners were flown to Guantanamo, terrorists repeatedly used the imagery of the orange-clad suspects, held in six-by-eight-foot open-air, wire-mesh cages, for recruiting purposes. As of May 2018, Guantanamo remains open with forty detainees held, five of whom were recommended for release by a high-level government panel, as well as twenty-six indefinite detainees who will likely never be charged, prosecuted, or let go.[32] President Donald Trump issued an executive order in January 2018 that directed the military to send even more prisoners to Guantanamo, ensuring that nearly seventeen years after it opened, it is no closer to being shuttered.[33]

Fear of terrorism also drove the White House to adopt policies that not only were illegal but also violated basic American values. Torture, and in particular waterboarding, of terrorist suspects became frighteningly routine. The CIA operated a secret rendition, interrogation, and torture program with black sites in Afghanistan, Lithuania, Poland, Romania, and Thailand. These unethical and illegal efforts brought marginal national security gain. There is little evidence that information obtained through torture prevented any attacks against the United States.[34] The use of such measures instead had a damaging cascade effect when horrifying pictures emerged of U.S. soldiers in Iraq using the same torture methods against detainees at Abu Ghraib, a notorious prison complex west of Baghdad where Saddam Hussein had imprisoned and tortured his political enemies.[35]

The diplomatic and reputational costs of these policies have been tremendous. A Carr Center for Human Rights Policy at Harvard University study found that the use of torture "incited extremism in the Middle East, hindered cooperation with U.S. allies, exposed American officials to legal repercussions, undermined U.S. diplomacy, and offered a convenient justification for other governments to commit human rights abuses."[36] Concerns over the use of torture jeopardized relationships that were critical for the war on terrorism, stalling military cooperation, extradition treaties, and access to foreign airports, air bases, and airspace.[37] For example, in 2003, the Netherlands planned to send troops to Afghanistan to support the U.S.-led mission, until public opposition to torture delayed parliamentary authorization for the deployment for three years.[38] The Finnish parliament deferred the ratification of an extradition treaty between the United States and European Union, and both Ireland and Great Britain enacted strict requirements for landing U.S. military planes on their soil.[39]

There were also more direct financial costs for America's obsessive focus on terrorism. More than forty countries were recruited to play a role in the Iraq invasion and occupation, and many received compensation. In addition, the United States began subsidizing counterterrorism efforts around the globe. Pakistan alone has received more than $34 billion in economic and security assistance since 2002.[40] This is the same country that remained home to Osama bin Laden for nearly a decade and provided sanctuary to Taliban insurgents fighting U.S. troops in Afghanistan. It is not hard to imagine the many ways $34 billion, or a fraction of that total, could have been spent on more modest counterterrorism efforts.

Finally, there are larger foreign policy opportunity costs. The war on terrorism undermined other long-standing U.S. foreign policy objectives, such as democracy promotion—an issue that moved to the forefront of Bush's second-term foreign policy agenda. But Bush quickly found those efforts thwarted by his war on terror prerogatives. In Ethiopia, during the run-up to national elections that would be dominated by allegations of electoral fraud, prime minister Meles Zenawi's government expelled several major U.S. democracy-promotion organizations. The Bush administration complained but ultimately offered little protest. After all, Ethiopia played a crucial role in the U.S. fight against Islamist rebels in Somalia. American leaders pushed for legislative elections in Gaza in 2006, but out of fear of upsetting counterterrorism allies in Israel and Egypt, they rejected the outcome when Hamas, a U.S.-designated "foreign terrorist organization," prevailed. Similar episodes played out with Kazakhstan and Azerbaijan, two countries led by authoritarian strongmen but critical players in the U.S. war in Afghanistan.[41]

Few post-9/11 foreign policy decisions, however, would prove more disastrous than U.S. involvement in Afghanistan. By the fall of 2001, the initial U.S. objective there was achieved: the Taliban had been removed from power in Kabul, and al-Qaeda training camps in southern Afghanistan had been eliminated. However, after Osama bin Laden and his senior aides were allowed to escape to Pakistan and the Taliban became a structured insurgent force, U.S. attention waned, particularly in the face of herculean economic, political, and developmental hurdles involved in rebuilding Afghanistan. The United States refused to work with Afghan political leaders to broker a diplomatic settlement with the Taliban. After all, the war on terrorism had been predicated on destroying terrorist organizations, not making deals with them.[42] With focus moving to the next front in the war on terror, Iraq, critical military assets—including elite special operations forces and Predator drones—were diverted to the Persian Gulf. As a result, the political and security situation inside Afghanistan began to fester, and the Taliban insurgency reemerged.[43]

By 2009, the Taliban had made significant inroads in reestablishing itself as a viable insurgent group. While the Taliban still posed little threat to the United States—and had few operational ties to al-Qaeda—U.S. leaders were practically powerless in resisting the call to do something to stabilize Afghanistan. President Barack Obama sent nearly fifty thousand additional U.S. troops into the country in order to break the Taliban's momentum—an effort that did nothing to bring the war closer to conclusion, as Afghanistan remains mired in civil war today. The human toll of the war has been more than twenty-three hundred U.S. troops and at least thirty-two thousand Afghan civilians.[44] As of this book's publication, the war in Afghanistan—and the Taliban insurgency—continues, making the seventeen-year war the longest in American history. Amazingly, its price tag now exceeds that of the war in Iraq.

Invading Iraq

While the war on terrorism dominated the attention of the Bush administration in the days and weeks after 9/11, it was the ill-fated decision to invade Iraq in March 2003 that created a true foreign policy catastrophe. The U.S. invasion and occupation has led—directly and indirectly—to more than one million deaths.[45] Another 7.6 million people have been displaced by the war.[46] A decade and a half after Saddam Hussein was toppled, Iraq suffered the highest number of terror attacks and terror fatalities in the world, and a host of terrorist organizations, militias, and proxy forces continued to destabilize the country.

Close to 4,500 U.S. active-duty, national guard, and reserve service members died fighting in Iraq.[47] Another 110 U.S. private citizens were killed in Iraq while supporting the war effort.[48] In addition to the ultimate sacrifice of U.S. troops are the unknown yet essential contributions of private contractors in America's wars. For every U.S. troop in-country, there was at least one military contractor providing support, with the total number peaking at 164,000 in 2008.[49] More than 1,500 of these contractors lost their lives—approximately one-third of whom were American citizens.[50]

Beyond the human toll, the financial costs of the Iraq War have been stratospherically high. Before the 2003 invasion, secretary of defense Donald Rumsfeld pegged the total bill for the war at "something under $50 billion." When the White House economic adviser Lawrence Lindsey projected the war's cost at 1 or 2 percent of gross domestic product—$100 to $200 billion—he was summarily pushed out of his job.[51] Andrew Natsios, the director of USAID, said that the costs of reconstruction would top out at around $1.7 billion, and deputy secretary of defense Paul Wolfowitz claimed that Iraq could "finance its own reconstruction, and relatively soon."[52]

In fact, the high end of Lindsey's estimate was off by a factor of four. The United States spent more than $819 billion on the invasion, occupation, and reconstruction of Iraq between 2003 and 2017.[53] This number includes only direct war spending, which peaked at

$12 billion a month in 2008. Reconstruction efforts alone, such as building roads and repairing water systems, and providing assistance to small businesses reached more than $170 billion—one hundred times higher than Natsios's estimate.[54] By comparison, the first Gulf War cost $61 billion and was largely subsidized by Germany, Japan, and Persian Gulf states.[55] According to one independent government investigation, that total is actually nearly equal to the amount of money spent between 2003 and 2011 on reconstruction efforts in Iraq.[56]

The direct costs to American taxpayers for U.S. involvement in Iraq and Afghanistan have—so far—reached $3.8 trillion.[57] That works out to approximately $20,000 paid by each individual taxpayer.[58] This staggering figure includes all war-related costs, veterans costs, and interest payments related to war borrowing made through November 2017. The sum is more than the United States spent on any of its previous wars, except World War II ($4.5 trillion in current dollars)—and the meter continues to run.[59]

The Long-Term Costs, Now and Forever: $7 Trillion

As enormous as these numbers are, they do not do full justice to the outsized costs of America's military response to 9/11. The tally for America's war on terror did not simply stop when active combat ended or when public attention moved on to something else. It continues to mount today as interest accrues on wartime borrowing, as veterans still require treatment, and as their families shoulder the mantle of their care. Neta Crawford, codirector of the Costs of War Project at Brown University, likens these additional expenses to an iceberg: "Some of it is visible, but most goes unseen. With climate change, people think that all icebergs melt, but this one doesn't melt; in fact, it only gets bigger."[60] Beyond the immediate toll for U.S. troops and their families, as well as for Iraq, Afghanistan, and their neighbors, these long-term expenditures will impact every U.S. government program for the rest of the twenty-first century.

Unlike for previous U.S. conflicts, the Bush administration and Congress chose to finance the wars in Iraq and Afghanistan not through short-term tax increases but rather by borrowing money.[61] Going to war in Iraq and Afghanistan on a credit card added about $2 trillion to the national debt. In fact, at least one-third of the federal debt accrued after 2003 is directly attributable to just these two conflicts.[62] American taxpayers—and their children and grandchildren—will be servicing this debt for decades to come. In fact, they are actually paying for it now. The increased debt burden from the war contributed to an increase in interest rates, which, by 2010, were estimated to be 0.35 percentage points higher as a direct result of deficit-financed war spending. This higher interest rate in turn raised fixed mortgage rates, costing the average American homeowner an extra $600 a year in mortgage payments.[63]

Based on current estimates, when the interest accrued on wartime borrowing and future borrowing is combined, the total costs of Iraq and Afghanistan could reach $7 trillion through 2056.[64]

However, it is the direct costs in government spending that may be the most enduring legacy of the war on terrorism. Hundreds of billions of dollars will continue to be needed to care for those who have returned from war. In all, more than 2.7 million active-duty, national guard, and reserve members served in Afghanistan and Iraq between 2001 and 2017.[65] By way of comparison, fewer American troops and reservists were deployed during the Vietnam War (2.6 million) and the Korean War (1.8 million)—and more than half of all post-9/11 troops were deployed more than once.[66] These multiple deployments have been shown to significantly increase the likelihood of troops suffering from combat-related trauma.[67] In fact, the average wounded veteran from Iraq and Afghanistan has an astounding 7.3 recognized disabilities.[68]

All of this comes with a significant and underappreciated cost. In 2001, the United States was spending $1.76 billion on disability benefits for veterans of the Gulf War, a conflict that took 148 American lives and left fewer than one thousand service members wounded.[69] Now consider for a moment the amount of spending that will be required for veterans of the wars in Iraq and Afghanistan, which left 6,800 killed and more than 52,000 wounded.[70] Already the annual disability compensation given to vets of the war on terrorism is $15 billion. These payments will rise exponentially over the next several decades.[71]

The families of service members killed on active duty or from service-related injuries and those receiving VA disability benefits at the time of death are also eligible for pensions of at least $1,200 a month.[72] It bears noting that eighty-eight dependents still receive benefits from the Spanish-American War, which ended in 1898. And astonishingly, 151 years after the surrender at Appomattox, the VA still pays benefits to an eighty-seven-year-old daughter of a Civil War veteran. As of August 2017, Irene Triplett was receiving $73.13 every month from her father's pension.[73] Since life expectancy in the United States has nearly doubled since the Civil War, there will be many Irene Tripletts who will be receiving monthly tax-free pension checks into the twenty-second century and beyond.

These costs are already piling up. In 2001, $91 billion was appropriated annually for both the Military Personnel and the Defense Health programs. In 2015, that number had risen to $160 billion.[74] These costs are, in many ways, qualitatively different from those of previous conflicts because of the nature of modern wartime injuries. While the most common malady for returning vets is hearing loss, the defining physical and mental injuries from the wars in Iraq and Afghanistan have been traumatic brain injury (TBI) and posttraumatic stress disorder (PTSD).[75] Between 15 to 23 percent of returning service members have a TBI, while one in five have suffered from PTSD.[76] Such injuries create lifelong infirmities—and enduring costs. In 2014 and 2015, the federal government spent $116 million on TBI care for Iraq and Afghanistan veterans, and the VA estimates that TBI will cost another $500 million total for post-9/11 veterans from 2016 to 2025.[77] While $3.3 billion was spent in 2012 for veterans suffering from PTSD, demand will increase because both traumas can go undiagnosed for years, with symptoms manifesting themselves decades later.[78] Then there are the indirect expenses. Through 2010, $2.2 billion has been lost in earnings by military veterans because of traumas and disabilities.[79] Moreover, PTSD can be transferred to family members (called "secondary traumatic stress"), the long-term consequences of which are unknown.[80]

It is nearly impossible to accurately quantify the impact that the war on terrorism has had on state and federal budgets or the U.S. economy. Nearly 60 percent of veterans had family responsibilities, and more than one million children had a parent deployed overseas.[81] Children whose parents were sent to Iraq or Afghanistan—compared to children of civilian parents—perform worse in school, experience greater anxiety or clinical depression, and attempt suicide at greater rates. They are also frequently required to fulfill parental or nursing responsibilities.[82] In fact, 1.1 million Americans serve as military caregivers for veterans of post-9/11 wars, at an estimated $5.9 billion in lost productivity.

In total, Linda Bilmes of Harvard University estimates that through 2056, the costs for disability, medical, and administrative costs of caring for post-9/11 veterans will total more than $1 trillion—and that is without taking into account lost productivity or the personal and emotional responsibilities borne by families, neighbors, and local communities. In short, the financial burden of America's overreaction to 9/11 will be borne by multiple generations of Americans for decades to come—and not just those who served.[83]

What Might Have Been, Part I

What if the reaction to 9/11 had been more modest? What if the focus of the Bush administration had been on strengthening homeland security but eschewing a strategy of preemptive war? Perhaps the greatest tragedy of the post-9/11 period is the millions of deaths that could have been prevented with the money spent on America's wars.

Take for example, one of the more unusual elements of the global war on terror: a public health initiative pushed by President Bush while he was making the case to go to war in Iraq. In his January 2003 State of the Union Address, in which he uttered the notorious (and inaccurate) claim that the "the British Government has learned that Saddam Hussein recently sought significant quantities of uranium from Africa," Bush unveiled the President's Emergency Plan for AIDS Relief (PEPFAR). The need for action could not have been more pressing. In 2002, three million people died from AIDS, five million more were stricken by the disease, and forty-two million had been infected in total—effectively a death sentence given the lack of available antiretroviral treatments. That year, only fifty thousand out of 29.4 million HIV-positive people living in sub-Saharan African had received these life-extending medicines.[84]

Bush asked Congress to authorize $15 billion over five years for PEPFAR—nearly $10 billion of which was new money—to combat the disease in fourteen of the most afflicted countries in Africa and the Caribbean. Bush's request represented a more than 1,400 percent increase in U.S. funding for international HIV/AIDS programs.[85] As he later recounted, "I hoped it would serve as a medical version of the Marshall Plan."[86] It more than achieved that goal.

Within just the first four years after Bush unveiled the program, PEPFAR's activities and spending on HIV care, prevention, and treatment averted 1.2 million deaths in twelve countries: Botswana, Cote d'Ivoire, Ethiopia, Kenya, Mozambique, Namibia, Nigeria, Rwanda, South Africa, Tanzania, Uganda, and Zambia.[87] A four-year Institute of Medicine review concluded that PEPFAR had been "globally transformative" and had "saved and improved the lives of millions."[88]

What is most remarkable about PEPFAR is its relatively paltry sum of $15 billion. Contrast that with the trillions of dollars spent in Iraq and Afghanistan, for far more dubious benefit. Just a fraction of that money could have done a world of good elsewhere. For example, providing universal health care is one of the best public health strategies for immediately helping the world's poor. Studies have shown that, at a cost of approximately $6.7 billion, expanding existing and proven health programs could, for example, reduce the number of deaths from pneumonia and diarrhea.[89] An expenditure of $9.6 billion on maternal nutrition and mineral and vitamin supplementation (less than two months of what it cost to fight the Iraq War) could have averted the deaths of nine hundred thousand children under five years old across the developing world.[90] Similarly, insecticide-treated bed nets (ITNs) have been shown to reduce deaths from malaria infections (which killed more than 740,000 people each year between 2000 and 2005) by up to 44 percent.[91] At the time, each ITN cost less than three dollars and lasted three years.[92] For a few million dollars above what the United States was contributing to the effort, a hundred thousand lives, or more, could have been saved.

Noteworthy progress could have also been made in improving childhood nutrition. In 2000, the World Health Organization warned that 3.4 million children died each year from being underweight.[93] This is a public health challenge that just a small financial contribution could have significantly impacted. For example, a 2002 World Bank program in Senegal recruited health workers to counsel and monitor mothers of children under the age of three. For just $23 million over four years, more than two hundred thousand participating children were prevented from growing up underweight and thus dying prematurely.[94] Similar results occurred in Colombia, where from 2001 to 2005, fifteen-dollar monthly grants to households resulted in increased food consumption and improved nutritional quality for young children.[95] Although extraordinary gains have been made in recent years on a host of public health issues, if just a small portion of the money spent on promoting democracy and fighting terrorism in the Middle East had been spent on helping people live happier, healthier, and longer lives, it could have made a world of difference.

These global investments are not simply worthwhile acts of charity and compassion. Rather, when people's quality of life is improved—when they are less worried about feeding their family and when children go to school—it increases stability, improves economic performance, and limits the potential for conflict. This makes America safer, since more stable and peaceful countries are less likely to serve as safe havens for transnational terrorists or to be at war with allies that U.S. troops would be obligated to protect. Former Marine general—and later secretary of defense—James Mattis expressed this sentiment best to Congress in 2013: "If you don't fund the State Department fully, then I need to buy more ammunition."[96] Few people, unfortunately, were listening to Mattis, including his future commander in chief, Donald Trump, who in his first two budgets as president, proposed slashing spending for the State Department and USAID by more than 25 percent a year.[97]

What Might Have Been, Part II

Beyond the global effect, the $3.8 trillion spent in Iraq and Afghanistan could have transformed the lives of the American people. As we detailed earlier, the risks and systemic harms that pose the greatest threats to Americans are neither foreign terrorist masterminds nor malicious hackers. Rather, Americans are killed in vastly greater numbers by disease, guns, and narcotics. They are hurt by failing infrastructure, poor schools, and growing levels of income inequality. If the United States had redirected even a fraction of the hundreds of billions spent "fighting terrorism" toward reducing the challenges that Americans face at home, not only would Americans be safer, but their quality of life would be dramatically better too.

Start with the number-one killer of Americans: noncommunicable diseases (NCDs). In 2004, 2.14 million people died from NCDs like cancer, heart disease, and respiratory disease.[98] One critical preventive factor for reducing the prevalence of NCDs and the onset of all diseases and ailments is ensuring affordable access to health care. The number of Americans who lacked health care coverage increased from 38.7 million in 2000 to 45.8 million in 2004.[99] At the time, public health groups estimated that expanding coverage to all the uninsured would cost an additional $48 billion—or four months of funding the war in Iraq.[100] Expanding health care coverage nationwide would have prevented 17,000 premature deaths annually—or one life for every 830 newly insured Americans.[101]

We know that U.S. deaths from gun violence would have been diminished if Congress and state legislatures had passed more restrictive gun laws. However, had money been spent on expanding mental health coverage to better ensure that people receive diagnosis and treatment for severe depression, that too would have substantially decreased gun deaths. In 2007, a legislative proposal garnered wide support from mental health providers and organizations because of its promise to do just that. The Community Mental Health Services Improvement Act would have given grants to mental health providers to expand and improve coverage, instituting programs such as "telemental health" services for underserved areas. The proposal would have required approximately $100 million a year in funding, but Congress never even voted on it. Hiring extra police officers would also have led to more illegal gun seizures and a reduction in overall gun crimes.[102] The money spent during just one day on the Iraq War in 2008 could have put nine thousand more state and local police officers on the streets in high-gun-violence communities.[103]

While the United States spent $170 billion rebuilding Iraq's and Afghanistan's roads, water systems, and energy systems, its own crumbling critical infrastructure was in dire need of repairs and upgrades. The American Society of Civil Engineers (ASCE) releases a report card every four years on the status of U.S. infrastructure. In 2001, the ASCE graded U.S. infrastructure with a D+ overall and estimated that $1.3 trillion was needed over the next five years to bring the country's infrastructure to an "acceptable level."[104] Needless to say, no such funds were allocated, and in the ASCE's next report in 2003, it listed $1.6 trillion as the amount needed.[105] Its following report in 2009 raised the number to $2.2 trillion.[106] As a consequence of this underinvestment, between 2002 and 2015, the United States fell eleven spots in the overall international ranking of infrastructure quality, from five to sixteen.[107]

For one concrete example of how infrastructure spending in the middle of the first decade of the twenty-first century would have improved Americans' well-being, go no further than the water you and your children drink. In February 2001, the Environmental Protection Agency (EPA) estimated that the cost to maintain, upgrade, or replace aging water and wastewater infrastructure over the ensuing twenty years would amount to approximately $151 billion.[108] This includes $83.2 billion to repair or replace aging water lines, the deterioration of which poses significant health risks, including elevated lead and copper levels in the blood stream of children. That same year, the EPA estimated that $19.4 billion was needed immediately for water treatment to protect Americans from developing chronic health effects, including cancer and birth defects, after unnecessary exposure to nitrates and other chemical contaminants.[109] Needless to say, with the United States focused on wars in the Middle East, such funding was not forthcoming. Not surprisingly, by 2009 the EPA reported that the price tag for fixing America's water supply had more than doubled, from $151 billion in 2001 to $334.8 billion.[110]

A congressional report at the time, *War at Any Price? The Total Economic Costs of the War beyond the Federal Budget*, offered a menu of alternatives for the Iraq conflict that was running a tab of $435 million every single day.[111] The same money spent on surging 30,000 U.S. troops to Iraq in 2007 could have added 5,500 teachers to U.S. classrooms. It could have also enrolled 57,500 low-income children in the Head Start program. The money could have also helped 150,000 low-income students through Pell Grants, a lifeline for poor adults seeking to go to college.[112]

Finally, there are the enormous opportunity costs of the war on terrorism. Economists have often demonstrated that defense spending has, at best, a temporary and limited positive impact on the economy. For every $1 billion spent on defense, 11,200 direct and indirect military-related jobs are created. The same amount creates 5,600 more jobs if spent on clean energy, 6,000 more if spent on health care, and 15,500 more if spent on education. By one estimate, if the money spent in Iraq and Afghanistan through 2014 had been channeled into clean-energy industries, health care, and education, two million more Americans would have been gainfully employed during that time period.[113] These domestic investments to improve and protect Americans' lives were never seriously considered during the same time that Americans were fighting and dying in Iraq.

At the end of the day, few people would look back on the war on terrorism as a raging success or, at the very least, a good return on investment. In fact, the U.S. reaction to September 11 is perhaps the greatest "own goal"—when a soccer or hockey team unintentionally scores its own net—in American history.

Ironically, the United States should have listened more closely to the man responsible for 9/11. Osama bin Laden often said that one of the key goals in attacking America was to produce an overreaction that would mire the United States and its allies in a war with the Muslim world. Bin Laden, who argued that the Soviet war in Afghanistan "had bled Russia for ten years, until it went bankrupt," even claimed in a September 2007 video message that "the mistakes of Brezhnev [who had ordered Soviet troops in Afghanistan] are being repeated by Bush."[114]

If al-Qaeda's actions on 9/11 were intended to fundamentally weaken the United States economically and politically, it succeeded beyond the terrorist organization's wildest imaginations.

Conclusion

The world as we have created it is a process of our thinking. It cannot be changed without changing our thinking.

—*Albert Einstein*

On December 1, 2009, President Obama traveled to the U.S. Military Academy at West Point to deliver a major speech on Afghanistan. For nearly eight years, the United States had been waging war there, but the conflict hardly looked to be any closer to a conclusion. If anything, the opposite was true: the Taliban insurgency was expanding its reach, the Afghan government had become increasingly dysfunctional, and U.S. military commanders were demanding more troops to throw into the fight. After a months-long review of U.S. policy, in which Obama had been placed under extraordinary public pressure by military leaders, many of his advisers and, a host of foreign policy pundits to increase America's military commitment in Afghanistan, the president was finally ready to announce his plans.

It was not a surprise.

"As Commander-in-Chief," he told the assembled cadets, "I have determined that it is in our vital national interest to send an additional 30,000 U.S. troops to Afghanistan. After eighteen months, our troops will begin to come home. These are the resources that we need to seize the initiative, while building the Afghan capacity that can allow for a responsible transition of our forces out of Afghanistan." Though Obama acknowledged that al-Qaeda did not have a significant presence in Afghanistan and that the Afghan government was not in immediate danger of being overthrown, he nonetheless told Americans that he was "convinced that our security is at stake in Afghanistan and Pakistan" and that the U.S. must follow through on a strategy "to disrupt, dismantle, and defeat al Qaeda."[1]

According to the president, "Af-Pak," as it became known, "is the epicenter of violent extremism practiced by al Qaeda. It is from here that we were attacked on 9/11, and it is from here that new attacks are being plotted as I speak. This is no idle danger; no hypothetical threat." As long as Afghanistan was insecure, argued Obama, so too was America.

The president, however, did not point to any specific threats emanating from Afghanistan but rather from those across the border in Pakistan. His argument boiled down to the simplistic notion that 9/11 had been plotted and organized in Afghanistan and that even though al-Qaeda had a relative safe haven in Pakistan, it could return to Afghanistan to create a new one. It had been eight years since 9/11 and there had been no major terrorist attack on U.S. soil. Obama had run for office on a platform of ramping down America's war on terrorism. Yet now, ten months into his presidency, he was escalating that conflict.

Obama's decision was more a function of politics than sound policy. In an effort to burnish his foreign policy bona fides during the presidential campaign, he promised more attention to the war in Afghanistan—without giving much thought to what that attention would look like. Once in office, the young president was put under concerted pressure to abide by the military's wishes for more soldiers and the resources for a counterinsurgency strategy. On Afghanistan, the chickens had come home to roost.

However, what is most interesting and surprising about Obama's remarks is what came at the end of his speech. He explicitly criticized a U.S. foreign policy focused on searching for monsters to destroy and the lack of national attention to challenges at home.

"We've failed to appreciate the connection between our national security and our economy," declared the president. "In the wake of an economic crisis, too many of our neighbors and friends are out of work and struggle to pay the bills. Too many Americans are worried about the future facing our children. Meanwhile, competition within the global economy has grown more fierce. So we can't simply afford to ignore the price of these wars," as he noted the trillions of dollars spent prosecuting the war on terror.

But the president went even further. "We must rebuild our strength here at home. Our prosperity provides a foundation for our power. It pays for our military. It underwrites our diplomacy. It taps the potential of our people, and allows investment in new industry. And it will allow us to compete in this century as successfully as we did in the last."

He said American security and leadership "does not come solely from the strength of our arms" but also from "workers and businesses," from "entrepreneurs and researchers," "from the teachers that will educate our children," and from "the service of those who work in our communities at home."

Obama would frequently return to these themes during his presidency. In his first National Security Strategy, unveiled in May 2010, Obama pledged renewed American leadership but also greater focus on domestic policy because "what takes place within our borders will determine our strength and influence beyond them."[2]

Defining the U.S. economy as "the wellspring of American power," Obama called for new "investments" in "a quality education for our children; enhancing science and innovation; transforming our energy economy to power new jobs and industries; lowering the cost of health care; . . . reducing the federal deficit"; and creating "a more resilient nation" that is better able to withstand natural and man-made threats.[3]

In 2011, when Obama followed through on his pledge to draw down troops from Afghanistan within eighteen months, he told the American people, "it is time to focus on nation building here at home."[4] During his 2012 State of the Union Address, he pledged to "take the money we're no longer spending at war, use half of it to pay down our debt, and use the rest to do some nation-building right here at home."[5] While campaigning against Mitt Romney later that year, Obama added, "Let's rebuild our infrastructure, . . . our roads and our bridges, . . . broadband lines and high speed rail. Let's expand our ports and improve our airports." And once again he asked the American people, "Why wouldn't we do some nation-building here at home?"[6]

The disconnect is dizzying and is one of the more compelling examples of the pathology of threat inflation. Obama clearly recognized the need for America to focus on pressing domestic challenges and noted their connection to national power. But only in America could the president expand a military commitment against a largely phantom threat, while at the same time decrying the deleterious impact of pursuing such policies. Unsurprisingly, Obama's efforts to recast U.S. foreign policy and focus less on distant and foreign threats and more on the challenges America faced at home fell on deaf ears.

Indeed, the 2016 presidential campaign made clear that America had returned to an era in which fear was the key driver of domestic politics. From literally the moment that Donald Trump announced his candidacy for president on June 16, 2015, his campaign was defined by xenophobia and fear-based rhetoric that grossly mischaracterized and inflated foreign threats. This ran the gamut from "rapist" Mexican immigrants and Islamic State terrorists posing as refugees to foreign governments—allies and rivals alike—that were allegedly ripping off America blind.

While Trump's pledge to "build a wall" along the U.S.-Mexican border put his candidacy on the map, it was his call in December 2015 for a total ban on Muslim immigration—in the wake of a mass shooting in San Bernardino, California, by two radicalized jihadist terrorists—that solidified his support within the Republican Party. Trump's proposal was certainly radical, but it also followed a familiar and growing pattern of anti-Muslim attitudes within the GOP.

During the 2016 Republican primary campaign, the former pediatric surgeon and later Housing and Urban Development secretary Ben Carson determined that Islam was inconsistent with the Constitution, adding, "I would not advocate that we put a Muslim in charge of this nation."[7] Sen. Ted Cruz advocated "empower[ing] law enforcement to patrol and secure Muslim neighborhoods before they become radicalized."[8] Sen. Marco Rubio proposed monitoring "anyplace—whether it's a cafe, a diner, an internet site—where radicals are being inspired," without revealing how such a seemingly infinite number of places could be identified or how those who happened to be there would receive Fourth Amendment constitutional protections.[9] In an unhinged speech at the Republican National Convention, Newt Gingrich declared, "We are at war with radical Islamists," who he claimed would somehow acquire weapons of mass destruction. "Instead of losing 3,000 people in one morning," said the former Speaker of the House, "we could lose more than 300,000."[10]

Even the relatively moderate former Florida governor Jeb Bush joined practically every other Republican officeholder in America in calling for a ban on Syrian Muslim refugees entering the country. It was a far cry from his brother, George W. Bush, who in the days after September 11 ventured to a Washington, DC, mosque and called for tolerance toward Muslim American communities.[11]

Trump's top foreign policy adviser and later his short-lived national security adviser—retired lieutenant general Michael Flynn—embraced and informed Trump's anti-Islamic views. "Fear of Muslims is RATIONAL [*sic*]," he tweeted out at one point during the campaign. He also coauthored an incendiary book that, among many unfounded claims, asserted, "We are under attack, not only from nation-states directly, but also from al-Qaeda, Hezbollah, ISIS, and countless other terrorist groups. . . . Suffice to say, the same sort of cooperation binds together jihadis, Communists, and garden-variety tyrants."[12] These imagined links between all U.S. adversaries was a willful distortion of reality yet consistent with the Trump campaign's apocalyptic threat inflation. As the former New York City mayor Rudy Giuliani put it starkly at the Republican National Convention, unless Trump won in November, "there's no next election, this is it."[13]

In ordinary political moments, such divisive and bigoted rhetoric would have been a national scandal—and the death knell of a presidential campaign. But the 2016 campaign offered a depressing reminder of the extent to which fearmongering remained a potent political weapon.

Once in office, Trump did not let up. Days after his inauguration, he signed an executive order (EO) banning all refugees from entering the country for 120 days and blocking travelers from seven Muslim-majority countries for 90 days. "We want to ensure that we are not admitting into our country the very threats our soldiers are fighting overseas," Trump said in seeking to justify the ban. Homeland Security secretary (and later White House chief of staff) John Kelly echoed these sentiments, arguing that the EO was necessary because "this way we can ensure the system is doing what it is designed to do, which is protect the American people."[14] It should be noted that the chances of an American being killed by a refugee in a terrorist attack is about one in 3.6 billion. In contrast, the odds of being struck by lightning are one in seven hundred thousand—being struck twice is one in nine million.[15] In fact, between 1975 and the day Trump signed his EO, only three refugees had committed deadly terrorist attacks within the United States. They had all been from Cuba.[16]

Nonetheless, Trump defended the White House's decision to announce the travel ban without warning or guidance to the Transportation Security Administration and U.S. Border Patrol on the grounds that "if the ban were announced with a one week notice, the 'bad' would rush into our country during that week. A lot of bad 'dudes' out there!"[17]

Though numerous federal courts struck down the ban, the White House issued another order that was eventually upheld by the Supreme Court. The court's decision notwithstanding, the economic and reputational damage to the United States from Trump's actions is quite clear. When the ban was put into effect in January 2017, residents of seven Muslim-majority countries, including some dual-citizenship Americans, were detained and questioned at airports across America for hours on end. Translators who served alongside U.S. troops in Afghanistan and Iraq had been forced to return to the countries where their lives, and those of their families, were placed in danger because of the support they had provided to the U.S. military.[18]

Even American citizens flying from San Francisco to New York City were stopped by Customs and Border Protection agents while deplaning and required to show their "documents," which is a violation of the Fourth Amendment.[19] More directly, pulling away America's welcome mat damaged the U.S. economy and tourism industry, hurt colleges and universities that relied on foreign students, and undermined health care services for Americans in poor rural areas, where often only foreign-born doctors and nurses will work. In just the first week after the ban had been announced, the United States saw a $200 million drop in business travel. For 2017, while tourism boomed around the world, international bookings for travel to the United States fell by 4 percent, costing the United States more than $4.6 billion and forty thousand jobs.[20] At the same time, newly empowered immigration enforcement officials began systematically rounding up undocumented immigrants across the United States—even those who had never been accused or convicted of a crime and had lived peacefully in America for years. As this book prepared to go to print, the Trump administration implemented a policy of forcibly separating migrant children from their parents, including those seeking asylum in the United States. Public outcry forced the White House to reverse course, and a federal judge ordered the administration to immediately reunify children—some younger than five years old—with their parents. However, the harm to America's standing in the world—as well as the chilling effect on tourism and immigration—is impossible to ignore.

Trump's focus on overseas security threats was felt elsewhere. His first budget proposal, titled "A New Foundation for American Greatness," called for more than $50 billion in new military spending, along with dramatic reductions in domestic spending initiatives, from cuts to job-training and employment-assistance programs to massive cuts for government agencies that focus on worker safety and environmental protection.[21]

Trump also implemented what he called an "America First" foreign policy that eschewed long-standing alliances, international agreements, and global cooperation. Trump spent far more time berating NATO allies for their spending on national defense than he did extolling the virtues of the nearly seventy-year security relationship. He pulled the United States out of the Paris Climate Change Treaty, walked away from the multilateral nuclear-nonproliferation agreement with Iran (with no better, or alternative strategy), and enacted unilateral tariffs that risked sparking a global trade war. Though, not to fear, the president proclaimed, "trade wars are good, and easy to win."[22] Later, in July 2018, when asked who is America's "biggest foe globally right now," Trump amazingly responded that it is the European Union.[23]

Trump's first secretary of state, Rex Tillerson, in his maiden major foreign policy speech spoke of the importance of putting national interests ahead of values like democracy and human rights—rather than viewing them as operating hand in hand. Internally, he enacted decimating personnel cuts and sidelined career diplomats, which led to a historic exit of Foreign Service officers and a precipitous drop in agency morale. Trump also proposed massive cuts to the State Department budget, including a 29 percent reduction in foreign operations and foreign-aid programs. At the United Nations, he ended support for international family-planning programs. Perhaps worst of all, Trump openly embraced antidemocratic leaders, such as Rodrigo Duterte in the Philippines, Recep Tayyip Erdoğan in Turkey, an increasingly authoritarian Xi Jinping in China, Viktor Orban in Hungary, and most controversially, Vladimir Putin in Russia.

Trump's domestic policies were not much better at making America great again. His initial legislative gambit was a failed attempt to repeal Obamacare and rip health insurance away from tens of millions of Americans. However, the administration continues to take steps to undermine the legislation and, in effect, weaken health care coverage for millions of Americans.[24] On issues like the rising opioid epidemic, his administration did little; on gun violence, nothing. Environmental and labor regulations were slashed, and infrastructure spending—an issue with bipartisan support—went nowhere in Congress. Trump's one big legislative victory was a massive trillion-and-a-half-dollar tax cut that disproportionately benefited the wealthiest Americans. The bill, however, was projected by the Congressional Budget Office to increase the federal deficit by nearly $2 trillion and is estimated by the economists at the San Francisco Federal Reserve to have had between minimal and zero impact on economic growth.[25] This legislation makes it increasingly difficult for Congress to find future budgetary resources needed to tackle the country's growing set of domestic challenges.[26]

Trump constantly pointed to billions of dollars in new defense spending that was aimed at confronting foreign dangers that either did not exist or were at best minor threats to Americans. At the same time, he cut the legs out from under the domestic elements of American power. Rather than making the country safer, his proposals have had the exact opposite effect. Nation building at home, it seemed, would have to wait another day.

A Better Way

As this book has shown, threat inflation and the inevitable counterproductive and costly policies that it leads to are the road to a weaker, more insecure, and less safe America. Worst of all, this mindset ignores the clear and present threats lurking among us—ones that kill Americans on a regular basis and at rates far higher than in most other developed countries. Beyond such life-and-death issues are the daily impact of weakening Americans' quality of life and the ability of workers and businesses to compete in a globalized economy. This diminished safety, security, and well-being is a collective, if often unconscious, choice of American citizens and their elected leaders. But these constant self-inflicted wounds—enabled by the Threat-Industrial Complex's misleading portrayal of the world—should not be America's future.

If America is ever to change course and adopt the policies that will truly keep its people safe, it first needs to recognize that it has a problem. In May 2014, former secretary of defense Robert Gates provided a stellar example of what owning up to this reality sounds like. Bob Schieffer, the host of CBS's *Face the Nation*, posed to Gates the kind of question that Sunday-morning talk shows were seemingly invented to ask: "Do you see Russia as posing the greatest national security threat to this country at this point?" Gates replied with refreshing and unusual frankness. He said, "I think the greatest national security threat to this country at this point is the two square miles that encompasses the Capitol Building and the White House." According to Gates, who worked for eight presidents, including as CIA director and secretary of defense, "If we can't get some of our problems solved here at home, . . . some compromises on the Hill that move the country forward, then I think these foreign threats recede significantly into—as far as being a risk to the well-being and the future of this country."[27]

That Gates's honest observation was unprecedented and made only after he had retired from public service demonstrates how narrow our national discussion about "national security" has become. So how do we change the dominant threat-inflation narrative documented throughout this book?

The primary transmitter of foreign-threat inflation is, first and foremost, the president's bully pulpit. In the fall of 2016, President Obama guest edited a special issue of *Wired* magazine and made an observation that is all too rarely heard from the commander in chief. "The next time you're bombarded with over-the-top claims about how our country is doomed or the world is coming apart at the seams, brush off the cynics and fearmongers. Because the truth is, if you had to choose any time in the course of human history to be alive, you'd choose this one. Right here in America, right now."[28]

If there is one problem with Obama's statement, it is that it came in the fall of 2016—at the tail end of the second term of his presidency. Presidents have an enormous impact on how Americans see the world. Too often their inclination, when it comes to foreign affairs and national security, is to focus on reasons to be fearful rather than optimistic. Politicians will and should talk about foreign dangers and challenges, but they are responsible for placing such discussions in a proper context. Portrayals of overseas threats should not be accompanied by hopeful platitudes about the future but rather recognition that there are plenty of reasons to be enthusiastic about the present—and that these reasons for optimism far outweigh reasons for concern.

Change must not only come from the executive branch. Every spring, for more than twenty years, congressional intelligence committees have held a series of "global threat" briefings. There intelligence and Pentagon officials routinely describe a world of ever-increasing chaos in which Americans perpetually face more and more lethal foreign threats. To counterbalance this exclusively one-sided portrayal, Senate and House foreign affairs committees should hold annual U.S. foreign policy "opportunity briefings." State Department and USAID officials, plus outside experts, would be called on to describe positive advances in world affairs and to offer recommendations for how the United States can further consolidate and advance them.

Beyond public hearings, Congress holds tremendous power to shape foreign policy perspectives with its mandated reporting requirements. The House and Senate foreign relations committees should require the State Department (with contributions from other agencies) to produce a public report that is dedicated to documenting positive global trends. This would include the decline in global conflict, long-term improvements in democratization, the continuing and unprecedented decline of extreme poverty rates, and steady international gains in education and life expectancy.

As noted earlier, presidential debates are tremendously skewed toward terrorism and the Middle East when they address foreign policy. This is unsurprising given that debate moderators—almost always TV news hosts—choose the questions and thereby frame how the candidates will respond. The Commission on Presidential Debates should agree to use moderators who are respected and balanced experts in foreign policy (when that is the focus of a debate), not simply TV news readers. Moreover, the commission should crowdsource foreign policy topics and questions from prospective voters and nongovernmental experts. Without such changes, these highly watched and influential events will remain overwhelmingly focused on foreign threats and continue to promote fear, not understanding.

Media

Even though President Trump derides any disagreeable information as "fake news," prominent media outlets still play a vital role in framing the world for Americans. More accurate context and balanced viewpoints are particularly important when covering terrorism. One study of how the media covered eighty-nine terror attacks committed within the United States between 2011 and 2015 found that attacks carried out by Muslims received 44 percent of all coverage, even though Muslims perpetrated just 12.4 percent of them. Attacks by a foreign-born Muslim were more than ten times as likely to have a story written about them than if the perpetrator had been a right-wing extremist or their motivations were unknown.[29] This is happening despite the fact that between 2008 and 2017, of the 387 extremist killings in the United States, 71 percent were committed by right-wing extremists and 26 percent by Islamic extremists.[30] Given this disproportionate coverage, almost half of all Americans supported Trump's travel ban, mistakenly thinking it would protect them from terrorist attacks.

Print, digital, and television media need to change the way they cover and contextualize terrorism. As things stand, to quote the terrorism scholar Brian Michael Jenkins, "warnings of imminent doom have an advantage over those counseling calm. Fear sells."[31] One way to correct this skewed perspective is for the media to make greater use of terrorism scholars who do peer-reviewed, data-driven research. Few of these individuals are ever invited to speak on cable news. Producers instead rely on the same group of retired military officers or homeland security officials, many of whom are employed by private-sector companies that are de facto members of the Threat-Industrial Complex. Beyond expanding the number and diversity of "expert" voices, news organizations should push themselves to make more evidence-based and data-driven arguments. Journalists are often rightly skeptical of politicians' claims about domestic issues. They should employ the same skepticism the next time a TV talking head claims that World War III could be upon us.

Media outlets should also highlight relevant financial and professional interests of experts appearing on their shows. Presently, news hosts occasionally mention that those pundits who appear exclusively on their networks manage companies that have U.S. government contracts. But news shows overwhelmingly omit the fact that TV pundits frequently have direct financial interests in whatever issue is being discussed. The business press provides a best practice worth emulating: when financial analysts appear on shows or write corporate profiles, they disclose whether they hold positions in the companies mentioned or have plans to initiate one within the next seventy-two hours. If a terrorism expert or retired admiral is asked for advice on a news program, either the host should state explicitly or it should appear on screen what government or private-sector links that individual has related to the issue being discussed.

Think Tanks

Think tank experts provide a significant and respected source of information that politicians and the media use when engaging in foreign-threat inflation. But many of these individuals have financial interests or affiliations that—perhaps even unconsciously—shape the focus and tone of their research findings. When publishing these conclusions, think tanks should be required to reveal the consulting contracts and outside sources of income for their employees that are related to their field of research. In addition, any potential financial or professional conflicts of interest should be listed on their personal bio pages.[32] Meanwhile, think tanks should transparently outline their financial support and what percentage of their overall funding individual donors contribute. Transparency groups, such as Transparify, should continue to "name and shame" organizations that refuse to divulge their donors or detail how money received is being spent and to rank them by their relative levels of openness.[33]

Philanthropic foundations have tremendous influence over the foreign policy topics on which think tank fellows and university professors write. These grant-giving institutions make clear the issue areas that they will support and the types of publications and even likely conclusions they expect to receive in a proposal for funding. Among prominent funders, there are requests for research into nuclear nonproliferation, torture, drone strikes, the erosion of civil liberties, the chronically unstable Middle East, or advances in threatening robotics or big data. Rarely is support given for research that disagrees with the severity of such purported threats or more crucially that views the world in less alarmist terms. These organizations fund research into the destructive policies that flow from foreign-threat inflation, but they all too rarely question the overarching narrative that makes these policies possible. Philanthropic foundations, particularly progressive-oriented organizations, should make it a priority to seek out and support new voices and perspectives that go against the conventional national security narrative.

You

Finally, changing the national security narrative requires Americans to be better informed about the world around them. This begins by recognizing the fear-based appeals of the Threat-Industrial Complex. When a politician or general refers to a foreign threat as "existential" or justifies the next war as essential to "safeguard your children," understand that these emotive claims are intended to scare, not inform, you. Fear is peddled to elicit public support or acquiescence for policies that, far too often, will not make you safer, freer, healthier, or happier.

One way to better educate yourself is to bookmark, or follow on social media, websites that provide nonpartisan, factual information about the world. Our top-dozen such sites would include Our World in Data, Gapminder, OECD Library, Wikipedia (for almost any issue, it provides the most accurate information, with citations for deeper exploration), Human Security Report Project, Uppsala Conflict Data Program, World Health Organization, Centers for Disease Control and Prevention, Center for Systematic Peace, Gun Violence Archive, Global Terrorism Database, and HumanProgress. These websites provide a free, constantly updated, and accurate characterization of domestic and international affairs that are consistently misrepresented by the Threat-Industrial Complex.

Not only will community engagement provide essential context about the never-ending threats peddled each news cycle, but getting involved with organizations like the American Red Cross or other volunteer groups will provide a sense of control over your and your family's safety. If it is within your means, travel is perhaps the best way to ease one's fears of the outside world.[34] In the absence of political leadership that assuages our misplaced fears, take the initiative to play that role yourself. Whether your "audience" is your family, Facebook friends, or the classroom, you can combat the Threat-Industrial Complex by sharing not only comforting words and resilient rhetoric but also evidence and information that puts the alleged threats into perspective. This will not make you naïve or Pollyannaish but rather empowered and accurate.

National Security for American Citizens

Changing how Americans think about "national security" is critical and long overdue but not simply because of the foreign policy implications. Change must begin at home with the fundamental recognition that the foundations of American power—and in turn national security—are eroding and must be repaired. That means that political attention and resources must be directed toward the domestic risks and systemic harms that threaten Americans and undermine their quality of life far more frequently and consequentially than any combination of foreign dangers does.

The revamped approach to national security offered here does not contain an exhaustive list of policy recommendations but rather highlights five of the most pressing challenges that Americans face. We also focus on those policy interventions that have demonstrably worked in the past and that should be politically tenable for government officials and policy makers who often claim that their number-one priority is to protect the American people.

Health Care

As discussed in "That Which Harms Us," the gravest threat to Americans is noncommunicable diseases (NCDs), which prematurely kill nearly nine out of ten of all Americans every year. What is so frustrating about NCDs is how easily preventable they are and the extent to which eating healthier, quitting smoking, moderating drinking, and increasing exercise or any physical activity would save lives, save money, improve economic productivity, and heighten the quality of life for hundreds of millions of Americans. Policy interventions for tackling NCDs are relatively cheap and straightforward.

For example, a 20 percent tax on sugary drinks would dramatically reduce the number of Americans suffering from diabetes and cardiovascular diseases. A one-cent-an-ounce tax on these drinks (twelve to sixteen cents per beverage) would also result in $17 billion in savings on health care costs over ten years.[35]

A 30 percent subsidy on the cost of fresh fruits and vegetables could significantly increase consumption for the forty million poor Americans enrolled in the highly effective Supplemental Nutrition Assistance Program (SNAP).[36] Numerous evidence-based studies have shown that eating more fruits and vegetables is associated with lower rates of mortality for all NCDs and cancer.

Since 1995, smoking rates have fallen 40 percent among adults and 35 to 70 percent for high school students, and the main reason is very simple: taxes on cigarettes were increased.[37] Further increasing the tax on cigarettes by one dollar a pack could prevent an estimated two million smoking-related and premature deaths every year.[38] Such a tax, applied nationally, would generate an extra $8.6 billion in tax revenue that could be used to fund tobacco-cessation programs.[39] In addition, limiting the advertising and marketing of cigarettes would also keep more kids from picking up a habit that will likely shorten their lives.[40]

Finally, changes in the tax code that incentivize companies to create programs encouraging their employees to exercise, to offer healthy vending machine options, and to provide financial incentives for participation in health and wellness programs, such as gym-membership reimbursement, would significantly reduce the number of Americans who fall victim to an NCD. It would also improve their quality of life and that of their families. None of these are onerous policy changes; they have all been shown to work and would more than pay for themselves within several years via lower health care costs and stronger economic growth.

Gun Violence

Gun deaths claim more than thirty-eight thousand Americans every year, cost hundreds of billions of dollars in lost productivity and health care expenditures, and cause untold suffering for those affected by it. Gun ownership, however, is so embedded in American society that it is politically difficult for the United States to reduce this self-inflicted and preventable carnage.

But there are still cost-effective and even politically feasible ways to make gun deaths rarer. That process can only begin with better information. Between 2004 and 2015, an equal amount of federal research funds went to gun violence as to drowning, even though the former kills eight times as many Americans annually.[41] A vast expansion of research monies for the Centers for Disease Control and National Institutes of Health to study gun violence would tell policy makers more about the backgrounds of murderers and how they obtained their weapons—and provide a policy road map for keeping guns out of the hands of likely perpetrators.[42]

But what we do know is that the easy availability of guns is strongly associated with America's increasing suicide rate from firearms.[43] States with mandatory waiting periods and universal background checks have significantly lowered suicide rates. When those laws are reversed, suicide and also homicide rates spike.[44] Gun locks, mandatory gun safes when children are present in a home, restrictions on the size of gun magazines, taking firearms away from people accused of domestic violence, treating what are now seen as accidental gun deaths as criminal neglect, and even public education programs are all steps that, though unlikely to dramatically lower gun deaths, would certainly save lives. Most of these modest and sensible initiatives also enjoy overwhelming public support.[45]

Drug Deaths

The fastest growing threat to Americans is drugs and primarily opioids—such as heroin, fentanyl, and prescription pain relievers. With seventy-two thousand fatalities annually, drugs now kill nearly as many people as guns and cars combined.[46] More money for and access to drug treatment, including diversion programs for people arrested for drug possession, would reduce these numbers significantly. Every dollar invested in effective drug prevention in secondary schools saves up to eighteen dollars in long-term substance-abuse costs.[47] Mandating greater federal and state regulation of opioid prescription guidelines and placing tighter controls on the importation of powerful synthetic opioids, such as fentanyl, would dry up the supply of drugs that are often legally prescribed.

Even increased political focus on job creation and economic development would reduce drug deaths. One study of every county in the United States between 1999 and 2014 found that as the county's unemployment rate increased by one percentage point, the opioid death rate per one hundred thousand rose by 0.19 (3.6 percent), while overdose visits to emergency rooms increased by 70 percent.[48] Of course, creating more jobs and spurring economic growth have enormous societal benefits beyond simply reducing drug use.

Infrastructure

America's crumbling infrastructure hinders economic prosperity and job growth, burdens business owners, and puts lives needlessly at risk. The price tag to create a modern twenty-first-century infrastructure in the United States will run in the trillions of dollars, but the ripple effect of such public investment would be transformative. It would create millions of jobs, spur innovation, increase productivity, and alleviate the daily stresses that Americans face when commuting and traveling.

Raising the federal gas tax by just one quarter to a mere 43.4 cents per gallon would create $291 billion in new revenue over the next decade, which could be used to expand and upgrade mass transit. Congress and state legislatures could pursue other ways to raise revenue for new spending, from establishing an infrastructure bank and incentivizing the private sector to partner in infrastructure improvements to taking advantage of relatively low interest rates and beginning new public-works projects. Ironically, while there is bipartisan support for improving national infrastructure, the first eighteen months of the Trump administration saw virtually no tangible progress in addressing the worsening situation. This unwillingness to act will only ensure that America continues to become less economically competitive compared to other developed countries—and ultimately individual Americans will pay the price in lower wages and greater economic anxiety.

Education

The primary way for maintaining America's economic competitiveness, better ensuring that citizens have healthier and more fulfilling lives, lifting families out of poverty, and reducing income inequality is through education. America already spends more per pupil on education than any other developed country in the world does, so throwing more money at the problem is not necessarily the ideal solution. But redirecting resources to areas of greatest need could do a world of good. Increasing access for universal prekindergarten and helping low- and middle-income students pay for college are relatively inexpensive initiatives that could have an enormously positive impact. Today, attending community college is the primary way that low-income and minority students can address historical underachievement; yet by one estimate, there is four thousand times more public funding for four-year research universities per student than for two-year community colleges. In addition, modest federal initiatives that in recent years have encouraged administrators to transform their curriculums and rewarded high-performing schools should be continued and fully supported.[49]

Improving educational outcomes must, however, be about more than classrooms and degrees. Workers who have lost their jobs to the relentless trilogy of algorithms, robotics, and globalization need greater access to job training and connections to potential employers that will help them find new, well-paying jobs. Unfortunately, the United States spends a smaller proportion of its wealth on work retraining than does any other OECD country, except for Mexico and Chile.[50] Correcting that imbalance would help create a workforce that is better able to compete against similarly advanced economies.

Countless American politicians will tell you that their number-one priority—and their most sacred obligation—is to keep the American people safe. Putting aside the fact that the number-one priority of any American politician should be to uphold the Constitution, this national devotion to safety has, over the past seventeen years, led to one destructive, expensive, and counterproductive policy after another. But if American politicians are being honest about protecting the American people from harm, then they need to be focused on the foregoing five issue areas. Redirecting a fraction of the money currently maintaining America's military might to modest policy interventions at home is the single best way to truly keep Americans safe.

A Foreign Policy for a Better World and a Safer America

The cynic might argue that in the quarter century since the end of the Cold War, America has become the world's most powerful nation—with the strongest military and economy and unparalleled global influence. In short, "if it ain't broke, don't fix it." But an America that is militarily overcommitted, that defines its national security interests in the broadest manner imaginable, and that gives inadequate attention to far more pressing problems at home while focusing obsessively on phantom threats overseas will likely not remain a great power forever. Overstretch abroad and inertia at home will inevitably take its toll. While it is essential that America rebuild the domestic foundations of national power, it also must recalibrate its approach to foreign policy.

That process can only begin with the realization that the dramatic global economic, political, and social improvements that have occurred since the end of the Cold War—and have made America safer and the world a demonstrably better place—have less to do with America's massive military than we have been led to believe.

The reality of post-Cold War American foreign policy is that U.S. military strength has been most powerful when it has not been used. Security alliances in Europe and Asia have increased regional security and reduced the likelihood of war. Coercive diplomacy with Iran and Syria has led to nonproliferation agreements that have reduced the threat of weapons of mass destruction being used. Security assistance, training, and education have helped professionalize militaries in virtually every corner of the world. Finally, the more modest use of military force and support for peacekeeping operations—both direct and indirect—in the Balkans, the Middle East, and Central Africa have been among the biggest contributors to international peace and security.

Force is generally seen in Washington as the default elixir to that which threatens America. In reality, when the United States employs its military (for example, in Iraq and Afghanistan), it usually does as much to weaken American national security as promote it.

Instead, it is the quiet work of diplomacy, foreign assistance, and support for international organizations that has been more consequential and enduring for U.S national security interests. The work of civilian agencies, U.S. diplomats and negotiators, and nongovernmental organizations as well as direct support for international organizations has helped to improve global living standards, spur economic innovation and growth, and promote democracy and adherence to the rule of law.

The focus of U.S. leaders going forward should be to consolidate the extraordinary progress detailed in this book and orient American foreign policy toward ensuring that these advances continue and become more difficult to reverse. This does not mean that the United States should pull up the drawbridge to the rest of the world—far from it. But it does mean placing greater emphasis on soft power over hard power and inexpensive diplomacy and development assistance over costly and open-ended military engagements.

First and foremost, America must increase its national investment in the nonmilitary elements of foreign policy. As we wrote several years ago, "American foreign policy needs fewer people who can jump out of airplanes and more who can convene roundtable discussions and lead negotiations."[51]

The increases in military spending and cuts to the foreign-operations budget are examples of the misguided priorities that drive national security decision-making. If anything, the State Department, the Agency for International Development (USAID), the Millennium Challenge Corporation, and the National Endowment for Democracy, among others, should not be fighting for budget scraps but should be fully resourced by Congress and the president. In addition, the Overseas Private Investment Corporation, Export-Import Bank, and International Finance Corporation incentivize U.S. firms to invest in supposedly dangerous foreign locales. More public support for such efforts could encourage business leaders and their employees to push back on the narrative that the world is defined by instability and upheaval and could bring greater awareness among Americans of their economic and political potential.

USAID in particular has been hollowed out by budget cuts, reorganization, and a lack of attention and interest from policy makers.[52] Currently, the United States spends approximately 0.18 percent of its GDP on development assistance.[53] That is far behind other OECD countries, many of which match or surpass the long-standard benchmark for advanced nations of 0.7 percent, which is also reflected in the UN Millennium Development Goals. Considering the benefit to American foreign policy of a world that is freer, wealthier, and better educated, the United States should be number one when it comes to support for global development. Do not just take our word for it. As the former commander of U.S forces in Afghanistan Gen. John Allen has noted, "In many respects, USAID's efforts can do as much—over the long term—to prevent conflict as the deterrent effect of a carrier strike group or a marine expeditionary force."[54]

Conversely, when it comes to defense spending, policy makers should be looking at ways to save money and reduce America's military footprint. This is particularly true of the Army, which is by far the largest service branch and remains a formidable fighting force. But the nature of conflict in the twenty-first century does not lend itself to a future in which national militaries engage in large set-piece battles, which the Army remains currently structured to do. In recent years, the Army has been focused on counterinsurgency and post-conflict stabilization operations—neither of which falls within its core competencies. Rather, the comparative advantage of the U.S. military lies elsewhere: its extraordinary power-projection capabilities, relative air and naval superiority, offensive cyber programs, alliances and overseas bases, special operations forces, and integration of information technology into war-fighting capabilities.

Instead of maintaining an oversized active-duty ground force, the Pentagon should reduce the Army's size and shift more of its capabilities to the reserve component (the Army Reserve and Army National Guard), which played such an important role in the Iraq and Afghanistan conflicts. A more streamlined active-duty force could be reoriented to discrete tasks, such as projecting force quickly and lethally, while the reserves could build up skills in areas such as peacekeeping, building partner capacity, civil-society support, and cyber operations.

Such steps would bring significant budgetary savings. Humans are costly and rarely more so than when they serve in the military. Between 2001 and 2016, military compensation increased by 44 percent, and military health care costs went up by 114 percent. Much of these expenses were localized in the Army.[55] As we have documented in "An Alternative Post-9/11 History," those costs, particularly the latter, will undoubtedly increase in the future. The money saved by shifting toward a larger reserve force would allow greater investments in the areas where the United States needs to maintain and expand its comparative military advantage: the Navy, the Air Force, information technology, space systems, and unmanned platforms and robotics.[56]

But there is one other key reason to consider reducing the size of the active force. Since the U.S. military is so disproportionately larger than every other aspect of American power, all challenges to the United States are perceived through the lens of a military solution. If your biggest national security tool is a hammer, there is a natural inclination to view all overseas challenges as if they are nails. Reducing the size of the Army and increasing the use of reserve and national guard forces (which creates political dilemmas since such forces are largely made up of civilians) would not end all U.S. military misadventures, but it could make them more politically difficult to initiate and sustain.

Finally, policy makers should be focused on strengthening the architecture of international institutions—and global norms—that provide a platform for promoting U.S. interests and are essential for maintaining global peace and security. This, of course, means continuing strong U.S. support and engagement in the United Nations and its affiliated agencies, such as UNICEF, the UN Development Program, and the UN Department of Peacekeeping. The hundred thousand UN peacekeepers deployed in support of fourteen peace operations around the world not only are relatively cheap—one U.S. soldier in Afghanistan costs $2.1 million a year, while the annual reimbursement rate for one peacekeeper is less than $16,000 annually—but also reduce the potential and length of civil wars.[57]

But strengthening international institutions also includes support for—among others—the International Atomic Energy Agency (IAEA), which, notwithstanding the Trump administration's withdrawal from the agreement in May 2018, is still actively verifying the Iran nuclear deal at a staggeringly low price tag of $11 million a year. It means standing up the World Trade Organization, which is an essential global body for resolving trade disputes among member states that at one time might have led to conflict, and the International Criminal Court (ICC), of which the United States is not a member but should be.[58] Though American policy makers often dismiss the importance of the ICC, research has shown that it plays an important deterrent role. Members of the court are nearly 50 percent less likely than nonmember states to kill civilians when fighting civil wars.[59]

Then there are the regional organizations like the Organization of American States (OAS), the African Union (AU), the Association of

South Eastern Asian Nations (ASEAN), and other regional groups. In the post-Cold War era, these groups have been a crucial impediment to regional conflict and have also spearheaded greater respect for the rule of law and human rights. In Europe, the allure of participation in the European Union has pushed countries in eastern Europe, the former Soviet Union, and even Turkey to do away with the death penalty and pass laws providing greater protections for minority communities. In Latin America, the OAS has worked to avert conflict between Ecuador and Colombia, and the AU has conducted successful peacekeeping missions in Somalia and South Sudan (in collaboration with the UN).

Finally, the United States must continue to be engaged in international technical organizations that promulgate and maintain universally applied rules on the global commons. This includes everything from outer space and international air to maritime travel, telecommunications, and the internet. With growing demands on these domains from governments, businesses, and consumers—asteroid mining and suborbital tourism could be coming in our lifetimes, for example—U.S. participation can both shape the direction of these organizations and assure that their rules remain consistent with U.S. national interests.

Beyond these international and regional organizations are the global norms—both written and unwritten—that strongly influence international behavior. The international coalition that was assembled to push Iraqi troops out of Kuwait in 1991 not only upheld international law but put teeth in the international norm against cross-border invasion, occupation, and seizure of territory. Nuclear-nonproliferation efforts received a significant boost from the international diplomatic initiatives—and the UN Security Council–backed multilateral sanctions regime—that pressured Iran to recommit itself to the Nuclear Non-Proliferation Treaty and to place its nuclear program under intrusive IAEA inspections. The lever of U.S. military force compelled Syria's Assad regime in 2013 to turn over its known chemical-weapons program to the Organization for the Prohibition of Chemical Weapons and to sign the Chemical Weapons Convention.

Greater adherence to these international norms and rules has not ended the potential for countries to invade their neighbors or to develop prohibited weapons of mass destruction, but the growing international consensus around these issues has made it more costly for countries to openly violate them. Certainly, the Gulf War did not stop Russian-backed forces from forcibly annexing Crimea from Ukraine in 2014, but the international response ensured that Moscow paid a significant price. Since the war in Ukraine, Russia has become more isolated diplomatically while international sanctions have contributed to significant capital flight, negative GDP growth, and currency devaluation.[60]

One of the ironies of the punishment meted out to Russia is that the leading voice of condemnation came from the United States—the same nation that in 2003 flagrantly violated international law and global norms when it assembled a meager coalition of willing nations to invade and occupy Iraq. The United States often pushes hardest for other countries to abide by international norms while remaining the least inclined to consistently do so itself. This hypocrisy is one of the many benefits that come from being an unrivaled and largely unthreatened global superpower. This lesson has not been lost on Russia and China and their regional and global ambitions.

There are consequences for such actions, both direct and indirect. For example, the Senate has refused to consider the ratification of the 1982 Convention on the Law of the Sea (UNCLOS), which has been ratified by 168 countries, including China and Russia.[61] The treaty defines universal legal standards for fishing, shipping, and mining, while also codifying sensible and safe navigation principles that are adhered to by most of the world. Every senior U.S. military official—especially those serving in the Navy—have strongly endorsed UN-CLOS ratification for decades on the grounds that it would give the United States a seat at the table in crafting global rules for resolving maritime disputes and conducting routine naval operations. By staying outside the international laws and norms outlined in UNCLOS, the United States has less leverage and authority in maritime issues.

The repeated use of unilateral force and the creation of coalitions of the willing may fulfill certain near-term American interests but in the long term will make it more difficult to create international consensus in condemning actions that go against U.S. interests. An argument often heard in U.S. foreign policy debates is that when America conforms its behavior to international laws and institutions, it weakens national security. But the exact opposite is true. The more America universalizes international issues and the more it is able to create consensus around adherence to the rule of law, respect for human rights and electoral democracy, and condemnation of flaunting international laws, the more it makes America stronger and more respected.

In the wake of World War II, U.S diplomats and policy makers laid the foundation for a rules-based international system and a series of international organizations to administer allegiance to these precepts. To a largely underappreciated degree, the United States can point, more than seventy years later, to extraordinary success in that effort. This is perhaps the saddest and most misguided element of America's propensity for foreign-threat exaggeration: Americans fail to see and appreciate their abundant accomplishment in helping to create a world that is very much in America's image.

Much of this book was researched and written as Donald Trump was elected president, and admittedly, it is hard to feel positive about the future of international affairs with him residing in the White House. Since Trump took office, he has repeatedly shown contempt for the international system. Even worse, Trump's "America First" rhetoric posits that if a global problem does not directly impact the United States, he is not interested in dealing with it. When we first began working on this book, we could only imagine a black-swan event that would divert America and the world from the progress that has been made over the past several decades. Trump's election has the potential to be precisely that black swan.

Trump's ascendancy also comes at a time of growing concerns about the state of political freedom in the world. For all of the positive advances that we chart in this book, nowhere is the record more mixed—and is the potential for significant reversals greater—than on democracy and adherence to the rule of law. This refers not just to semiauthoritarian rulers turning into fully authoritarian rulers in China, Turkey, and Russia, among others. There is a growing crisis in Western democracy in which populism and xenophobia are pushing democratic nations toward the policies and politics of exclusion. This is happening in places like Hungary, Poland, Italy, the Philippines, Great Britain, and, of course, the United States.

There are still plenty of reasons to be bullish about the present and cautiously optimistic about the future. But we are also painfully aware that the past several decades of extraordinary progress are not destined to continue. It would be the height of hubris to suggest that the world can only move in one direction—forever better and brighter. Things can fall apart, and while we do not believe that we will return to the conflict-ridden, undemocratic, and economically stagnant world of thirty or forty years ago, progress can be halted and, in some cases, reversed. We wrote this book not just to point out how far we have come but also as a reminder that bad decisions and poor policy choices can do untold—and sometimes permanent—damage.

Reversing the international cooperation and active U.S. engagement that has defined the post–Cold War era is precisely one of those bad decisions that could have grave long-term consequences. On few issues is this more true than climate change, the effects of which will not be restricted to one nation. If there is the same level of commitment and cooperation in confronting rising temperatures and cresting seas that we have seen in improving literacy rates, wiping out disease, consolidating democratic gains, and limiting cross-border conflict, then the world can find a way to weather the proverbial storm. The United States has the ability and the global influence to lead that effort. The question today is whether it will.

As we've argued in this book, America should stop overdramatizing foreign threats—and deemphasize the role of the U.S military. But contra Trump, this is not a call for America to walk away from its traditional role as a global leader. We reject the notion, sometimes heard on both the far left and the far right, that America would be safer or wealthier if it played a less sustained role in the world. Particularly now, at a time of more explicit great-power competition and efforts by China and Russia to rewrite the rules and norms of the international system, it is more vital than ever that the United States—in concert with partners and allies—pushes back on such efforts. This does not mean military interventions or unilateral coercion. As this book has exhaustively demonstrated, those approaches have consistently failed at tremendous cost and political consequence since 9/11. What is needed is forward-leaning direct engagement and a spirit of cooperation with international political organizations, humanitarian and public health nonprofits, scientific and technical alliances, and multilateral industry forums. These are the underpinnings of the international system, from which Americans benefit every day. To abandon these organizations—and to abdicate America's global leadership role—to China or Russia will diminish the lives of not just the American people but all of the world's citizens.

Rather than huddle in fear at the happenings outside our borders, Americans should take pride in having helped build a world that is safer, freer, wealthier, healthier, and better educated than at any point in history—and make a commitment to continue the effort. At the same time, Americans must also look inward—to the inequalities and inadequacies at home—to ensure that their country is matching the human development progress that is so evident overseas. America's global influence will only be as strong as the foundations of national power at home.

We know the path forward for a better future, but it will rely on the decisions that are made by America's elected officials today. There is no reason that the extraordinary advances of the past quarter century cannot continue and that tomorrow will not be brighter than today. The choice is in our hands.

Notes

Introduction

Epigraph: Bertrand Russell, *An Outline of Intellectual Rubbish* (Girard, KS: Haldeman-Julius, 1943).

1. Based on author interview.

2. Holly Hedegaard, Margaret Warner, and Arialdi M. Miniño, "Drug Overdose Deaths in the United States, 1999–2015" (NCHS Data Brief No. 273, Centers for Disease Control and Prevention, February 2017).

3. Jim Norman, "North Korea, Cyberterrorism Top Threats to U.S.," Gallup, March 5, 2018.

4. Rasmussen Reports, "52% Say U.S. Less Safe Today than Before 9/11," November 6, 2017.

5. Dartmouth College / YouGov, "Survey on Foreign Policy and Overseas Security Commitment," May 2012.

6. OnTheIssues, "Jeb Bush on War & Peace," accessed August 25, 2016, www.ontheissues.org/celeb/Jeb_Bush_War_+_Peace.htm.

7. "Republican Candidates Debate in North Charleston, South Carolina," January 14, 2016, www.presidency.ucsb.edu/ws/index.php?pid=111395.

8. Jonathan Easley, "Trump Calls for Muslim Patrols, Torture in Wake of Brussels Attacks," *The Hill*, March 22, 2016; Colin Campbell, "Trump: You Have to 'Take Out' Terrorists' Families," *Business Insider*, December 2, 2015.

9. Niels Lesniewski, "Graham Says World 'Literally about to Blow Up,'" *Roll Call*, January 28, 2014.

10. Missy Ryan, "McCain Will Use Influential Senate Perch to Push for Expanded Middle East Response," *Washington Post*, January 24, 2015.

11. John Kelly, "Home and Away: DHS and the Threats to America, Remarks Delivered by Secretary Kelly at George Washington University Center for Cyber and

Homeland Security," April 18, 2017, www.dhs.gov/news/2017/04/18/home-and-away-dhs-and-threats-america.

12. White House, "Remarks by President Trump and Vice President Pence in Meeting with Members of Congress," June 20, 2018.

13. Christopher Hooton, " 'The ISIS of Biological Agents?': CNN Is Asking the Stupid Ebola Questions," *Independent*, October 7, 2014.

14. Department of Defense, "Remarks by Secretary Hagel at a Troop Event, San Diego, California," August 12, 2014; Senate Armed Services Committee, "Hearing of the Senate Armed Services Committee on the Nomination of Chuck Hagel to Be Secretary of Defense," January 31, 2013; Greg Sargent, "Tom Cotton: Terrorists Collaborating with Mexican Drug Cartels to Infiltrate Arkansas," *Washington Post*, October 7, 2014.

15. Adam Suchy, *Product Instability or Tip-Over Injuries and Fatalities Associated with Televisions, Furniture, and Appliances: 2014 Report* (Bethesda, MD: U.S. Consumer Product Safety Commission, August 2014); National Oceanic and Atmospheric Administration, "2016 Lightning Fatalities," May 2017, www.weather.gov/safety/lightning-fatalities16.

16. Jim Norman, "Four Nations Top U.S.'s Greatest Enemy List," Gallup, February 22, 2016.

17. Samantha Tatro, "Americans Split on View of U.S. Military Power in the World, Gallup Poll Finds," NBC San Diego, February 15, 2016.

18. "Transcript: ABC News Anchor David Muir Interviews President Trump," ABC News, January 25, 2017.

19. By 2018, the number of people living in extreme poverty was estimated to have fallen further to 8.1 percent of the global population. See World Poverty Clock, accessed May 7, 2018, http://worldpoverty.io.

20. Global Polio Eradication Initiative, "This Week," accessed July 4, 2018, http://polioeradication.org/polio-today/polio-now/this-week/; Angus Hervey, "11 Reasons Why 2015 Was a Great Year for Humanity," *Medium*, December 14, 2015, http://medium.com/future-crunch/11-reasons-why-2015-was-a-great-year-for-humanity-70db584db748; Centers for Disease Control, "Today's HIV/AIDS Epidemic," fact sheet, August 2016; World Health Organization, "Maternal Mortality," fact sheet, updated November 2015, www.who.int/mediacentre/factsheets/fs348/en/; World Health Organization, "Under-Five Mortality," accessed March 14, 2016, www.who.int/gho/child_health/mortality/mortality_under_five_text/en/; Centers for Disease

Control and Prevention, *CDC's Work to Eradicate Polio* (Atlanta: U.S. Department of Health and Human Services, September 2014).

A Safer and Freer World

Epigraph: White House, "Press Briefing by Press Secretary Sean Spicer," February 7, 2017.

1. William Wan, "Xi Visits Iowa, Where the Diplomatic Equivalent of Love Is in the Air," *Washington Post*, February 15, 2012.

2. U.S. Congress, House, Appropriations Committee, Defense Subcommittee, *Department of Defense FY 2013 Budget Request*, 112th Cong., 2nd sess. (February 16, 2012).

3. Monty G. Marshall, "Major Episodes of Political Violence, 1946–2015," Center for Systemic Peace, accessed May 6, 2018, www.systemicpeace.org/warlist/warlist.htm.

4. *The Impacts of Sequestration and/or a Full-Year Continuing Resolution on the Department of Defense: Hearing before the Committee on Armed Services, United States Senate*, 113th Cong. (February 12, 2013).

5. Ali Watkins, "Here's Twenty Years of Spy Chiefs Scaring the Hell Out of Congress," *Buzzfeed*, February 9, 2016.

6. *Impacts of Sequestration* (February 12, 2013).

7. Missy Ryan, "McCain Will Use Influential Senate Perch to Push for Expanded Middle East Response," *Washington Post*, January 24, 2015.

8. "OTH Video Interview: Lt Gen Steven Kwast," *Over the Horizon*, November 28, 2017.

9. In 2014, a survey by the Pew Research Center and *USA Today* found that 65 percent of respondents said the world was more dangerous than it was several years ago, and just 7 percent said the world has gotten safer. Pew Research Center, *As New Dangers Loom, More Think the U.S. Does "Too Little" to Solve World Problems* (Washington, DC: Pew Research Center, August 28, 2014).

10. "John McCain Reacts to Brussels Attacks," MSNBC, March 22, 2016.

11. Niels Lesniewski, "Graham Says World 'Literally about to Blow Up,' " *Roll Call*, January 28, 2014.

12. Therese Pettersson and Kristine Eck, "Organized Violence, 1989–2017," *Journal of Peace Research*, June 18, 2018, http://journals.sagepub.com/doi/full/10.1177/0022343318784101; Nils Petter Gleditsch, Peter Wallensteen, Mikael Eriksson, Margareta Sollenberg, and Håvard Strand, "Armed Conflict 1946–2001: A New Dataset," *Journal of Peace Research* 39, no. 5 (2002): 615–637.

13. The 2014 Russian-supported armed separatist violence in Ukraine was an internationalized civil war, the conflict type that has grown slightly over the past six years or so, from six in 2011 to nineteen in 2015. See Stockholm International Peace Research Institute, *SIPRI Yearbook 2011: Armaments, Disarmaments and International Security* (New York: Oxford University Press, 2011), 4.

14. Timothy Snyder, *Bloodlands: Europe between Hitler and Stalin* (New York: Basic Books, 2010), 7.

15. Max Hastings, *Catastrophe 1914: Europe Goes to War* (New York: Vintage Books, 2014).

16. Pettersson and Eck, "Organized Violence."

17. Reena Flores, "Chris Christie: 'We're Already in World War III,' " CBS News, December 16, 2015.

18. "Syria Death Toll: UN Envoy Estimates 400,000 Killed," Al Jazeera, April 23, 2016.

19. "How to Stop the Fighting, Sometimes," *Economist,* November 11, 2013. In part, this reduction in the lethality of conflict is due to tremendous advances in battlefield medicine. See Tanisha M. Fazal, "Dead Wrong? Battle Deaths, Military Medicine, and Exaggerated Reports of War's Demise," *International Security* 39, no. 1 (2014): 95–125.

20. UN High Commissioner for Refugees (UNHCR), *Global Trends: Forced Displacement in 2017* (Geneva: UNHCR, June 2018).

21. Central Intelligence Agency (CIA), *The World Factbook 2016–17* (Washington, DC: CIA, 2016).

22. Meaning one thousand noncombatants or more over a one-year period.

23. Jay Ulfelder, "Trends over Time in State-Sponsored Mass Killing," *Dart-Throwing Chimp* (blog), July 25, 2013, http://dartthrowingchimp.wordpress.com/2013/07/25/trends-over-time-in-state-sponsored-mass-killing.

24. United Nations, Department of Economic and Social Affairs, Population Division, *World Population Prospects: The 2017 Revision* (New York: United Nations, 2017), custom data acquired via website.

25. Syrian Centre for Policy Research (SCPR), *Alienation and Violence: Impact of Syria Crisis Report 2014* (Damascus: SCPR, March 10, 2015).

26. United Nations Educational, Scientific and Cultural Organization (UNESCO), *Education for All Global Monitoring Report 2011: The Hidden Crisis: Armed Conflict and Education* (Paris: UNESCO, March 1, 2011), 2; UNHCR, "Out-of-School Children in Refugee Settings, Education" (Issue Brief 2, UNHCR, July 2015), 3.

27. Institute for Economics and Peace (IEP), *Global Peace Index 2017* (Sydney: IEP, June 2017), 5, 54–59.

28. Clionadh Raleigh, "Civil War Risk in Democratic and Non-democratic Neighborhoods" (Post-Conflict Transitions Working Paper No. 17, World Bank, July 2007), 26.

29. Hearing before the Committee on Armed Services, United States Senate, to Receive Testimony on Worldwide Threats, 114th Cong. (February 9, 2016).

30. Marie Allansson, Erik Melander, and Lotta Themnér, "Organized Violence, 1989–2016," *Journal of Peace Research* 54, no. 4 (2017): 574–587; Gleditsch et al., "Armed Conflict 1946–2001." Data represented in Uppsala Conflict Data Program / Peace Research Institute Oslo's "Armed Conflict Dataset," version 17.2.

31. Amy F. Woolf, *Nonstrategic Nuclear Weapons*, CRS Report No. RL32572 (Washington, DC: Congressional Research Service, March 23, 2016); Robert S. Norris and Hans M. Kristensen, "U.S. Nuclear Weapons in Europe, 1954–2004," *Bulletin of the Atomic Scientists* 60, no. 6 (2004): 76–77; "Nuclear Notebook," *Bulletin of the Atomic Scientists*, accessed May 6, 2018, http://thebulletin.org/nuclear-notebook-multimedia; Arms Control Association, "The Lisbon Protocol at a Glance," updated March 2014.

32. Pettersson and Eck, "Organized Violence."

33. Michael J. Abramowitz, *Freedom in the World 2018: Democracy in Crisis* (Washington, DC: Freedom House, 2018).

34. Ibid. As of 2016, the figure is 61 percent of the sub-Saharan African population.

35. Ibid.

36. Jay Ulfelder, "Statistical Assessments of Coup Risk for 2015," *Dart-Throwing Chimp* (blog), January 17, 2015, http://dartthrowingchimp.wordpress.com/2015/01/17/statistical-assessments-of-coup-risk-for-2015.

37. Monty G. Marshall, "Polity IV Annual Time-Series, 1800–2016," data set, Center for Systemic Peace.

38. Ibid.

39. Max Roser, "Human Rights vs. Type of Political Regime," Our World in Data, accessed May 6, 2018, http://ourworldindata.org/grapher/human-rights-vs-the-political-regime.

40. "Daily Chart: Declining Trust in Government Is Denting Democracy," *Economist*, January 25, 2017.

41. The Uppsala Conflict Data Program categorizes Middle East and Africa conflicts. North Africa was separated using UN designations for North African

countries. Mark J. C. Crescenzi and Kelly M. Kadera, "Built to Last: Understanding the Link between Democracy and Conflict in the International System," *International Studies Quarterly* 60, no. 3 (2016): 565–572; Michael Poznansky and Matt K. Scroggs, "Ballots and Blackmail: Coercive Diplomacy and the Democratic Peace," *International Studies Quarterly* 60, no. 4 (2016): 731–741.

42. U.S. Department of State, Office of the Legal Adviser, "U.S. Collective Defense Arrangements," accessed May 6, 2018, www.state.gov/s/l/treaty/collective-defense; Allansson, Melander, and Themnér, "Organized Violence"; Gleditsch et al., "Armed Conflict 1946–2001." Data represented in Uppsala Conflict Data Program / Peace Research Institute Oslo's "Armed Conflict Dataset," version 17.2.

43. Havard Hegre, "Democracy and Armed Conflict," *Journal of Peace Research* 51, no. 2 (2014): 1–14; John R. O'Neal and Bruce M. Russett, "The Classical Liberals Were Right: Democracy, Interdependence, and Conflict, 1950–1985," *International Studies Quarterly* 41, no. 2 (1997): 267–294; Erica Chenoweth, "Terrorism and Democracy," *Annual Review of Political Science* 16 (May 2013): 355–378.

44. New America, "Part IV. What Is the Threat to the United States Today?," in *Terrorism in America after 9/11*, accessed July 22, 2018, www.newamerica.org/indepth/terrorism-in-america/what-threat-united-states-today.

45. Micah Zenko, "The State of Global Terrorism in 2015," *Politics, Power, and Preventive Action* (blog), Council on Foreign Relations, June 2, 2016, www.cfr.org/blog/state-global-terrorism-2015.

46. New America, "Part IV. What Is the Threat to the United States Today?"

47. U.S. Department of State, Bureau of Counterterrorism, *Patterns of Global Terrorism 2002* (Washington, DC: U.S. Department of State, April 2003), xviii; U.S. Department of State, Bureau of Counterterrorism, *Annex of Statistical Information: Country Reports on Terrorism 2017* (Washington, DC: U.S. Department of State, September 2018), 4.

48. Institute for Conflict Management, South Asia Terrorism Portal, "Fatalities in Terrorist Violence in Pakistan 2003–2018," accessed May 6, 2018, www.satp.org/satporgtp/countries/pakistan/database/casualties.htm.

49. Robert D. Kaplan, *The Coming Anarchy: Shattering the Dreams of the Post Cold War* (New York: Vintage, 2001); Samuel P. Huntington, *The Clash of Civilizations and the Remaking of World Order* (New York: Simon and Schuster, 1996); Joel Kotkin, *Tribes: How Race, Religion, and Identity Determine Success in the New Global Economy* (New York: Random House, 1992).

50. Huntington, *Clash of Civilizations*; John J. Mearsheimer, "Why We Will Soon Miss the Cold War," *Atlantic Monthly*, August 1990, 35–50.

51. Kaplan, *Coming Anarchy*; Daniel Patrick Moynihan, *Pandaemonium: Ethnicity in International Politics* (New York: Oxford University Press, 1994).

52. Yahya Sadowski, *The Myth of Global Chaos* (Washington, DC: Brookings Institution Press, 1998).

Healthier, Wealthier, Better Educated, and More Interconnected

Epigraph: Barack Obama, "Remarks by President Obama at YSEALI Town Hall," September 7, 2016.

1. Novus and Gapminder, "The Ignorance Survey: United States," 2013.

2. World Health Organization, "Global Health Observatory Data Repository: Polio (Pol3) Immunization Coverage Estimates by WHO Region," last updated July 17, 2017.

3. The remaining 22 percent said "neither of those." See Ipsos MORI (@IpsosMORI), "Only 13% of the public think the world is getting better (Belgians most gloomy = "must be the booze" says @benatipsosmori) #ipsosmorilive," Twitter, December 6, 2017, 2:36 p.m.

4. Chelsea Follet, "Five Graphs That Will Change Your Mind about Poverty," HumanProgress, March 14, 2017.

5. World Bank, "GDP Per Capita (Current US$)," accessed May 7, 2018, https://data.worldbank.org/indicator/NY.GDP.PCAP.CD.

6. Ronald Inglehart, Roberto Foa, Christopher Peterson, and Christian Welzel, "Development, Freedom, and Rising Happiness: A Global Perspective (1981–2007)," *Perspectives on Psychological Science* 3, no. 4 (2008): 268.

7. World Bank and International Monetary Fund, *Global Monitoring Report 2015/2016: Development Goals in an Era of Demographic Change* (Washington, DC: World Bank, 2016).

8. Marcio Cruz, James Foster, Bryce Quillin, and Philip Schellekens, *Ending Extreme Poverty and Sharing Prosperity: Progress and Policies* (Washington, DC: World Bank, October 2015).

9. World Bank, "Transcript: World Bank Group Opening Press Conference by President Jim Yong Kim at the 2017 WBG/IMF Annual Meetings," October 12, 2017.

10. World Bank, "Poverty & Equity: Iran (Poverty Headcount Ratio at $1.90 a Day (2011 PPP) (% of Population)," accessed July 4, 2018, https://data.worldbank.org/indicator/SI.POV.DDAY.

11. World Bank, "Poverty & Equity: El Salvador (Poverty Headcount Ratio at $1.90 a Day (2011 PPP) (% of Population)," accessed July 4, 2018, https://data.worldbank.org/indicator/SI.POV.DDAY; World Bank, "Ethiopia," accessed July 4, 2018, https://data.worldbank.org/indicator/SI.POV.DDAY.

12. World Bank, "Poverty & Equity Data Portal: Brazil," accessed July 4, 2018, https://data.worldbank.org/indicator/SI.POV.DDAY.

13. World Health Organization Regional Office for Africa, "Namibia: MDG Goal 1: Eradicate Extreme Poverty and Hunger—Other MDGs," accessed May 10, 2018, http://www.aho.afro.who.int/profiles_information/index.php/Namibia:MDG_Goal_1:_Eradicate_extreme_poverty_and_hunger_-_Other_MDGs; United Nations Development Program, *Poverty and Deprivation in Namibia 2015*, accessed July 4, 2018, www.na.undp.org/content/dam/namibia/docs/povred/undp_na_povred_npcreportsum_2015.pdf.

14. World Bank, "Bangladesh," accessed July 4, 2018, https://data.worldbank.org/country/bangladesh?view=chart.

15. Max Roser, "Hunger and Undernourishment," Our World in Data, 2017, http://ourworldindata.org/hunger-and-undernourishment; World Bank, "Prevalence of Undernourishment (% of Population)," accessed July 4, 2018, https://data.worldbank.org/indicator/SN.ITK.DEFC.ZS.

16. Max Roser, "Famines," Our World in Data, revised December 7, 2017, http://ourworldindata.org/famines.

17. David Cutler and Adriana Lleras-Muney, "Education and Health: Evaluating Theories and Evidence" (NBER Working Paper No. 12352, National Bureau of Economic Research, June 2006).

18. United Nations, *Statistical Annex: Millennium Development Goals, Targets and Indicators*, 2015, http://mdgs.un.org/unsd/mdg/Resources/Static/Products/Progress2015/StatAnnex.pdf.

19. Ibid.

20. Ibid.

21. UNESCO, "Literacy Rates Continue to Rise from One Generation to the Next," fact sheet 45, September 2017; World Bank, "Literacy Rate, Adult Total (% of People Ages 15 and Above)," accessed July 4, 2018, https://data.worldbank.org/indicator/SE.ADT.LITR.ZS.

22. United Nations, *Statistical Annex*; Esteban Ortiz-Ospina and Max Roser, "Global Rise of Education," Our World in Data, 2016, http://ourworldindata.org/global-rise-of-education.

23. World Bank, "Labor Force, Female (% of Total Labor Force)," accessed July 4, 2018, https://data.worldbank.org/indicator/SL.TLF.TOTL.FE.ZS.

24. Gudrun Østby and Henrik Urdal, "Education and Conflict: What the Evidence Says" (policy brief, Centre for the Study of Civil War, Peace Research Institute Oslo, February 2011).

25. United Nations Inter-agency Group for Child Mortality Estimation (UN IGME), as published in UNICEF, *Committing to Child Survival: A Promise Renewed—Progress Report* (New York: UNICEF, 2015).

26. Lucia Breierova and Esther Duflo, "The Impact of Education on Fertility and Child Mortality: Do Fathers Really Matter Less than Mothers?" (NBER Working Paper No. 10513, National Bureau of Economic Research, May 2004); Karen Grépin and Prashant Bharadwaj, "Maternal Education and Child Mortality in Zimbabwe," *Journal of Health Economics* 44 (2015): 97–117.

27. United Nations, *Millennium Development Goals Report, 2015* (New York: United Nations, 2015), 6; United Nations, *Trends in Maternal Mortality, 1990 to 2015* (New York: United Nations, 2015).

28. Guttmacher Institute, "Unintended Pregnancy Rates Declined Globally from 1990 to 2014," press release, March 5, 2018.

29. United Nations, *Statistical Annex*; World Health Organization, "HIV/AIDS Fact Sheet," November 2017.

30. World Health Organization, "Tuberculosis Fact Sheet," January 2018; World Health Organization, "Measles: Key Facts," January 22, 2018; Global Polio Eradication Initiative, "This Week," accessed July 4, 2018, http://polioeradication.org/polio-today/polio-now/this-week/.

31. Global Polio Eradication Initiative, *Global Polio Eradication: Progress 2000* (Geneva: World Health Organization, 2001); Centers for Disease Control and Prevention, "CDC's Work to Eradicate Polio," fact sheet, last updated September 2014.

32. Carter Center, "Guinea Worm Case Totals," last updated May 3, 2018, www.cartercenter.org/health/guinea_worm/case-totals.html.

33. Ibid.

34. World Bank, "Improved Sanitation Facilities (% of Population with Access)," 2016; Max Roser and Esteban Ortiz Ospina, "World Population Growth," Our World in Data, 2017, http://ourworldindata.org/world-population-growth. In

addition, an extraordinary 2.1 billion people enjoy better sanitation, in large part because the proportion of people living in urban slums in the developing world has fallen from 39 percent to 29 percent since 2000. See World Health Organization, "Poliomyelitis," fact sheet N144, April 2016; Global Polio Eradication Initiative, "Global Polio Eradication: Progress 2000"; Centers for Disease Control and Prevention, "CDC's Work to Eradicate Polio."

35. World Health Organization, "Key Facts from JMP 2015 Report," 2015.

36. World Health Organization, "General Assembly Proclaims the Decade of Action on Nutrition," April 1, 2016.

37. World Health Organization, "Life Expectancy Increased by 5 Years since 2000, but Health Inequalities Persist," news release, May 19, 2016. An overall decrease in conflict in most of the developing world also helps explain this increase; in 2015, a group of Iranian researchers determined that peace had a statistically significant effect on life expectancy, even holding all other factors constant. See Vahid Yazdi Feyzabadi, Aliakbar Haghdoost, Mohammad Hossein Mehrolhassani, and Zahra Aminian, "The Association between Peace and Life Expectancy: An Empirical Study of the World Countries," *Iranian Journal of Public Health* 44, no. 3 (2015): 341–351.

38. Laura Freschi, "The Millennium Development What?," *Aid Watch* (blog), NYU Development Research Initiative, September 21, 2010.

39. UNCTAD, *Investment Trends Monitor* 28 (January 2018); Institute of International Finance, *Capital Flows to Emerging Markets* (Washington, DC: Institute of International Finance, May 8, 2018).

40. Rasmane Ouedraogo and Elodie Marlet, "Foreign Direct Investment and Women Empowerment: New Evidence on Developing Countries" (Working Paper No. 18/25, International Monetary Fund, January 25, 2018).

41. Zornitsa Kutlina-Dimitrova and Csilla Lakatos, "The Global Costs of Protectionism" (Policy Research Working Paper No. 8277, World Bank, December 2017).

42. International Monetary Fund, Group of Twenty, *Global Prospects and Policy Challenges* (Washington, DC: International Monetary Fund, September 2016).

43. Solomon William Polachek, "Conflict and Trade," *Journal of Conflict Resolution* 24, no. 1 (1980): 55; Kristian Skrede, "Transnational Dimensions of Civil War," *Journal of Peace Research* 44, no. 3 (2007): 303–304.

44. Solomon W. Polachek, Carlos Seiglie, and Jun Xiang, "Globalization and International Conflict: Can Foreign Direct Investment Increase Cooperation among Nations?," in *The Oxford Handbook of the Economics of Peace and Conflict*, ed. Michelle R. Garfinkel and Stergios Skaperdas, 733–762 (Oxford: Oxford University Press, 2012).

45. Statista, "Smartphones Industry: Statistics & Facts," accessed May 7, 2018, www.statista.com/topics/840/smartphones; IDC, "Apple Tops Samsung in the Fourth Quarter to Close Out a Roller Coaster Year for the Smartphone Market, According to IDC," press release, February 1, 2017.

46. Ericsson, *Ericsson Mobility Report: Interim Update* (Stockholm: Ericsson, February 2018); Ericsson, "Mobile Subscriptions Worldwide Outlook," *Ericsson Mobility Report*, November 2017.

47. Peter Evans, "Afghanistan—Telecoms, Mobile and Broadband—Statistics and Analyses," Budde.com, November 16, 2016, www.budde.com.au/Research/Afghanistan-Telecoms-Mobile-and-Broadband-Statistics-and-Analyses.

48. IHS Markit, "Apple iPhone X (A1865) Preliminary Cost Summary," November 2017.

49. Dionne Searcey and Jaime Yaya Barry, "Inspired by the U.S., West Africans Wield Smartphones to Fight Police Abuse," *New York Times*, September 17, 2016, A2.

50. Julian Smith, "Third World IOU," *IQ*, October 6, 2015.

51. Tavneet Suri and William Jack, "The Long-Run Poverty and Gender Impacts of Mobile Money," *Science* 354, no. 6317 (2016): 1288.

52. Ibid., 1290.

53. Vishwa Mohan, "E-NAM: Changing the Way Farmers Sell Their Produce," *Times of India*, September 24, 2017.

54. Priya Jaisinghani and Mindy Hernandez, "Mobile Persuasion: Can Mobile Phones and Cutting-Edge Behavioral Science Improve Lives?," *Impact Blog*, United States Agency for International Development, April 5, 2014.

55. Steven Radelet, *The Great Surge: The Ascent of the Developing World* (New York: Simon and Schuster, 2016), 178.

56. Minahil Asim and Thomas Dee, "Mobile Phones, Civil Engagement, and School Performance in Pakistan" (NBER Working Paper No. 22764, National Bureau of Economic Research, October 2016).

57. Zeynep Taydas and Dursun Peksen, "Can States Buy Peace? Social Welfare Spending and Civil Conflicts," *Journal of Peace Research* 49, no. 2 (2012): 277–278; Alan Smith and Tony Vaux, *Education, Conflict, and International Development* (London: UK Department for International Development, 2003), 17–18.

58. Chia-yi Lee, "Oil and Terrorism: Uncovering the Mechanisms," *Journal of Conflict Resolution* 65, no. 5 (2016): 903–928.

59. World Health Organization, "World Hunger Again on the Rise, Driven by Conflict and Climate Change, New UN Report Says," September 15, 2017, www

.who.int/news-room/detail/15-09-2017-world-hunger-again-on-the-rise-driven-by-conflict-and-climate-change-new-un-report-says; UNESCO, *Global Education Monitoring Report, 2017/18: Accountability in Education: Meeting Our Commitments* (Paris: UNESCO, 2018), 124; UNAIDS, "Fact Sheet—Latest Statistics on the Status of the AIDS Epidemic," accessed May 7, 2018, www.unaids.org/en/resources/fact-sheet; UNICEF and World Health Organization, *Progress on Sanitation and Drinking Water: 2017 Update and MDG Assessment* (Geneva: UNICEF, 2017), 3. In fact, the biggest growing threats to global health are not hunger, pandemics, and parasites that dominate news coverage but, rather, cancer, heart disease, diabetes, and other noncommunicable diseases.

60. For a roadmap that the international community could use to save tens of millions of lives over the next dozen years, see Karin Stenberg, Odd Hanssen, Tessa Tan-Torres Edejer, et al., "Financing Transformative Health Systems towards Achievement of the Health Sustainable Development Goals: A Model for Projected Resource Needs in 67 Low-Income and Middle-Income Countries," *Lancet* 5, no. 9 (2017): e875–e887.

That Which Harms Us

1. Sparks, Nevada, Police Department, *Sparks Police Department Supplemental or Continuation Report*, October 21, 2013.

2. Mike Spies, "The Undoing of Eddie Ray Routh," *The Trace*, November 23, 2015.

3. Richard H. Ullman, "Redefining Security," *International Security* 8, no. 1 (1983): 129–153.

4. Forrestal made this assertion when he was secretary of the Navy. See Forrestal, testimony before the Senate Committee on Military Affairs, October 22, 1945, in *Hearings: Department of Armed Forces, Department of Military Security*, 79:1 (Washington, DC: U.S. Government Printing Office, 1945), 97.

5. George H. W. Bush, *National Security Strategy of the United States* (Washington, DC: White House, 1993), 2.

6. Barack Obama, *National Security Strategy of the United States* (Washington, DC: White House, 2010), 9.

7. Strikingly, there is a marked disparity between avoidable-death rates of urban and rural Americans: those in nonmetropolitan areas are more likely to die from each of the leading causes of preventable deaths than are their metropolitan compatriots. See Lena H. Sun, "Rural Americans Are More Likely to Die from the Top Five Causes

of Death," *Washington Post*, January 12, 2017; World Health Organization, *Noncommunicable Diseases Progress Monitor 2017* (Geneva: World Health Organization, September 2017), 201.

8. Emelia J. Benjamin, Salim S. Virani, Clifton W. Callaway, et al., "Heart Disease and Stroke Statistics—2018 Update," *Circulation* 137, no. 12 (2018): e67–e492.

9. Brian Wansink and Jeffery Sobal, "Mindless Eating: The 200 Daily Food Decisions We Overlook," *Eating and Behavior* 39, no. 1 (2007): 106–123.

10. Gitanjali M. Singh, Renata Micha, Shahab Khatibzadeh, Stephen Lim, Majid Ezzati, and Dariush Mozaffarian, "Estimated Global, Regional, and National Disease Burdens Related to Sugar-Sweetened Beverage Consumption in 2010," *Circulation* 132, no. 8 (2015): 639–666.

11. Matthew P. Pase, Jayandra J. Himali, Alexa S. Beiser, Hugo J. Aparicio, Claudia L. Satizabal, Ramachandran S. Vasan, Sudha Seshadri, and Paul F. Jacques, "Sugar- and Artificially Sweetened Beverages and the Risks of Incident Stroke and Dementia," *Stroke* 48, no. 5 (2017): 1139–1146.

12. Institute of Medicine and National Research Council, *U.S. Health in International Perspective: Shorter Lives, Poorer Health* (Washington, DC: National Academies Press, 2013).

13. Ashish P. Thakrar, Alexandra D. Forrest, Mitchell G. Maltenfort, and Christopher B. Forrest, "Child Mortality in the US and 19 OECD Comparator Nations: A 50-Year Time-Trend Analysis," *Health Affairs* 37, no. 1 (2018): 140–149.

14. Organization for Economic Co-operation and Development (OECD), *Obesity Update 2017* (Paris: OECD, 2017).

15. Craig M. Hales, Margaret D. Carroll, Cheryl D. Fryar, and Cynthia L. Ogden, "Prevalence of Obesity among Adults and Youth: United States, 2015–2016" (NCHS Data Brief no. 288, National Center for Health Statistics, October 2017).

16. The NIH categorizes individuals with a body mass index (BMI, weight divided by the square of height in meters) of twenty-five or over as overweight and individuals with a BMI of thirty or higher as obese. See OECD, *Obesity Update 2017*.

17. The State of Obesity, "Adult Obesity in the United States," accessed March 7, 2018, http://stateofobesity.org/adult-obesity.

18. Kenneth D. Kochanek, Sherry L. Murphy, Jiaquan Xu, and Elizabeth Arias, "Mortality in the United States, 2016" (NCHS Data Brief no. 293, National Center for Health Statistics, December 2017).

19. John Cawley, Chad Meyerhoefer, Adam Biener, Mette Hammer, and Neil Wintfeld, "Savings in Medical Expenditures Associated with Reductions in Body

Mass Index among U.S. Adults with Obesity, by Diabetes Status," *PharmacoEconomics* 33, no. 7 (2014): 707–722.

20. Ross A. Hammond and Ruth Levine, "The Economic Impact of Obesity in the United States," *Diabetes, Metabolic Syndrome and Obesity: Targets and Therapy* 3 (August 2010): 285–295.

21. Avi Dor, Christine Ferguson, Casey Langwith, and Ellen Tan, *A Heavy Burden: The Individual Costs of Being Overweight and Obese in the United States* (Washington, DC: Department of Health Policy, School of Public Health and Health Services, George Washington University, September 21, 2010); Victoria Stilwell, "Obesity Is Hurting the U.S. Economy in Surprising Ways," *Bloomberg,* March 5, 2015; and Eric A. Finkelstein, Marco daCosta Di Bonaventura, Somali M. Burgess, and Brent C. Hale, "The Costs of Obesity in the Workplace," *Journal of Occupational and Environmental Medicine* 52, no. 10 (2010): 971–976.

22. Hammond and Levine, "Economic Impact of Obesity"; Stilwell, "Obesity Is Hurting the U.S. Economy"; F. S. Luppino, L. M. de Wit, P. F. Bouvy, T. Stijnen, P. Cuijpers, B. W. Pennix, and F. G. Zitman, "Overweight, Obesity and Depression: A Systematic Review and Meta-analysis of Longitudinal Studies," *Archives of General Psychiatry* 67, no. 3 (2010): 220–229.

23. The State of Obesity, "Fast Facts on the State of Obesity in America," accessed March 7, 2018, http://stateofobesity.org/fastfacts.

24. General Richard B. Myers, "How Junk Food in Schools Affects the Military," *Politico*, September 24, 2012.

25. George H. W. Bush, *National Security Strategy of the United States* (Washington, DC: White House, 1991), 7.

26. Centers for Disease Control and Prevention, National Center for Health Statistics, "Provision Drug Overdose Death Counts," based on data available for analysis on September 5, 2018.

27. Josh Katz, "The First Count of Fentanyl Deaths in 2016: Up 540% in Three Years," *New York Times,* September 2, 2017; Holly Hedegaard, Margaret Warner, and Arialdi M. Miniño, "Drug Overdose Deaths in the United States, 1999–2016" (NCHS Data Brief No. 294, Centers for Disease Control and Prevention, December 2017).

28. Council of Economic Advisers, *The Underestimated Costs of the Opioid Crisis* (Washington, DC: White House, November 2017). The annual economic costs are certainly higher today, given the vast increase in users and overdoses.

29. David A. Nielsen, Amol Utrankar, Jennifer A. Reyes, Daniel D. Simons, and Thomas R. Kosten, "Epigenetics of Drug Abuse: Predisposition or Response," *Phar-*

macogenomics 13, no. 10 (2012): 1149–1160; National Institute on Drug Abuse, *Drugs, Brains, and Behavior: The Science of Addiction*, NIH Pub. No. 14-5605 (Bethesda, MD: National Institutes of Health, revised July 2014).

30. *Hearing of the Joint Economic Committee on Economic Aspects of the Opioid Crisis*, 115th Cong. (June 8, 2017).

31. Evan Osnos, "Making a Killing," *New Yorker*, June 27, 2016, 36.

32. Nese F. DeBruyne, *American War and Military Operations Casualties: Lists and Statistics* (Washington, DC: Congressional Research Service, April 26, 2017); Centers for Disease Control and Prevention, "Deaths Resulting from Firearm- and Motor-Vehicle-Related Injuries—United States, 1968–1991," *Morbidity and Mortality Weekly Report* 43, no. 3 (1994): 37–42; Centers for Disease Control and Prevention Web-Based Injury Statistics Query and Reporting System (WISQARS), "Injury Mortality Reports, 1981–1998," accessed May 6, 2018, http://webappa.cdc.gov/sasweb/ncipc/mortrate9.html; Centers for Disease Control and Prevention WISQARS, "Fatal Injury Reports, National and Regional, 1999–2013," accessed May 6, 2018, http://webappa.cdc.gov/sasweb/ncipc/mortrate10_us.html.

33. What factors have caused the collapse in major violent crimes is highly contested by criminologists and sociologists. Centers for Disease Control and Prevention, "FastStats—All Injuries," October 7, 2016, www.cdc.gov/nchs/faststats/injury.htm; Centers for Disease Control and Prevention WISQARS, "Firearm Deaths and Rates per 100,000 and Overall Firearm Gunshot Nonfatal Injuries and Rates per 100,000," accessed May 6, 2018, www.cdc.gov/injury/wisqars/leading_causes_death.html.

34. Ashish P. Thakrar, Alexandra D. Forrest, Mitchell G. Maltenfort, and Christopher B. Forrest, "Child Mortality in the US and 19 OECD Comparator Nations: A 50-Year Time-Trend Analysis," *Health Affairs* 37, no. 1 (2018): 140–149.

35. Centers for Disease Control and Prevention WISQARS, "Suicide Injury Deaths and Rates per 100,000," accessed May 6, 2018, www.cdc.gov/injury/wisqars/leading_causes_death.html.

36. David Owens, Judith Horrocks, and Allan House, "Fatal and Non-fatal Repetition of Self-Harm. Systematic Review," *British Journal of Psychiatry* 181 (2002): 193–999; Sabrina Tavernise, "To Reduce Suicide Rates, New Focus Turns to Guns," *New York Times*, February 13, 2013.

37. Andrew Anglemyer, "The Accessibility of Firearms and Risk for Suicide and Homicide Victimization among Household Members: A Systematic Review and Meta-analysis," *Annals of Internal Medicine* 160, no. 2 (2014): 101–110.

38. As the NRA head Wayne LaPierre warned in 2016, "these bad guys we are facing . . . they're trying to kill us." Rebecca Savransky, "NRA's LaPierre Blasts Dems' Gun Control Push," *The Hill*, June 19, 2016.

39. Federal Bureau of Investigation Uniform Crime Reporting Program (FBI UCR), "2016 Crime in the United States: Expanded Homicide Data Table 4: Murder Victims by Weapon, 2012–2016"; FBI UCR, "2015 Crime in the United States: Expanded Homicide Data Table 10: Murder Circumstances by Relationship, 2015."

40. FBI UCR, "2016 Crime in the United States: Expanded Homicide Data Table 6: Justifiable Homicide by Weapon, Private Citizen, 2012–2016."

41. EveryTown, "#NotAnAccident Index," accessed July 4, 2018, https://everytownresearch.org/notanaccident/.

42. Christopher Ingraham, "American Toddlers Are Still Shooting People on a Weekly Basis This Year," *Washington Post*, September 29, 2017

43. Michael Martinez and Tony Marco, "Mom Fatally Shot When Son, 2, Grabs Gun from Her Purse in Walmart," CNN, December 31, 2014; David Chang and Alison Burdo, "Mom at Home When 11-Year-Old Daughter Shot, Killed: Police," NBC, April 6, 2014; Jack Healy, Julie Bosman, Alan Blinder, and Julie Turkewitz, "One Week in April, Four Toddlers Shot and Killed Themselves," *New York Times*, May 5, 2016.

44. Centers for Disease Control and Prevention, "Unintentional Drowning: Get the Facts," fact sheet, April 28, 2016.

45. Matthew Hnatov, *Non-fire Carbon Monoxide Deaths Associated with the Use of Consumer Products 2012 Annual Estimates* (Bethesda, MD: Consumer Product Safety Commission, January 7, 2016).

46. Adam Suchy, *Product Instability or Tip-Over Injuries and Fatalities Associated with Televisions, Furniture, and Appliances: 2016 Report* (Bethesda, MD: U.S. Consumer Product Safety Commission, August 2016).

47. Adam Suchy, *Product Instability or Tip-Over Injuries and Fatalities Associated with Televisions, Furniture, and Appliances: 2014 Report* (Bethesda, MD: Consumer Product Safety Commission, September 25, 2014).

48. This includes jihadist, far-right-wing, and black nationalist terrorist attacks. See New America, "What Is the Threat to the United States Today?," accessed March 7, 2018, www.newamerica.org/in-depth/terrorism-in-america/what-threat-united-states-today.

49. John Kelly, remarks at "Home and Away: DHS and the Threats to America," George Washington University Center for Cyber and Homeland Security, April 18, 2017.

50. Donald J. Trump (@realDonaldTrump), "Terrorists are engaged in a war against civilization-it is up to all who value life to confront & defeat this evil," http://45.wh.gov/ardıny," Twitter, May 26, 2017, 4:26 p.m.

51. Michael Cohen, "It's Coming from Inside the House," in *A Dangerous World? Threat Perception and U.S. National Security*, ed. Christopher Preble and John Mueller (Washington, DC: CATO Institute, 2014), 155–169; Richard Haass, *Foreign Policy Begins at Home: The Case for Putting America's House in Order* (New York: Basic Books, 2013).

52. Christopher Ingraham, "This Is How Toxic Flint's Water Really Is," *Washington Post*, January 15, 2016.

53. Dina Gusovsky, "America's Water Crisis Goes Beyond Flint, Michigan," CNBC, March 24, 2016.

54. White House, *An Economic Analysis of Transportation Infrastructure Investment* (Washington, DC: White House, July 2014).

55. Jaeyoung Lee, BooHyun Nam, and Mohamed Abdel-Aty, "Effects of Pavement Surface Conditions on Traffic Crash Severity," *Journal of Transportation Engineering* 141, no. 10 (2015). According to Federal Administration Highway statistics, just 59 percent of America's public roads are in "good" condition. See Ranjitha Shivaram and Adie Tomer, "Do Our Infrastructure Systems Put People at Risk?," *The Avenue* (blog), Brookings Institution, May 10, 2018, www.brookings.edu/blog/the-avenue/2018/05/10/do-our-infrastructure-systems-put-people-at-risk/.

56. World Health Organization, *Global Status Report on Road Safety 2015* (Geneva: World Health Organization, October 2015).

57. Northeast Corridor Infrastructure and Operations Advisory Commission, *The Northeast Corridor and the American Economy* (Washington, DC: Northeast Corridor Commission, April 2014); Emily Nonko, "NYC Subway's Failures Threaten City's Financial Future, Says MTA Chief," *Curbed*, November 21, 2017.

58. Tyler Kelley, "Choke Point of a Nation," *New York Times*, November 27, 2016.

59. "America's Aging Dams Are in Need of Repair," *New York Times*, February 23, 2017.

60. Edward Alden and Rebecca Strauss, *How America Stacks Up: Economic Competitiveness and U.S. Policy* (New York: Council on Foreign Relations, 2016), 9.

61. OECD, *Country Note: Key Findings from PISA 2015 for the United States* (Paris: OECD, 2016), 18.

62. "Forty-Eighth Is Not a Good Place," editorial, *New York Times*, October 26, 2010; OECD, "United States Country Note," in *Education at a Glance 2013: OECD*

Indicators (Paris: OECD, 2013); and "OECD Education Rankings—2013 Update," *Signs of Our Times* (blog), April 10, 2008, https://ourtimes.wordpress.com/2008/04/10/oecd-education-rankings/.

63. National Center for Education Statistics, "The Nation's Report Card," accessed March 11, 2018, www.nationsreportcard.gov.

64. OECD, "United States Country Note," in *Education at a Glance 2014: OECD Indicators* (Paris: OECD, 2014).

65. Richard Perez-Pena, "U.S. Adults Fare Poorly in a Study of Skills," *New York Times*, October 8, 2013.

66. Anne Case and Angus Deaton, "Rising Morbidity and Mortality in Midlife among White Non-Hispanic Americans in the Twenty-First Century," *Proceedings of the National Academy of Sciences of the United States of America* 112, no. 49 (2015): 15078–15083.

67. Richard Dobbs, Anu Madgavkar, James Manyika, Jonathan Woetzel, Jacques Bughin, Eric Labaye, and Pranav Kashyap, *Poorer than Their Parents? A New Perspective on Income Inequality* (McKinsey & Company, July 2016).

68. Cohen, "It's Coming from Inside the House."

69. Bruce Stokes, *Global Publics More Upbeat about the Economy* (Washington, DC: Pew Research Center, June 5, 2017).

70. Rakesh Kochhar and Anthony Cilluffo, "How Wealth Inequality Has Changed in the U.S. since the Great Recession, by Race, Ethnicity and Income," Fact Tank, Pew Research Center, November 1, 2017.

71. Rakesh Kochhar and Richard Fry, "Wealth Inequality Has Widened along Racial, Ethnic Lines since End of Great Recession," Fact Tank, Pew Research Center, December 12, 2014.

72. Raj Chetty, Nathaniel Hendren, Patrick Kline, and Emmanuel Saez, "Where Is the Land of Opportunity? The Geography of Intergenerational Mobility in the United States," *Quarterly Journal of Economics* 129, no. 4 (2014): 1578.

73. World Inequality Database, accessed May 6, 2018, http://wid.world.

74. Estelle Sommeiller, Mark Price, and Ellis Wazeter, *Income Inequality in the U.S. by State, Metropolitan Area, and County* (Washington, DC: Economic Policy Institute, June 16, 2016).

75. United Nations Human Rights Office of the High Commissioner, "Statement on Visit to the USA, by Professor Philip Alston, United Nations Special Rapporteur on Extreme Poverty and Human Rights," December 15, 2017.

76. Andrew G. Berg and Jonathan D. Ostry, "Inequality and Unsustainable Growth: Two Sides of the Same Coin?" (IMF Staff Discussion Note, International Monetary Fund, April 8, 2011), 3.

77. Marina Azzimonti, "Does Partisan Conflict Deter FDI Inflows to the US?" (NBER Working Paper No. 22336, National Bureau of Economic Research, June 2016).

78. Bureau of Economic Analysis, *Technical Note: Gross Domestic Product Fourth Quarter of 2013 (Advance Estimate)* (Washington, DC: U.S. Department of Commerce, January 30, 2014); Council of Economic Advisers, *Economic Activity during the Government Shutdown and Debt Limit Brinksmanship* (Washington, DC: White House, October 2013).

79. Shaun Donovan, "The Economic Case for a Budget Deal That Lifts Sequestration," *White House Blog*, September 17, 2015.

80. William C. Thompson Jr., *One Year Later: The Fiscal Impact of 9/11 on New York City* (New York: Comptroller of the City of New York, 2002).

81. American Heart Association, "Heart Disease Death Rate Continues to Drop," December 9, 2015, https://news.heart.org/heart-disease-death-rate-continues-to-drop/.

82. Gina Kolata, "A Medical Mystery of the Best Kind: Major Diseases Are in Decline," *New York Times*, July 8, 2016.

83. Office of the Surgeon General, *The Health Consequences of Smoking—50 Years of Progress* (Washington, DC: U.S. Department of Health and Human Services, January 2014).

84. Centers for Disease Control and Prevention, National Center for Chronic Disease Prevention and Health Promotion, "Trends in Current Cigarette Smoking among High School Students and Adults, United States, 1965–2014," March 2016, www.cdc.gov/tobacco/data_statistics/tables/trends/cig_smoking/index.htm; and "Only 15 Percent of U.S. Adults Now Smoke, CDC Finds," Associated Press, May 24, 2016.

85. Pearl Bader, David Boisclair, and Roberta Ferrence, "Effects of Tobacco Taxation and Pricing on Smoking Behavior in High Risk Populations: A Knowledge Synthesis," *International Journal of Environmental Research and Public Health* 8, no. 11 (2011): 4118–4139.

86. Stephanie L. Mayne, Amy H. Auchincloss, Mark F. Stehr, David M. Kern, Ana Navas-Acien, Joel D. Kaufman, Yvonne L. Michael, and Ana V. Diez Roux,

"Longitudinal Associations of Local Cigarette Prices and Smoking Bans with Smoking Behavior in the Multi-ethnic Study of Atherosclerosis," *Epidemiology* 28, no. 6 (2017): 863–871; World Bank, *Curbing the Epidemic: Governments and the Economics of Tobacco Control* (Washington, DC: World Bank, 1999).

87. Theodore R. Holford, "Tobacco Control and the Reduction in Smoking-Related Premature Deaths in the United States, 1964–2012," *Journal of the American Medical Association* 311, no. 2 (2014): 164–171.

88. Insurance Institute for Highway Safety Highway Loss Data Institute, "General Statistics," accessed May 6, 2018, www.iihs.org/iihs/topics/t/general-statistics/topicoverview.

89. National Highway Traffic Safety Administration, "2016 Fatal Motor Vehicle Crashes: Overview" (Traffic Safety Facts Research Note, U.S. Department of Transportation, October 2017).

90. Ibid., 7.

91. "Death on Foot: Pedestrian Fatalities Skyrocket in U.S.," *Detroit Free Press,* May 8, 2018.

92. Liisa Ecola, Steven W. Popper, Richard Silberglitt, and Laura Fraade-Blanar, *The Road to Zero: A Vision for Achieving Zero Roadway Deaths by 2050* (Santa Monica, CA: RAND Corporation, 2018).

93. Martin Makary and Daniel Michael, "Medical Error—The Third Leading Cause of Death in the U.S.," *BMJ* 353 (May 2016).

94. Aaron E. Carroll, "Death by Medical Error: Adding Context to Scary Headlines," *New York Times*, August 15, 2016.

95. Liz Kowalczyk, "Fourteen Instances of Right Procedure, Wrong Patient in Mass.," *Boston Globe*, November 20 2016.

96. James Lieber, *How Medical Error Became America's Third Largest Cause of Death and What Can Be Done about It* (New York: OR Books, 2015).

97. Yusuke Tsugawa, Anupam B. Jena, Jose F. Figueroa, E. John Orav, Daniel M. Blumenthal, and Ashish K. Jha, "Comparison of Hospital Mortality and Readmission Rates for Medicare Patients Treated by Male vs. Female Physicians," *JAMA Internal Medicine* 177, no. 2 (2016): 206–213; Vanessa McMains, "Johns Hopkins Study Suggests Medical Errors Are Third-Leading Cause of Death in U.S.," Johns Hopkins University Hub, May 3, 2016, https://hub.jhu.edu/2016/05/03/medical-errors-third-leading-cause-of-death/.

98. Jonathan Chait, "Republicans Own Health Care Now. How Many People Will They Let Suffer?," *New York,* January 22, 2017.

The Grand American Tradition of Threat Inflation

Epigraph: Daniel Henninger, "George Bush Talks about 'The Next Attack on America,' " *Wall Street Journal*, October 27, 2006.

1. Eric F. Goldman, *The Crucial Decade—America 1945–1955* (New York: Knopf, 1965), 59.

2. Harry S. Truman, "Truman Doctrine," speech delivered before a joint session of Congress, March 12, 1947.

3. Ibid. Joseph Jones, who drafted the Truman Doctrine speech, later noted that geostrategic, humanitarian, and loyalty considerations were consciously omitted from Truman's address. Joseph M. Jones, *The Fifteen Weeks: February 21—June 5, 1947* (New York: Viking, 1951), 151–198.

4. Jones, *Fifteen Weeks*, 179; Public Law 80–75, May 22, 1947.

5. C. L. Sulzberger, *A Long Row of Candles: Memoirs and Diaries, 1934–1954* (New York: Macmillan, 1969), 364–365.

6. *Foreign Relations of the United States, 1945–1967*, vol. 23, *United States-Vietnam Relations, 1961–1963*, ed. Edward C. Keefer (Washington, DC: U.S. Government Printing Office, 1994), Document 4; Wolf Blitzer, "Search for the 'Smoking Gun,' " CNN, January 10, 2003.

7. Thomas Christensen, *Useful Adversaries: Grand Strategy, Domestic Mobilization, and Sino-American Conflict, 1947–1958* (Princeton, NJ: Princeton University Press, 1996).

8. Benjamin Friedman, "Alarms and Excursions: Explaining Threat Inflation in U.S. Foreign Policy," in *A Dangerous World? Threat Perception and US National Security*, ed. Christopher A. Preble and John E. Mueller (Washington, DC: CATO Institute, 2014), 289.

9. For an excellent overview of pre-Cold War threat inflation, see John A. Thompson, "The Exaggeration of American Vulnerability: The Anatomy of a Tradition," *Diplomatic History*, 16, no. 1 (1992): 23–43.

10. Sean Cleary, "From the Times to the Tomes: Remember the Maine, to Hell with Spain!," *American Experience*, Public Broadcasting Service, May 20, 2010.

11. Campbell Craig and Fredrik Logevall, *America's Cold War: The Politics of Insecurity* (Cambridge, MA: Harvard University Press, 2012), 117.

12. Harry S. Truman, "Radio and Television Address to the American People on the Situation in Korea," July 19, 1950.

13. Ibid.

14. Ibid.; U.S. Department of State, Office of the Historian, "NSC-68, 1950."

15. Craig and Logevall, *America's Cold War*, 136.

16. President's Science Advisory Committee, Security Resources Panel, *Deterrence and Survival in the Nuclear Age (the "Gaither Report" of 1957)* (Washington, DC: U.S. Government Printing Office, 1976).

17. Christopher A. Preble, "Who Ever Believed in the 'Missile Gap'? John F. Kennedy and the Politics of National Security," *Presidential Studies Quarterly* 33, no. 4 (2003): 801–826.

18. Richard, Reeves, "Missile Gaps and Other Broken Promises," *New York Times,* February 10, 2009; "Soviet Capabilities for Strategic Attack through Mid-1964," National Intelligence Estimate 11-8-59, February 9, 1960; and "Soviet Capabilities for Long Range Attack through Mid-1965," National Intelligence Estimate 11-8-60, August 1, 1960.

19. Memorandum regarding "Operation Candor," July 22, 1953; Stewart Alsop, "Eisenhower Pushes Operation Candor," *Washington Post*, September 21, 1953.

20. John F. Kennedy, "Inaugural Address," January 20, 1961.

21. Stephen Schwartz, *Atomic Audit: The Costs and Consequences of U.S. Nuclear Weapons since 1940* (Washington, DC: Brookings Institution, 1993), 186.

22. Robert S. McNamara, "Department of State Bulletin 57," October 9, 1967, 443–445; Amy F. Woolf, *U.S. Strategic Nuclear Forces: Background, Developments, and Issues* (Washington, DC: Congressional Research Service, 2018).

23. Lyndon B. Johnson, "The President's News Conference," July 28, 1965.

24. Ibid.

25. Ibid.

26. Lyndon B. Johnson, "Remarks of Welcome to Vietnamese Leaders upon Arriving at Honolulu International Airport," February 6, 1966.

27. Ibid.

28. Lyndon B. Johnson, "Address on Vietnam before the National Legislative Conference, San Antonio, Texas," September 29, 1967.

29. Ibid.

30. George W. Bush, "Graduation Speech at West Point," June 1, 2002.

31. U.S. Department of Defense, "U.S. Military Casualties—Vietnam Conflict Casualty Summary," Defense Casualty Analysis System, August 1, 2016.

32. John Tirman, "Why Do We Ignore the Civilians Killed in American Wars?," *Washington Post*, January 6, 2012.

33. Vietnamese estimates range from 2.1 million to 4.8 million Vietnamese exposed to Agent Orange, with at least 3 million suffering serious health problems from

exposure. See Michael F. Martin, *Vietnamese Victims of Agent Orange and U.S.-Vietnam Relations* (Washington, DC: Congressional Research Service, August 29, 2012).

34. As CIA analysts warned after investigating the impact of U.S. bombing in Southwest Cambodia, "[The Khmer Rouge] are using damage caused by B-52 strikes as the main theme of their propaganda. The cadre tell the people that the Government of Lon Nol has requested the airstrikes and is responsible for the damage and the 'suffering of innocent villagers.' . . . This approach has resulted in the successful recruitment of a number of young men. . . . Residents . . . say that the propaganda campaign has been effective with refugees and in areas . . . which have been subject to B-52 strikes." CIA, "Efforts of Khmer Insurgents to Exploit for Propaganda Purposes Damage Done by Airstrikes in Kandal Province," Intelligence Information Cable, May 2, 1973. See Ben Kiernan, "Recovering History and Justice in Cambodia," *Comparativ* 14, no. 5/6 (2004): 78.

35. Richard Nixon, "Address to the Nation on the Situation in Southeast Asia," April 30, 1970.

36. Craig and Logevall, *America's Cold War*, 269.

37. Anne Hessing Cahn, *Killing Détente: The Right Attacks the CIA* (University Park: Pennsylvania University Press, 1998); Micah Zenko, *Red Team: How to Succeed by Thinking like the Enemy* (New York: Basic Books, 2015), 76–83.

38. Craig and Logevall, *America's Cold War*, 286.

39. Ronald Reagan, "Speech to America," March 31, 1976.

40. Julian E. Zelizer, *Arsenal of Democracy: The Politics of National Security—From World War II to the War on Terrorism* (New York: Basic Books, 2010), 331.

41. Ibid., 267.

42. Jimmy Carter, "Address at Commencement Exercises at the University of Notre Dame," May 22, 1977.

43. Craig and Logevall, *America's Cold War*, 304; Jimmy Carter, "The State of the Union Address Delivered before a Joint Session of the Congress," January 23, 1980.

44. Carter, "The State of the Union Address Delivered before a Joint Session of the Congress," January 23, 1980.

45. Komer, testimony before the Subcommittee on Europe and the Middle East, House Committee on Foreign Affairs, April 2, 1980.

46. In April 2018, it became impossible for American citizens to know how many troops are in the Middle East, because the Pentagon suddenly stopped releasing data for Iraq, Afghanistan, and Syria. See Tara Copp, "Pentagon Strips Iraq, Afghanistan,

Syria Troop Numbers from Web," *Stars and Stripes*, April 9, 2018. For the last available data on troop numbers, see U.S. Department of Defense, Defense Manpower Data Center, "Military and Civilian Personnel by Service/Agency by State/Country," accessed June 1, 2018, www.dmdc.osd.mil/appj/dwp/data_reqs.jsp. For Pentagon contractor data for the Middle East, which is still being released quarterly, see U.S. Central Command, Quarterly Contractor Census Reports, accessed July 4, 2018, www.acq.osd.mil/log/ps/centcom_reports.html.

47. Sidney Blumenthal, *Pledging Allegiance: The Last Campaign of the Cold War* (New York: Harper Perennial, 1991), 13.

48. Ronald Reagan, "Address to the National Association of Evangelicals," March 8, 1983.

49. Ronald Reagan, "Excerpts from an Interview with Walter Cronkite of CBS News," March 3, 1981.

50. Amy Belasco, *Defense Spending and the Budget Control Act Limits* (Washington, DC: Congressional Research Service, May 19, 2015); Zelizer, *Arsenal of Democracy*, 307; Craig and Logevall, *America's Cold War*, 313; Ronald Reagan, "Interview with Garry Clifford and Patricia Ryan of People Magazine," December 6, 1983.

51. Schwartz, *Atomic Audit*, 494.

52. Reagan, "Excerpts from an Interview with Walter Cronkite"; Ronald Reagan, "Remarks at a Fundraising Dinner for Governor James R. Thompson, Jr., in Chicago, Illinois," July 7, 1981.

53. Ronald Reagan, "Address before a Joint Session of the Congress on the Program for Economic Recovery," February 18, 1981.

54. Ronald Reagan, "Remarks and a Question-and-Answer Session with Reporters on the Announcement of the United States Strategic Weapons Program," October 2, 1981.

55. Hans M. Kristensen and Robert S. Norris, "Nuclear Notebook," *Bulletin of the Atomic Scientists*, accessed January 3, 2017, http://thebulletin.org/nuclear-notebook-multimedia.

56. Daryl G. Kimball, "Looking Back: The Nuclear Arms Control Legacy of Ronald Reagan," Arms Control Association, July 1, 2004, www.armscontrol.org/act/2004_07-08/Reagan.

57. Hank Steuver, "Yes, 'The Day After' Really Was the Profound TV Moment 'The Americans' Makes It Out to Be," *Washington Post*, May 11, 2016.

58. Michael Weisskopf, "President's Popularity Near Peak, Poll Shows," *Washington Post*, November 17, 1985.

59. Ronald Reagan, "Radio Address to the Nation on Congressional Inaction on Proposed Legislation," August 11, 1984.

60. Craig and Logevall, *America's Cold War*, 322.

61. White House, "National Security Decision: Directive Number 32," May 20, 1982.

62. White House, "U.S. Relations with the USSR: National Security Decision Directive Number 75," January 17, 1983.

63. "Text of Reagan's Letter to Congress on Marines in Lebanon," *New York Times*, September 30, 1982.

64. Lou Cannon, *President Reagan: The Role of a Lifetime* (New York: PublicAffairs, 1991).

65. Ronald Reagan, "Remarks at a White House Meeting for Supporters of United States for the Nicaraguan Democratic Resistance," March 3, 1986.

66. Bob Woodward, *Veil: The Secret Wars of the CIA, 1981–1987* (New York: Simon and Schuster, 1987), 284; Stephen Kinzer, "Nicaraguan Says No Mines Are Left in Nation's Port," *New York Times*, April 13, 1984.

67. Department of Defense Authorization Act of 1983, Public Law 97–252.

68. While two hostages (the Reverend Benjamin Weir and Father Lawrence Jenco) were released during the weapons transfers, two more citizens (Frank Reed and Joseph Cicippio) were taken hostage.

69. Ronald Reagan, "Radio Address to the Nation on the Soviet Occupation of Afghanistan," December 28, 1985.

70. Stephen Kaufman, "Pressure to End Apartheid Began at Grass Roots in U.S.," U.S. Department of State Bureau of International Information Programs, December 16, 2013, https://geneva.usmission.gov/2013/12/17/pressure-to-end-apartheid-began-at-grass-roots-in-u-s/.

71. Even as a presidential candidate, Reagan warned of the limited American support for new interventions: "For too long, we have lived with the 'Vietnam Syndrome.'" Ronald Reagan, "Remarks before the Veterans of Foreign Wars Convention, Chicago, Illinois: Restoring the Margin of Safety," August 18, 1980.

72. Ronald Reagan, *National Security Strategy of the United States* (Washington, DC: White House, May 1982); and Ronald Reagan, *National Security Strategy of the United States* (Washington, DC: White House, January 1988).

73. Reagan, *National Security Strategy* (1988).

74. Blumenthal, *Pledging Allegiance*, 319.

75. Bill Peterson, "A Campaign of Distortions, Untruths," *Washington Post*, September 25, 1988.

76. Presidential debate, September 25, 1988; Bush's "Revolving Door" and "Tank Ride" campaign commercials, 1988, accessed July 4, 2018, www.livingroomcandidate. org/commercials/1988/revolving-door#4121 and www.livingroomcandidate.org/commercials/1988/tank-ride#4119.

77. George H. W. Bush, speeches and press conferences between October 15, 1990, and February 5, 1991.

78. Gallup, "Presidential Approval Ratings—Gallup Historical Statistics and Trends," accessed May 6, 2018, www.gallup.com/poll/116677/presidential-approval-ratings-gallup-historical-statistics-trends.aspx.

79. Joel Brinkley, "U.S. Looking for New Course as Superpower Conflict Ends," *New York Times*, February 2, 1992.

The Threat-Industrial Complex

Epigraph: James Risen, *Pay Any Price: Greed, Power, and Endless War* (New York: Mariner, 2014), 203.

1. Jennifer L. Merolla and Elizabeth J. Zechmeister, *Democracy at Risk: How Terrorist Threats Affect the Public* (Chicago: University of Chicago Press, 2009). In 2018, Merolla, along with Kerstin Fisk and Jennifer M. Ramos, demonstrated that priming Americans with a short fictional news report of terrorist plots made them approximately 30 percent more supportive of drone strikes, compared to those who were not primed with threatening information. See Kerstin Fisk, Jennifer L. Merolla, and Jennifer M. Ramos, "Emotions, Terrorist Threat, and Drones," *Journal of Conflict Resolution*, first published May 3, 2018.

2. *The Fiscal Year 2019 National Defense Authorization Budget Request from the Department of Defense: Hearing before the Armed Services Committee*, 115th Cong. (April 12, 2018).

3. Stephen M. Walt, "Imbalance of Power," *Foreign Policy*, May 22, 2009.

4. Dwight D. Eisenhower, "Farewell Address to the Nation," January 17, 1961.

5. Scott Eidelman, Christian S. Crandall, and Jennifer Pattershall, "The Existence Bias," *Journal of Personality and Social Psychology* 97, no. 5 (2009): 765–775.

6. Glenn Greenwald, "NSA Collecting Phone Records of Millions of Verizon Customers Daily," *Guardian*, June 6, 2013.

7. Barton Gellman and Greg Miller, " 'Black Budget' Summary Details U.S. Spy Network's Successes, Failures and Objectives," *Washington Post*, August 29, 2013.

8. Amnesty International, *Two Years after Snowden: Protecting Human Rights in an Age of Mass Surveillance* (London: Amnesty International, June 4, 2015); Scott Shane,

"No Morsel Too Minuscule for All-Consuming N.S.A.," *New York Times*, November 2, 2013.

9. Jason Leopold, "Revealed: NSA Pushed 9/11 as Key 'Sound Bite' to Justify Surveillance," *Al Jazeera America*, October 30, 2013.

10. Keith Alexander, "National Conversation on the Defense of Our Nation and Protection of Civil Liberties and Privacy: A Technical Perspective," presentation, accessed May 6, 2018, www.propublica.org/documents/item/802262-us-13-alexander-keynote.html#document, 14; Office of the Director of National Intelligence, "Remarks by General Keith Alexander, Director, National Security Agency at AFCEA's Conference," IC on the Record Database, June 28, 2013, www.intelligence.gov/ic-on-the-record-database/results/41-remarks-by-general-keith-alexander,-director,-national-security-agency-at-afcea's-conference.

11. 159 Cong. Rec. H5024 (July 24, 2013) (statement of Rep. Mike J. Rogers).

12. Justin Elliott and Theodoric Meyer, "Claim on 'Attacks Thwarted' by NSA Spreads Despite Lack of Evidence," *ProPublica*, October 23, 2013.

13. Bailey Cahall, Peter Bergen, David Sterman, and Emily Schneider, "Do NSA's Bulk Surveillance Programs Stop Terrorists?," *New America,* January 13, 2014; Matthathias Schwartz, "The Whole Haystack," *New Yorker*, January 26, 2015; and Ellen Nakashima, "NSA Cites Case as Success of Phone Data-Collection Program," *Washington Post*, August 8, 2013. In November 2015, federal judge Richard Leon noted in his opinion that the federal government "does *not* cite a single instance in which analysis of the NSA's bulk metadata collection actually stopped an imminent attack" and noted "the utter lack of evidence that a terrorist attack has ever been prevented because searching the NSA database was faster than other investigative tactics." *Klayman v. Obama*, 957 F. Supp. 2d 1, 60–61 (D.D.C. 2013).

14. *Continued Oversight of the Foreign Intelligence Surveillance Act: Hearing before the Senate Judiciary Committee*, 113th Cong. (October 2, 2013).

15. National Security Agency/Central Security Service, "What We Do," accessed February 8, 2018, www.nsa.gov/what-we-do.

16. Walter Pincus, "Eisenhower's Farewell Speech Has Wise Words on Split Government and Militarism," *Washington Post*, December 13, 2010.

17. Marybeth Peterson Ulrich, " 'Cashing In' Stars: Does the Professional Ethic Apply in Retirement?," *Strategic Studies Quarterly* 9, no. 3 (2015): 102–125.

18. Bryan Bender, "From the Pentagon to the Private Sector," *Boston Globe*, December 26, 2010. Another estimate "found 70 percent of the 108 three-and-four star generals and admirals who retired between 2009 and 2011 took jobs with defense

contractors or consultants." Citizens for Responsibility and Ethics in Washington, *Strategic Maneuvers: The Revolving Door from the Pentagon to the Private Sector* (Washington, DC: Citizens for Responsibility and Ethics in Washington, 2012).

19. Sam Skolnik, "Revolving Door between Trump Pentagon, Contractors Spins Faster," *Bloomberg Government*, February 1, 2018.

20. Moshe Schwartz, John F. Sargent Jr., and Christopher T. Mann, *Defense Acquisitions: How and Where DOD Spends Its Contracting Dollars* (Washington, DC: Congressional Research Service, July 2, 2018).

21. Ibid.

22. Heidi M. Peters, Moshe Schwartz, and Lawrence Kapp, *Department of Defense Contractor and Troop Levels in Iraq and Afghanistan: 2007–2017* (Washington, DC: Congressional Research Service, April 28, 2017).

23. Center for Responsive Politics, "Defense: Lobbying, 2017," OpenSecrets.org, accessed May 15, 2017, www.opensecrets.org/lobby/indus.php?id=d&year=2017.

24. Michael Beschloss, "Inside the Vaults—The Writing of Eisenhower's 'Military-Industrial Complex' Speech," YouTube, February 11, 2011, www.youtube.com/watch?v=APmlPtDrQEo.

25. David Barstow, "Behind TV Analysts, Pentagon's Hidden Hand," *New York Times*, April 20, 2008.

26. "Bush: 'I'm the Decider' on Rumsfeld,' " CNN, April 18, 2006.

27. U.S. Department of Defense Inspector General, *Review of Matters Related to the Office of the Assistant Secretary of Defense (Public Affairs) Retired Military Analyst Outreach Activities* (Alexandria, VA: Inspector General, Department of Defense, November 21, 2011), 16.

28. David Barstow, "Behind TV Analysts, Pentagon's Hidden Hand," *New York Times*, April 20, 2008.

29. Ibid.

30. Determined upon reviewing more than one hundred LexisNexis transcripts of retired military analysts' media appearances.

31. Center for Responsive Politics, "Huntington Ingalls Industries," OpenSecrets.org, accessed May 15, 2017, www.opensecrets.org/orgs/summary.php?id=D000064813&cycle=2012.

32. Eric Lipton and Brooke Williams, "How Think Tanks Amplify Corporate America's Influence," *New York Times*, August 7, 2016.

33. Ibid.

34. Ibid.

35. Seth Cropsey, Bryan McGrath, and Timothy A. Walton, *Sharpening the Spear: The Carrier, the Joint Force, and High-End Conflict* (Washington, DC: Hudson Institute, October 8, 2015), 30, 3.

36. Lipton and Williams, "How Think Tanks Amplify."

37. Ibid.

38. Bryan Clark and Jesse Sloman, *Deploying beyond Their Means: America's Navy and Marine Corps at a Tipping Point* (Washington, DC: Center for Strategic and Budgetary Assessments, November 2015), 20.

39. Ibid.

40. Ibid., 27.

41. Lipton and Williams, "How Think Tanks Amplify."

42. Thomas Donnelly and Roger Zakheim, "The Myth of the U.S. Military 'Readiness Myth,' " *National Review*, August 15, 2016.

43. Ibid.

44. Ibid.

45. "Why Aren't We Safer? Failure to Reform," *Primetime Live*, ABC, September 11, 2006.

46. "The Media on the Media," *New York Magazine*, July 24, 2016.

47. Ibid.

48. The number of foreign bureaus for cable news stations is down from fifty-three in 2010 to forty-eight in 2015, including bureaus dropped by CNN, Fox News, and MSNBC. Pew Research Center, *State of the News Media 2016* (Washington, DC: Pew Research Center, June 15, 2016).

49. In 2007, foreign stories accounted for 30 percent of CNN's news, compared to 21 percent on Fox and 25 percent on MSNBC. In 2013, CNN still led with 23 percent foreign coverage compared to 15 percent on Fox and only 7 percent on MSNBC. Mark Jurkowitz, Paul Hitlin, Amy Mitchell, Laura Houston Santhanam, Steve Dams, Monica Anderson, and Nancy Vogt, *The Changing TV News Landscape* (Washington, DC: Pew Research Center, March 17, 2013).

50. In the Republican undercard debates: 89; in Republican primary debates: 320; in Democratic primary debates: 135. American Presidency Project, "Presidential Debates 1960–2016," accessed July 4, 2018, www.presidency.ucsb.edu/debates .php.

51. Jim Naureckas, "CNN's Debate on 'Terror' Omitted the Kind That Kills the Most Americans," FAIR, December 16, 2015.

52. Leslie Savan, "Right-Wing Fear-Mongering Is Far More Contagious than Ebola," *Nation*, October 8, 2014; Joe Coscarelli, "Ebola Coverage Goes Extra Dumb on CNN, Fox News," *New York*, October 6, 2014.

53. Gerard Flynn and Susan Scutti, "Smuggled Bushmeat Is Ebola's Back Door to America," *Newsweek*, August 21, 2014. As the medical anthropologist Theresa MacPhail commented, "That *Newsweek* story, in my opinion, is just really bad journalism. Where were their facts, statistics, evidence?" John Horgan, "Ebola 'Fear Mongering' Critiqued by Medical Anthropologist," *Scientific American*, September 3, 2014.

54. Liz Hamel, Jamie Firth, and Mollyann Brodie, "Kaiser Health Policy News Index: Special Focus on Ebola," Henry J. Kaiser Family Foundation, October 16, 2014.

55. Centers for Disease Control and Prevention, "Cases of Ebola Diagnosed in the United States," last updated December 16, 2014, www.cdc.gov/vhf/ebola/outbreaks/2014-west-africa/united-states-imported-case.html.

56. Saeed Ahmed and Dorrine Mendoze, "Ebola Hysteria: An Epic, Epidemic Overreaction," CNN, October 20, 2014; Alan Yuhas, "Panic: The Dangerous Epidemic Sweeping an Ebola-Fearing US," *Guardian*, October 20, 2014; Laura Wagner, "New Jersey Governor Facing Lawsuit from Nurse Quarantined during Ebola Scare," National Public Radio, October 22, 2015.

57. World Health Organization, *Ebola Situation Report* (Geneva: World Health Organization, March 25, 2015).

58. Data Team, "Ebola in Africa: The End of a Tragedy?," *Economist*, January 14, 2016; Rucker Reals, "This Morning from CBS News, Dec. 23, 2016," CBS News, December 23, 2016; World Health Organization, "Final Trial Results Confirm Ebola Vaccine Provides High Protection against Disease," news release, December 2016.

59. Citizens for a Nuclear Free Iran, "General," TV commercial, 2015.

60. Anti-Defamation League, "The Iranian Nuclear Threat: Why It Matters," accessed May 15, 2017, www.adl.org/education/resources/fact-sheets/the-iranian-nuclear-threat-why-it-matters.

61. Department of Justice, "Foreign Agents Registration Act," accessed March 15, 2018, www.fara.gov.

62. See, for example, Catherine Ho, "Trump Adviser and Former Rep. Jack Kingston Hired to Lobby for Syrian Opposition Group," *Washington Post*, October 4, 2016.

63. The Center for Media and Democracy's PR Watch, "How PR Sold the War in the Persian Gulf," accessed May 15, 2017, www.prwatch.org/books/tsigfy10.html.

64. The *Times* did acknowledge that concurrent with its reporting based on Mandiant's research, the newspaper had also hired Mandiant "to investigate a sophisti-

cated Chinese-origin attack on its news operations." David Sanger, David Barboza, and Nicole Perloth, "Chinese Army Unit Is Seen as Tied to Hacking against U.S.," *New York Times*, February 18, 2013, A1. The same thing happened two months later, when the media reported Crowdstrike's published claims of the hacker groups Cozy Bear and Fancy Bear hacking Ukrainian military servers. Shane Harris, "Cyber Experts Cite Link between DNC Hacks and Aggression against Ukraine," *Wall Street Journal*, December 22, 2016.

65. Good Harbor Security Risk Management, home page, accessed May 6, 2018, www.goodharbor.net.

66. Richard A. Clarke and Robert Knake, *Cyber War* (New York: HarperCollins, 2010). In 1993, the RAND Corporation published a comparable hyperbolic warning with the report: John Arquilla and David Ronfeldt, *Cyberwar Is Coming!* (Santa Monica, CA: RAND Corporation, 1993). It still has not arrived.

67. "Richard Clarke on the Growing 'Cyberwar' Threat," *Fresh Air*, National Public Radio, April 19, 2010.

68. Ellen Nakashima, "The Latest Hot Job in the Washington Revolving Door? Cybersecurity," *Washington Post*, March 17, 2015; Carter Dougherty and Jesse Hamilton, "Ex-NSA Chief Pitches Banks Costly Advice on Cyber-Attacks," *Bloomberg*, June 20, 2104.

69. Sean Froelich, "Ex-NSA Chief Warns of Cyberspace Dangers," *U.S. News and World Report*, November 2, 2015; Randy Komisar, "An Interview with General Keith Alexander on Cybersecurity, Snowden, and IronNet," *TechCrunch*, March 1, 2016.

70. Cyber Squirrel 1, home page, accessed July 12, 2018, http://cybersquirrel1 .com.

71. Martin Miller, " '24' and "Lost" Get Symposium on Torture," *Los Angeles Times*, February 14, 2007.

72. "Republican Presidential Debate in South Carolina," *New York Times*, May 15, 2007, www.nytimes.com/2007/05/15/us/politics/16repubs-text.html.

73. Tung Yin, "Jack Bauer Syndrome: Hollywood's Depiction of National Security Law" (University of Iowa Legal Studies Research Paper Number 09-13, March 2009).

74. Dianne Feinstein, "Feinstein Releases Statement on 'Zero Dark Thirty,' " press release, December 19, 2012.

75. Tricia Jenkins, *The CIA in Hollywood: How the Agency Shapes Film and Television* (Austin: University of Texas Press, 2012).

76. "Hollywood a Longtime Friend of the CIA," *Los Angeles Times*, May 26, 2012.

77. John A. Rizzo, *Company Man: Thirty Years of Controversy and Crisis in the CIA* (New York: Scribner, 2014), 63–65.

78. David L. Robb, *Operation Hollywood: How the Pentagon Shapes and Censors the Movies* (Amherst, NY: Prometheus Books, 2004), 38.

79. World Bank DataBank, "People Using at Least Basic Drinking Water Services (% of Population)," accessed July 4, 2018, https://data.worldbank.org/indicator/SH.H2O.BASW.ZS.

80. Carter Center, "Guinea Worm Case Totals," last updated May 3, 2018, www.cartercenter.org/health/guinea_worm/case-totals.html.

81. Michael Lemonick, "It's Doomsday Clock Time Again," *Observations* (blog), *Scientific American*, January 26, 2016.

82. Rachel Becker, "The Doomsday Clock Is the Gimmick We Need to Think about Nuclear Tensions," *The Verge*, January, 25, 2018. See also Michael A. Cohen, "Stop the (Doomsday) Clock," *Boston Globe*, January 26, 2018.

83. Daniel Kahneman, *Thinking, Fast and Slow* (New York: Farrar, Straus and Giroux, 2011), 282.

84. Quoted in William Safire, *Before the Fall: An Inside View of the Pre-Watergate White House* (Garden City, NY: Doubleday, 1975), 8.

An Alternative Post-9/11 History

Epigraph: Lyndon B. Johnson, "The President's Inaugural Address," January 20, 1965.

1. "Philadelphia Fans Set Fire, Damage Property after Super Bowl Win," Reuters, February 5, 2018.

2. Jason Diamos, "Hockey: Rangers' Game Halted for President's Speech," *New York Times*, September 21, 2001.

3. George W. Bush, *Decision Points* (New York: Broadway Books, 2011), 191–192.

4. 9/11 Memorial, "Ground Zero Recovery Timeline," accessed May 6, 2018, http://timeline.911memorial.org/#Timeline/3.

5. George W. Bush, "Address to a Joint Session of Congress and the American People," September 20, 2001.

6. Bob Woodward, *Bush at War* (New York: Simon and Schuster, 2003), 108–109.

7. Anthony DiMaggio, *When Media Goes to War: Hegemonic Discourse, Public Opinion, and the Limits of Dissent* (New York: Monthly Review, 2010), 14–15.

8. George W. Bush, "State of the Union Address," January 29, 2002.

9. George W. Bush, "Graduation Speech at West Point, United States Military Academy, West Point, NY," June 1, 2002.

10. Amy Zegart, *Spying Blind: The CIA, the FBI, and the Origins of 9/11* (Princeton, NJ: Princeton University Press, 2007).

11. National Commission on Terrorist Attacks upon the United States, *The 9/11 Commission Report: Final Report of the National Commission on Terrorist Attacks upon the United States* (Washington, DC: U.S. Government Printing Office, 2004); *Visa Security and Overstays: How Secure Is America? Hearing before the Subcommittee on Border and Maritime Security of the Committee on Homeland Security, House of Representatives,* 113th Cong. (May 21, 2013); U.S. Department of Transportation, Office of Inspector General, "Letter to the U.S. Office of Special Counsel Regarding Alleged Aviation Security Violations," March 18, 2003, www.oig.dot.gov/library-item/30374.

12. Bipartisan Policy Center, National Security Preparedness Group, *Tenth Anniversary Report Card: The Status of the 9/11 Commission Recommendations* (Washington, DC: Bipartisan Policy Center, September 2011).

13. National Commission on Terrorist Attacks, *9/11 Commission Report*, 5.

14. Federal Aviation Administration, "Airlines Meet FAA's Hardened Cockpit Door Deadline," press release, April 2003.

15. National Commission on Terrorist Attacks, *9/11 Commission Report*, 390.

16. Natalie Gontcharova, "Soon, You May Not Be Able to Use Your Driver's License to Get on a Plane," *Huffington Post*, May 18, 2017.

17. National Commission on Terrorist Attacks, *9/11 Commission Report*.

18. Lawrence Wright, "The Agent," *New Yorker*, July 20, 2006.

19. According to the Office of Management and Budget, homeland security spending included intelligence and warning, border and transportation security, domestic counterterrorism, protection of critical infrastructure and key assets, defense against catastrophic threats, and emergency preparedness and response. Bart Hobijn and Erick Sager, "What Has Homeland Security Cost? An Assessment: 2001–2005," *Current Issues in Economics and Finance* 13, no. 2 (2007): 1–7.

20. John Mueller and Mark Stewart, "Terror, Security, and Money: Balancing the Risks, Benefits, and Costs of Homeland Security," paper presented at the annual convention of the Midwest Political Science Association, Chicago, IL, April 1, 2011.

21. *Fifteen Years after 9/11: A Preliminary Balance Sheet: Testimony of Brian Michael Jenkins before the Committee on Armed Services, U.S. House of Representatives,* 114th Cong. (September 21, 2016).

22. Alexander Meleagrou-Hitchens, Seamus Hughes, and Bennett Clifford, *The Travelers: American Jihadists in Syria and Iraq* (Washington, DC: George Washington University Program on Extremism, February 2018).

23. Samuel G. Freedman, "Six Days after 9/11, Another Anniversary Worth Honoring," *New York Times*, September 7, 2012, A15. In 2015, the International Centre for the Study of Radicalisation estimated that one hundred Americans had joined Sunni militant organizations in Syria and Iraq. In September 2016, FBI director James Comey testified before a Senate committee that the number of Americans who have tried to travel to the region is "in the dozens." That is compared to almost four thousand who have traveled from western Europe, most of whom came from France (twelve hundred). There are 3.3 million Muslims in the United States and 4.7 million in France. See Peter R. Neumann, "Foreign Fighter Total in Syria/Iraq Now Exceeds 20,000: Surpasses Afghanistan Conflict in the 1980s," International Centre for the Study of Radicalisation, January 26, 2015; Besheer Mohamed, "A New Estimate of the U.S. Muslim Population," Fact Tank, Pew Research Center, January 6, 2016; and Conrad Hackett, "5 Facts about the Muslim Population in Europe," Fact Tank, Pew Research Center, July 19, 2016. For studies on the depiction of Muslims in American media and the effects on public perception, see Christopher Blair, *Terrified: How Anti-Muslim Fringe Organizations Became Mainstream* (Princeton, NJ: Princeton University Press, 2015); and Muniba Saleem, Sara Prot, Craig A. Anderson, and Anthony F. Lemieux, "Exposure to Muslims in Media and Support for Public Policies Harming Muslims," *Communication Research* 44, no. 6 (2015): 841–869.

24. George Tenet, with Bill Harlow, *At the Center of the Storm: My Years at the CIA* (New York: HarperCollins, 2007), 230.

25. Peter Baker, *Days of Fire: Bush and Cheney in the White House* (New York: Knopf Doubleday, 2013).

26. George W. Bush, "Remarks by the President to Employees at the Federal Bureau of Investigation," September 25, 2001.

27. George W. Bush, "Remarks Announcing the Most Wanted Terrorist List," October 10, 2001.

28. Baker, *Days of Fire*; George W. Bush, "State of the Union Address," January 29, 2002.

29. Bush, "State of the Union Address." At the time, East Timor, Kosovo, and South Sudan had yet to become countries, and Montenegro and Serbia had not yet split; there were therefore 192 countries on September 20, 2001.

30. While those who are detained at Guantanamo Bay are citizens of forty-nine different countries, the majority were arrested in Afghanistan and Pakistan. See "The Guantanamo Docket: The Detainees," *New York Times*, October 20, 2016. In "Report on Guantanamo Detainees," Mark Denbeaux and Joshua Denbeaux find that only 5 percent of the detainees were arrested by U.S. forces, while 86 percent were captured by Pakistan or the Northern Alliance and turned over to U.S. custody. Mark Denbeaux and Joshua Denbeaux, *Report on Guantanamo Detainees: A Profile of 517 Detainees through Analysis of Department of Defense Data*, Seton Hall Public Law Research Paper No. 46 (Newark, NJ: Seton Hall University School of Law, 2006).

31. "Shackled Detainees Arrive in Guantanamo," CNN, January 11, 2002. A 2006 study by Seton Hall University Law School found that over 80 percent of prisoners at Guantanamo, whom Donald Rumsfeld referred to as the "worst of the worst," were not captured by U.S. troops on the battlefield but by Pakistanis and Afghans, often for bounty payments or personal vendettas. See Mark Denbeaux, Joshua W. Denbeaux, and John Gregorek, *Second Report on the Guantanamo Detainees: Inter- and Intra-Departmental Disagreements about Who Is Our Enemy*, Seton Hall Public Law Research Paper No. 893047 (Newark, NJ: Seton Hall University School of Law, 2006).

32. Andrei Scheinkman, Alan McLean, Jeremy Ashkenas, Archie Tse, and Jacob Harris, "The Guantanamo Docket: The Detainees," *New York Times,* May 2018.

33. Executive Order No. 13823, 83 FR 4831, 4831–4832 (2018).

34. CIA director John Brennan famously said that the answer to this question was "unknowable." CIA, "Remarks as Prepared for Delivery CIA Director John O. Brennan Response to SSCI Study on the Former Detention and Interrogation Program," December 11, 2014.

35. Stephen Farrell, "Abu Ghraib," *New York Times*, February 21, 2009.

36. Douglas A. Johnson, Alberto Mora, and Averell Schmidt, "The Strategic Costs of Torture," *Foreign Affairs*, September–October 2016, 122.

37. For example, see "Letter from Retired Military Leaders Urging Obama to Declassify Senate Torture Report," Human Rights First, May 1, 2014; "Letter from Retired Military Leaders Urging Presidential Candidates to Reject the Use of Torture," Human Rights First, September 14, 2015; and "Letter from Retired Military Leaders to President Obama on Guantanamo and the Senate Torture Report," Human Rights First, January 21, 2014.

38. Johnson, Mora, and Schmidt, "Strategic Costs of Torture."

39. Ibid.

40. *Direct Overt U.S. Aid Appropriations for and Military Reimbursements to Pakistan, FY2002–FY2018* (Washington, DC: Congressional Research Service, November 28, 2017); Burcu Savun and Jude C. Hays, "Foreign Aid as a Counterterrorism Tool: Aid Delivery Channels, State Capacity, and NGOs" (APSA 2011 Annual Meeting Paper, 2011).

41. Thomas Carothers, *U.S. Democracy Promotion during and after Bush* (Washington, DC: Carnegie Endowment for International Peace, 2007).

42. Gideon Resnick, "Seven Times the Taliban Was Supposedly Defeated," *Daily Beast*, September 29, 2015.

43. David Rohde and David Sanger, "How a 'Good War' in Afghanistan Went Bad," *New York Times,* August 12, 2007.

44. Neta C. Crawford, *Costs of War: Update on the Human Costs of War for Afghanistan and Pakistan, 2001 to Mid-2016* (Providence, RI: Watson Institute of International and Public Affairs at Brown University, August 2016); United Nations Assistance Mission in Afghanistan, *Afghanistan: Protection of Civilians in Armed Conflict Annual Report 2017* (Kabul: United Nations Assistance Mission in Afghanistan, February 2018).

45. Physicians for Social Responsibility, *Body Count: Casualty Figures after 10 Years of the "War on Terror"* (Washington, DC: Physicians for Social Responsibility, March 2015).

46. Watson Institute for International and Public Affairs at Brown University, "Costs of War: Summary of Findings," accessed May 7, 2018, http://watson.brown. edu/costsofwar/papers/summary.

47. Department of Defense, "Operation Iraqi Freedom (OIF) U.S. Casualty Status: Fatalities as of: July 3, 2018," accessed July 4, 2018, www.defense.gov/casualty.pdf.

48. U.S. Department of State, Bureau of Counterterrorism, *Annex of Statistical Information: Country Reports on Terrorism 2016*, July 2017.

49. Heidi M. Peters, Moshe Schwartz, and Lawrence Kapp, *Department of Defense Contractor and Troop Levels in Iraq and Afghanistan: 2007–2017* (Washington, DC: Congressional Research Service, April 28, 2017).

50. U.S. Department of Labor, "About the Defense Base Act Case Summary Reports," accessed May 7, 2018, www.dol.gov/owcp/dlhwc/lsaboutdbareports.htm. This is only an estimate, because the Department of Labor does not provide comprehensive data for U.S. citizens killed supporting U.S. wars. See Micah Zenko, "Mercenaries Are the Silent Majority of Obama's Military," *Foreign Policy*, May 18, 2016.

51. Bob Davis, "Bush Economic Aide Says the Cost of the Iraq War May Top $100 Billion," *Wall Street Journal*, September 16, 2002.

52. Miles O'Brien and Donald Rumsfeld, "Rumsfeld Briefs Press," CNN, January 19, 2003; James Fallows, "Invading Iraq: What We Were Told at the Time," *Atlantic*, March 19, 2013.

53. Neta C. Crawford, *United States Budgetary Costs of Post-9/11 Wars through FY2018: A Summary of the $5.6 Trillion in Costs for the US Wars in Iraq, Syria, Afghanistan and Pakistan, and Post-9/11 Veterans Care and Homeland Security* (Providence, RI: Watson Institute of International and Public Affairs at Brown University, November 2017), 8.

54. Watson Institute, "Costs of War: Summary of Findings"; Special Inspector General for Iraq Reconstruction, *Learning from Iraq* (Washington, DC: Special Inspector General for Iraq Reconstruction, March 2013), 55; Special Inspector General for Afghanistan Reconstruction, *Quarterly Report to the United States Congress* (Washington, DC: Special Inspector General for Iraq Reconstruction, October 30, 2016), 85.

55. "Gulf War Fast Facts," CNN, August 2, 2016.

56. Special Inspector for Iraq Reconstruction, *Learning from Iraq*.

57. Crawford, *United States Budgetary Costs of Post-9/11 Wars through FY2018*, 3. Note that we do not include Costs of War Project homeland security spending in our total figure.

58. Calculated based on the median average of American taxpayers in the seventeen years since 9/11: 190 million.

59. Stephen Daggett, *Costs of Major U.S. Wars* (Washington, DC: Congressional Research Service, June 29, 2010).

60. Neta Crawford, interview with the authors, October 20, 2016.

61. During the Korean War, President Truman raised the top marginal tax rate to 92 percent, while President Johnson raised it to 77 percent in 1967 during the height of the Vietnam War. Linda Bilmes, "The Credit Card Wars: Post-9/11 War Funding Policy in Historical Perspective" (statement in congressional briefing, Watson Institute for International and Public Affairs at Brown University, November 8, 2017).

62. Joseph E. Stiglitz and Linda J. Bilmes, "Estimating the Costs of War: Methodological Issues, with Applications to Iraq and Afghanistan," in *The Oxford Handbook of the Economics of Peace and Conflict*, ed. Michelle R. Garfinkel and Stergios Skaperdas (Oxford: Oxford University Press, 2012), 275–317.

63. Ryan D. Edwards, *Post-9/11 War Spending, Debt, and the Macroeconomy* (Providence, RI: Watson Institute for International and Public Affairs at Brown University, June 22, 2011), 12–13.

64. Crawford, *United States Budgetary Costs of Post-9/11 Wars through FY2018*. Note again that we do not include Costs of War Project homeland security spending in our total figure.

65. Watson Institute for International and Public Affairs at Brown University, "Costs of War: U.S. Veterans and Military Families," September 2016; and Peters, Schwartz, and Kapp, *Department of Defense Contractor and Troop Levels*.

66. Nese DeBruyne, *American War and Military Operations Casualties: Lists and Statistics* (Washington, DC: Congressional Research Service, April 26, 2017).

67. Ibid.; Committee on the Assessment of the Readjustment Needs of Military Personnel, Veterans, and Their Families, *Returning Home from Iraq and Afghanistan: Assessment of Readjustment Needs of Veterans, Service Members, and Their Families* (Washington, DC: Institute of Medicine, March 12, 2013); Anna Kline, Maria Falca-Dodson, Bradley Sussner, Donald S. Ciccone, Helena Chandler, Lanora Callahan, and Miklos Losonczy, "Effects of Repeated Deployment to Iraq and Afghanistan on the Health of New Jersey Army National Guard Troops: Implications for Military Readiness," *American Journal of Public Health* 100, no. 2 (2010): 276–283; and Melissa A. Polusny, Christopher R. Erbes, Paul A. Arbisi, Paul Thuras, Shannon M. Kehle, Michael Rath, Cora Courage, Madhavi K. Reddy, and Courtney Duffy, "Impact of Prior Operation Enduring Freedom/Operation Iraqi Freedom Combat Duty on Mental Health in a Predeployment Cohort of National Guard Soldiers," *Military Medicine* 174, no. 4 (2009): 353–357.

68. Veterans Benefits Administration, Department of Veterans Affairs, *Annual Benefits Report: Fiscal Year 2015* (Washington, DC: Veterans Benefits Administration, Department of Veterans Affairs, updated May 2016), 7.

69. Veterans Benefits Administration, Department of Veterans Affairs, *Annual Benefits Report: Fiscal Year 2001* (Washington, DC: Veterans Benefits Administration, Department of Veterans Affairs, updated May 2002), 81; Veterans Benefits Administration, *Annual Benefits Report: Fiscal Year 2015*, 18.

70. U.S. Department of Defense, Defense Casualty Analysis System, "Operation Enduring Freedom (OEF)," accessed July 4, 2018, https://dcas.dmdc.osd.mil/dcas/pages/report_oef_type.xhtml; U.S. Department of Defense, Defense Casualty Analysis System, "Operation Iraqi Freedom (OIF)," accessed July 4, 2018, https://dcas.dmdc.osd.mil/dcas/pages/report_oif_woundall.xhtml.

71. Veterans Benefits Administration, *Annual Benefits Report: Fiscal Year 2015*, 20.

72. Veterans Benefits Administration, Department of Veterans Affairs, "Compensation: Dependency and Indemnity Compensation—Effective 12/1/14," December 1, 2014.

73. Irene Triplett's father, Mose Triplett, actually served in the Confederacy for over two years, until joining a Union regiment in North Carolina in August 1864. As Triplett's grandson told a reporter in 2014, "[Mose] served his time out with the Union so he would get a pension." Michael M. Phillips, "Still Paying for the Civil War: Veterans' Benefits Live on Long after Bullets Stop," *Wall Street Journal*, May 9, 2014; Clint Davis, "Woman, 87, Still Gets Monthly $73 VA Pension from Father's Civil War Service," abc2news WMAR Baltimore, August 25, 2017; Office of Public Affairs, Department of Veterans Affairs, "America's Wars," fact sheet, May 2016.

74. Neta C. Crawford, *US Budgetary Costs of Wars through 2016: $4.79 Trillion and Counting: Summary of Costs of the US Wars in Iraq, Syria, Afghanistan and Pakistan and Homeland Security* (Providence, RI: Watson Institute of International and Public Affairs at Brown University, September 2016).

75. Defense and Veterans Brain Injury Center, "TBI & the Military," last updated July 3, 2018, http://dvbic.dcoe.mil/tbi-military.

76. Ann C. McKee and Meghan E. Robinson, "Military-Related Traumatic Brain Injury and Neurodegeneration," *Alzheimer's & Dementia: The Journal of the Alzheimer's Association* 10, no. 3 (2014): S242–S253; National Center for PTSD, Department of Veterans Affairs, "How Common Is PTSD?," last updated October 3, 2016.

77. Erin Bagalman, *Health Care for Veterans: Traumatic Brain Injury* (Washington, DC: Congressional Research Service, March 9, 2015).

78. Institute of Medicine, *Treatment for Posttraumatic Stress Disorder in Military and Veteran Populations: Final Assessment* (Washington, DC: National Academies Press, 2014); Bagalman, *Health Care for Veterans*; "Only Half the Vets with PTSD Are Getting Treatment: Report," CBS News, June 20, 2014.

79. Paul Heaton, David S. Loughran, and Amalia Miller, *Compensating Wounded Warriors: An Analysis of Injury, Labor Market Earnings, and Disability Compensation Among Veterans of the Iraq and Afghanistan Wars* (Santa Monica, CA: RAND Corporation, 2012).

80. Tara Galovski and Judith A Lyons, "Psychological Sequelae of Combat Violence: A Review of the Impact of PTSD on the Veteran's Family and Possible Interventions," *Aggression and Violent Behavior* 9, no. 5 (2004): 477–501; Rachel Dekel and Hadass Goldblatt, "Is There Intergenerational Transmission of Trauma? The Case of Combat Veterans' Children," *American Journal of Orthopsychiatry* 78, no. 3 (2008): 281–289.

81. Institute of Medicine, *Preventing Psychological Disorders in Service Members and Their Families: An Assessment of Programs* (Washington, DC: National Academies Press, 2014).

82. American Psychological Association Task Force on Military Deployment Services for Youth, Families and Service Members, *The Psychological Needs of US Military Service Members and Their Families: A Preliminary Report* (Washington, DC: American Psychological Association, February 2007); Patricia Lester, Kris Peterson, James Reeves, et al., "The Long War and Parental Combat Deployment: Effects on Military Children and At-Home Spouses," *Journal of the American Academy of Child and Adolescent Psychiatry* 49, no. 4 (2010): 310–320; Emily Wax-Thibodeaux, "When Veterans Return, Their Children Also Deal with the Invisible Wounds of War," *Washington Post,* April 16, 2015; Martha Teichner, "Collateral Damage: The Mental Health Issues Facing Children of Veterans," CBS News, March 16, 2014.

83. Linda Bilmes, "The Financial Legacy of Afghanistan and Iraq: How Wartime Spending Decisions Will Constrain Future U.S. National Security Budgets," *Economics of Peace and Security Journal* 9, no. 1 (2014): 8–9; Rajeev Ramchand, Terri Tanielian, Michael P. Fisher, et al., *Hidden Heroes: America's Military Caregivers* (Santa Monica, CA: RAND Corporation, 2014); "Military Caregivers Share the Costs of War," *RAND Review*, RAND Corporation, October 30, 2017.

84. World Health Organization, Joint United Nations Programme on HIV/AIDS, *AIDS Epidemic Update: December 2002* (Geneva: UNAIDS, November 26, 2002).

85. George W. Bush, "Address before a Joint Session of the Congress on the State of the Union," January 28, 2003; Todd Summers and Jennifer Kates, *Trends in U.S. Government Funding for HIV/AIDS: Fiscal Years 1981 to 2004* (Menlo Park, CA: Kaiser Family Foundation, March 2004), 8–9.

86. Bush, *Decision Points,* 333.

87. Eran Bendavid and Jayanta Bhattacharya, "The President's Emergency Plan for AIDS Relief in Africa: An Evaluation of Outcomes," *Annals of Internal Medicine* 150, no. 10 (2009): 688–695.

88. "PEPFAR's Glowing Report Card, 10 Years Later," editorial, *Washington Post,* February 25, 2013.

89. Igor Rudan, Harish Nair, Ana Marušić, and Harry Campbell, "Reducing Mortality from Childhood Pneumonia and Diarrhoea: The Leading Priority Is Also the Greatest Opportunity." *Journal of Global Health* 3, no. 1 (2013).

90. World Health Organization, *The Case for Investing in Public Health* (Geneva: World Health Organization, 2014).

91. World Health Organization, *2016 World Malaria Report* (Geneva: World Health Organization, 2016); World Health Organization, "WHO Releases New Guidance on Insecticide-Treated Mosquito Nets," news release, August 16 2007.

92. Warren Stevens, Virginia Wiserman, Juan Ortiz, and Desmond Chavasse, "The Costs and Effects of a Nationwide Insecticide-Treated Net Programme: The Case of Malawi," *Malaria Journal* 4, no. 22 (2005); Jan Kolaczinski and Kara Hanson, "Costing the Distribution of Insecticide-Treated Nets: A Review of Cost and Cost-Effectiveness Studies to Provide Guidance on Standardization of Costing Methodology," *Malaria Journal* 5, no. 37 (2006).

93. World Health Organization, *World Health Report: Overview* (Geneva: World Health Organization, 2000).

94. Harold Alderman, Biram Ndiaye, Sebastian Linnemayr, and Abdoulaye Ka, "Effectiveness of a Community-Based Intervention to Improve Nutrition in Young Children in Senegal: A Difference in Difference Analysis," *Public Health Nutrition* 12, no. 5 (2008): 668.

95. Orazio Attanasio and Alice Mesnard, *The Impact of a Conditional Cash Transfer Program on Consumption in Colombia* (London: Center for the Evaluation of Development Policies, Institute for Fiscal Studies, April 2005), 1, 17.

96. *U.S. Central Command and U.S. Special Operations Command: Hearing before the Committee on Armed Services, U.S. Senate*, 113th Cong. (March 5, 2013). Mattis continued, "I think it's a cost-benefit ratio, the more we put into the State Department's diplomacy, hopefully the less we have to put into a military budget."

97. Office of Management and Budget, *America First: A Budget Blueprint to Make America Great Again* (Washington, DC: U.S. Government Publishing Office, March 2017); Office of Management and Budget, *Efficient, Effective, Accountable: An American Budget* (Washington, DC: U.S. Government Publishing Office, February 2018).

98. World Health Organization, Department of Measurement and Health Information, "Table 1. Estimated Total Deaths ('000), by Cause and WHO Member State, 2004," Excel file, February 2009.

99. Carmen DeNavas-Walt, Bernadette D. Proctor, and Cheryl Hill Lee, *Income, Poverty, and Health Insurance Coverage in the United States: 2004* (Washington, DC: U.S. Census Bureau, August 2005).

100. Jack Hadly and John Holahan, *The Cost of Care for the Uninsured: What Do We Spend, Who Pays, and What Would Full Coverage Add to Medical Spending?* (Washington, DC: Kaiser Commission on Medicaid and the Uninsured, May 10, 2004), 5; Jack Hadley, John Holahan, Teresa Coughlin, and Dawn Miller, "Covering the Uninsured in 2008: Current Costs, Sources of Payment, and Incremental Costs," *Health Affairs* 27, no. 5 (2008): w412–w413.

101. Olga Khazan, "One Simple Trick to Live Longer," *Atlantic*, May 6, 2014; Benjamin D. Sommers, Sharon K. Long, and Katherine Baicker, "Changes in Mortality after Massachusetts Health Care Reform: A Quasi-experimental Study," *Annals of Internal Medicine* 160, no. 9 (2014): 585–593.

102. National Institute of Justice, Office of Justice Programs, U.S. Department of Justice, "Gun Violence Programs: Directed Police Patrols," last updated June 5, 2013.

103. Joint Economic Committee, *War at Any Price? The Total Economic Costs of the War beyond the Federal Budget* (Washington, DC: Joint Economic Committee, U.S. Congress, February 2008).

104. American Society of Civil Engineers, *Report Card for America's Infrastructure: 2003 Progress Report* (Reston, VA: American Society of Civil Engineers, 2003).

105. Ibid.

106. American Society of Civil Engineers, *Report Card for America's Infrastructure* (Reston, VA: American Society of Civil Engineers, 2009).

107. Edward Alden and Rebecca Strauss, *How America Stacks Up: Economic Competitiveness and U.S. Policy* (New York: Council on Foreign Relations, 2016), 43.

108. Environmental Protection Agency, *Drinking Water Infrastructure Needs Survey: Second Report to Congress* (Washington, DC: Environmental Protection Agency, 2001).

109. Environmental Protection Agency, "Fact Sheet: EPA's 2003 Drinking Water Infrastructure Needs Survey and Assessment," 2005.

110. Environmental Protection Agency, "Fact Sheet: EPA's 2007 Drinking Water Infrastructure Needs Survey and Assessment," 2009.

111. Joint Economic Committee, *War at Any Price?*

112. Eliana Garces, Duncan Thomas, and Janet Currie, "Longer-Term Effects of Head Start," *American Economic Review* 92, no. 4 (2004): 999–1012.

113. Heidi Garret-Peltier, *The Job Opportunity Costs of War* (Providence, RI: Watson Institute of International and Public Affairs at Brown University, August 19, 2014).

114. Daveed Gartsenstein-Ross, "Don't Get Cocky, America," *Foreign Policy*, May 2, 2011.

Conclusion

Epigraph: The quotation is also sometimes phrased, "The significant problems we face cannot be solved at the same level of thinking that was used when we created them." See Alice Calaprice, *The Ultimate Einstein Quotable* (Princeton, NJ: Princeton University Press, 2011), 476–477.

1. Barack Obama, "Address to the Nation on the Way Forward in Afghanistan and Pakistan," December 1, 2009. All following quotations from the speech are from this source.

2. Barack Obama, *National Security Strategy of the United States* (Washington, DC: White House, May 2010).

3. Ibid.

4. Barack Obama, "Remarks by the President on the Way Forward in Afghanistan," June 22, 2011.

5. Barack Obama, "State of the Union Address," January 24, 2012.

6. Barack Obama, "Remarks by the President at a Campaign Event in Roanoke, Virginia," July 13, 2012.

7. *Meet the Press*, NBC News, September 20, 2015.

8. Arnie Seipel and Sam Sanders, "Cruz: 'Empower Law Enforcement to Patrol and Secure Muslim Neighborhoods,' " National Public Radio, March 22, 2016.

9. *The Kelly File*, Fox News, November 19, 2015.

10. Newt Gingrich, "Speech at the Republican National Convention," July 21, 2016.

11. *The Kelly File*, Fox News, November 19, 2015.

12. Michael T. Flynn and Michael Ledeen, *The Field of Fight: How We Can Win the Global War against Radical Islam and Its Allies* (New York: St. Martin's, 2016).

13. Rudy Giuliani, "Speech at the Republican National Convention," July 18, 2016.

14. U.S. Department of Homeland Security, "Media Availability on Executive Order with Secretary Kelly and DHS Leadership," January 31, 2017.

15. Alex Nowrasteh, "Terrorism and Immigration: A Risk Analysis" (Policy Analysis No. 798, CATO Institute, September 13, 2016); Chris Nichols, "Mostly True: Odds of Fatal Terror Attack in U.S. by a Refugee? 3.6 Billion to 1," *PolitiFact*, February 1, 2017.

16. Lauren Leatherby, "Trump Clampdown: Four Charts on the US Refugee Programme," *Financial Times*, January 27, 2017.

17. Donald J. Trump (@realDonaldTrump), "If the ban were announced with a one week notice, the 'bad' would rush into our country during that week. A lot of bad 'dudes' out there!," Twitter, January 30, 2017, 8:31 a.m.

18. "After Helping U.S. Military, Iraqi Refugee Is Detained at JFK," *Boston Globe*, January 28, 2017.

19. Garrett Epps, "Papers, Please," *Atlantic*, February 27, 2017.

20. Ben Popken, "Tourism to U.S. under Trump Is Down, Costing $4.6B and 40,000 Jobs," NBC News, January 23, 2018.

21. "The Key Spending Cuts and Increases in Trump's Budget," *New York Times*, May 22, 2017.

22. Donald J. Trump (@realDonaldTrump), "When a country (USA) is losing many billions of dollars on trade with virtually every country it does business with, trade wars good, and easy to win. Example, when we are down $100 billion with a certain country and they get cute, don't trade anymore-we win big. It's easy!," Twitter, March 2, 2018, 5:50 a.m.

23. CBS, "Transcript: Face the Nation," July 15, 2018.

24. Congressional Budget Office, "H.R. 1528, Obamacare Repeal Reconciliation Act of 2017," July 19, 2017.

25. Tim Mahedy and Daniel J. Wilson, "Fiscal Times in Good and Bad," *FRBSF Economic Letter*, July 9, 2018, www.frbsf.org/economic-research/publications/economic-letter/2018/july/procyclical-fiscal-policy-tax-cuts-jobs-act/.

26. Joint Committee on Taxation, "Estimated Budget Effects of the Conference Agreement for H.R. 1, The 'Tax Cuts and Jobs Act,' " U.S. Congress, December 18, 2017, 8; Niv Elis, "GOP Tax Law Will Add $1.9 Trillion to Debt: CBO," *The Hill*, April 9, 2018.

27. *Face the Nation*, CBS News, May 11, 2014.

28. Barack Obama, "Now Is the Greatest Time to Be Alive," *Wired*, October 12, 2016.

29. Erin M. Kearns, Allison Betus, and Anthony Lemieux, "Yes the Media Do Underreport Some Terrorist Attacks. Just Not the Ones Most People Think Of," *Washington Post*, March 13, 2017.

30. Anti-Defamation League, *Murder and Extremism in the United States in 2017* (New York: Anti-Defamation League, January 2018).

31. Brian Michael Jenkins, "Taking the 'Terror' Out of Terrorism Requires Outsmarting Fear," *The RAND Blog*, RAND Corporation, March 16, 2017.

32. Peter W. Singer, "Writing about Defense, but at What Price? The Ethics of Thinktankers' Public Commentary and Private Profit," op-ed, Brookings Institution, December 13, 2010.

33. Stephen M. Walt, "Hacks and Hired Guns," *Foreign Policy*, September 19, 2014; Stephen M. Walt, "A Modest Proposal," *Foreign Policy*, November 20, 2009; Transparify, *How Transparent Are Think Tanks about Who Funds Them 2016?*, June 29, 2016, https://static1.squarespace.com/static/52e1f399e4b06a94c0cdaa41

/t/5773022de6f2e1ecf70b26d1/1467154992324/Transparify+2016+Think+Tanks+Report
.pdf.

34. A greater percentage of Americans than ever before—an estimated 46
percent—now have valid passports, allowing them to travel abroad. "How Many
Americans Have a Passport?," *Expeditioner*, December 11, 2016, www.theexpedi-
tioner.com/2010/02/17/how-many-americans-have-a-passport-2; U.S. Department
of State, "Passport Statistics," accessed May 10, 2018, http://travel.state.gov/content/
passports/en/passports/statistics.html.

35. Y. Claire Wang, Pamela Coxson, Yu-Ming Shen, Lee Goldman, and Kirsten
Bibbins-Domingo, "A Penny-Per-Ounce Tax on Sugar-Sweetened Beverages Would
Cut Health and Cost Burdens of Diabetes," *Health Affairs* 31 (2012): 199–207.

36. World Health Organization, *Fiscal Policies for Diet and Prevention of Noncommunicable Diseases: Technical Meeting Report* (Geneva: World Health Organization,
May 2015), http://apps.who.int/iris/bitstream/10665/250131/1/9789241511247-eng.
pdf?ua=1; Food and Nutrition Service, Department of Agriculture, Food and Nutrition Service, *Healthy Incentives Pilot (HIP) Final Report* (Washington, DC: Food
and Nutrition Service, July 2013), www.fns.usda.gov/sites/default/files/HIP-Final
.pdf.

37. On average, sixty-two cents for every dollar of cigarette tax is assessed by states,
and the remaining thirty-eight cents is assessed by the federal government. Jennifer
Maloney and Saabira Chaudhuri, "Against All Odds, the U.S. Tobacco Industry Is
Rolling in Money," *Wall Street Journal*, April 23, 2017.

38. Cancer Action Network, American Cancer Society, *Saving Lives, Saving
Money: A State-by-State Report on the Health and Economic Impact of Tobacco Taxes*
(Washington, DC: Cancer Action Network, 2011).

39. Ibid.

40. Scott P. Novak, Sean F. Reardon, Stephen W. Raudenbush, and Stephen L.
Buka, "Retail Tobacco Outlet Density and Youth Cigarette Smoking: A Propensity-
Modeling Approach," *American Journal of Public Health* 96 (2006): 670–676.

41. "Funding and Publication of Research on Gun Violence and Other Leading
Causes of Death," *JAMA* 317, no. 1 (2017): 84–85.

42. RAND Corporation, *The Science of Gun Policy: A Critical Synthesis of Research
Evidence on the Effects of Gun Policies in the United States* (Santa Monica, CA: RAND
Corporation, 2018).

43. American Foundation for Suicide Prevention, "Suicide Statistics," accessed
May 10, 2018, http://afsp.org/about-suicide/suicide-statistics.

44. Law Center to Prevent Gun Violence, "Waiting Periods," accessed May 10, 2018, http://lawcenter.giffords.org/gun-laws/policy-areas/gun-sales/waiting-periods/.

45. Pew Research Center, *Opinions on Gun Policy and the 2016 Campaign* (Washington, DC: Pew Research Center, August 26, 2016).

46. Centers for Disease Control and Prevention, National Center for Health Statistics, "Provision Drug Overdose Death Counts," based on data available for analysis on September 5, 2018.

47. U.S. Department of Health and Human Services, *Substance Abuse Prevention Dollars and Cents: A Cost-Benefit Analysis* (Washington, DC: U.S. Department of Health and Human Services, 2008); and White House Office of National Drug Control Policy, "Fact Sheet: A 21st Century Drug Policy," April 24, 2013.

48. Alex Hollingsworth, Christopher J. Ruhm, and Kosali Simon, "Macroeconomic Conditions and Opioid Abuse" (NBER Working Paper No. 23192, National Bureau of Economic Research, February 2017).

49. Heather Dunn, "10 Interesting Facts Comparing Community Colleges & 4-Year Institutions," *CampusLogic Blog*, March 24, 2016, http://campuslogic.com/blog/interesting-facts-comparing-community-colleges-4-year-institutions.

50. Vivek Wadhwa and Edward Alden, "The Government Failed U.S. Workers on Global Trade. It Must Do Better on Technology," *Washington Post*, November 3, 2016.

51. Micah Zenko and Michael A. Cohen, "Clear and Present Safety," *Foreign Affairs*, March–April 2012.

52. Noam Unger and Margaret L. Taylor, with Frederick Barton, *Capacity for Change: Reforming U.S. Assistance Efforts in Poor and Fragile Countries* (Washington, DC: Brookings Institution and Center for Strategic and International Studies, April 2010).

53. In 2016, the United States disbursed $34.4 billion in official development assistance, just 0.19 percent of its gross national income that year. Curt Tarnoff and Marian L. Lawson, *Foreign Aid: An Introduction to U.S. Programs and Policy* (Washington, DC: Congressional Research Service, April 25, 2018); World Bank, "United States," accessed May 10, 2018, http://data.worldbank.org/country/united-states.

54. "Exclusive Interview with CENTCOM's Lt. Gen. John R. Allen," *FrontLines* (USAID), April–May 2011.

55. Bipartisan Policy Center, *The Military Compensation Conundrum: Rising Costs, Declining Budgets, and a Stressed Force Caught in the Middle* (Washington, DC: Bipartisan Policy Center, September 2016).

56. Michael Cohen, "A Reality-Based Army," *Democracy* 33 (Summer 2014), https://democracyjournal.org/magazine/33/a-reality-based-army/.

57. Seth G. Jones, *Rolling Back the Islamic State* (Santa Monica, CA: RAND Corporation, 2017), 221; United Nations Peacekeeping, "How We Are Funded," accessed May 4, 2018, http://peacekeeping.un.org/en/how-we-are-funded; Andrea Ruggeri, Han Dorussen, and Theodora-Ismene Gizelis, "Winning the Peace Locally: UN Peacekeeping and Local Conflict," *International Organization* 71, no. 1 (2017): 163–185; Virginia Page Fortna, "Does Peacekeeping Keep Peace? International Intervention and the Duration of Peace after Civil War," *International Studies Quarterly* 48 (2014): 269–292.

58. International Atomic Energy Agency, *Verification and Monitoring in the Islamic Republic of Iran in Light of United Nations Security Council Resolution 2231 (2015)* (Vienna: International Atomic Energy Agency, February 22, 2018).

59. U.S. Government Accountability Office, *Iran Nuclear Agreement: The International Atomic Energy Agency's Authorities, Resources, and Challenges*, GAO-16-565 (Washington, DC: U.S. Government Accountability Office, June 9, 2016); Hyeran Jo and Beth A. Simmons, "Can the International Criminal Court Deter Atrocity?," *International Organization* 70, no. 3 (2016): 443–475.

60. Rebecca M. Nelson, *U.S. Sanctions and Russia's Economy* (Washington, DC: Congressional Research Service, February 17, 2017); Olga Tanas, "Russian Economy Crawled to Growth with Recession in Rearview," *Bloomberg Markets*, March 31, 2017; World Bank, "Russia's Recovery: How Strong Are Its Shoots?" (Russia Economic Report 38, November 2017).

61. United Nations Office of Legal Affairs, "Chronological Lists of Ratifications of, Accessions and Successions to the Convention and the Related Agreements," last updated April 3, 2018, www.un.org/Depts/los/reference_files/chronological_lists_of_ratifications.htm.

Index

Tenet, George, 139

terrorism: Bush on, 133, 134, 139; case
study of American reaction to news
reports of, 216n1; domestic vigilance
after 9/11 attacks, 134; European
attacks, 5, 15; exaggeration of risk
from, 2, 107, 118; foreign reporting
dominated by, 15, 24; global
increase in incidents of, 24–25; in
Iraq since 2003, 144; jihadist
recruitment based on opposition to
U.S. policies, 91; media coverage
recommendations, 168–170;
presidential debates (2016) on topic
of, 120, 168; recruiting campaigns
by terrorists, 140, 224n23; since
9/11, number of U.S. citizens killed
by, 2, 24; Trump on, 15. *See also*
September 11, 2001 terrorist attacks

Thailand, 23, 140–141

think tanks' relationship with
military-industrial complex, 102,
111, 113–118, 170–171

Thirty Years' War, 15

Thomas, Chris, 125

Threat-Industrial Complex (TIC), 76,
101–130; Americans' participation
in, 130; conflicts of interest of
retired military officials, 109–113,
169, 217–218n18; defense
contractors' role, 105, 109–110;
Doomsday Clock, 129–130;
financial motivation of, 123–124;
global water crisis as exaggeration,
128–129; Hollywood's portrayal of
"dangers" to Americans, 126–128;
lingua franca of, 14, 104; media's
reporting on "dangers" to
Americans, 102–103, 118–120;

national consensus forming around,
104; need to recognize fear-based
appeals of, 9, 114, 166, 171; think
tanks' relationship with military-
industrial complex, 102, 111, 113–118,
170–171

threat inflation: Clapper's and
Dempsey's congressional testimony
as, 12–13; consequences of, 165–166,
178; data disproving claims of,
14–19, 169; disconnect between
reality of and discourse on, 6–7, 14,
125, 159; effect on creating a world
in America's image, 187; in foreign
policy discourse, 77, 167; human
penchant for believing, 101;
philanthropic foundations' role in,
171; presidential campaign (2016)
and, 160–161; reasons for focus on,
36–37, 104–105; in response to 9/11
terrorist attacks, 2, 9; steady
narrative feeding, 3–4, 17, 122.
See also bully pulpit of U.S.
presidents; media; *specific presidents*

Threat Matrix, 139

Tillerson, Rex, 164

tobacco and smoking risks, 68–69,
173, 174

torture and enhanced interrogation
techniques, 112, 126–127, 140–141,
171

totalitarianism, 21

tourism, 163

traffic accidents and fatalities, 59, 69,
207n55

Transparify, 170–171

Transportation Security
Administration (TSA), 136–137,
162